ANDY KAUFMAN REVEALED!

BEST FRIEND TELLS ALL

ANDY KAUFMAN REVEALED!

BOB ZMUDA
with MATTHEW SCOTT HANSEN

WITH A BACKWORD FROM JIM CARREY

LITTLE, BROWN AND COMPANY

BOSTON   NEW YORK   LONDON

First Edition

Library of Congress Cataloging-in-Publication Data

Zmuda, Bob.
    Andy Kaufman revealed! : best friend tells all / by Bob
Zmuda with Matthew Scott Hansen ; with a backword
from Jim Carrey. — 1st ed.
        p.   cm.
    Includes index.
    ISBN 0-316-68123-7
    1. Kaufman, Andy, 1949–1984. 2. Comedians — United
States Biography. 3. Actors — United States Biography.
I. Hansen, Matthew Scott. II. Title.
PN2287.K28Z68   1999
792.7'028'092 — dc21
[B]   99-26579

10 9 8 7 6 5 4 3

MV-NY

Printed in the United States of America

In memoriam

To Andy, Stan, and Laz

(Kaufman, if you're still alive, I'll kill you.)

All roads lead to Andy.

DANA CARVEY

ANDY KAUFMAN REVEALED!

Prologue

The three of us stood outside the funeral home, the varnished faces of the beautifully carved wooden doors glistening in the warm midmorning sun. I stared at the wrought-iron handles. We were the first group to arrive; we paused before stepping inside. Lynne Margulies, Andy's girlfriend, was on my right and Joe Troiani, a friend since childhood, was on my left.

In a ritual we had observed because Andy would have wanted it that way, Joe and I had gone out on the town the night before, taking in the live sex shows down on 42nd Street — just in case this whole thing was real. As we gazed at the entrance to the building that just might contain the earthly remains of my best friend, Andy Kaufman, I continued to pray that it was just a terrible joke Andy had managed to perpetrate on everyone, including me, the closest tie to the human race that he had. Maybe he would surprise us. We kept waiting for the punch line. I knew there was no limit to how far he'd take a joke. Denial was a very useful tool for the three of us at that moment.

Joe noticed my hesitation and blank expression and took it to mean that I was hiding something, perhaps holding back as I attempted to contain my laughter. *Zmuda's in on the joke, gotta be.* Joe had known me for more than twenty years and normally his read would have been accurate, but this time he was witnessing something he'd never seen in me and therefore couldn't identify: complete shock. It affected my behavior by giving off false signs that not only was everything fine, it was *cool*. Nothing was further from the truth.

"Hey, let's see a body," cracked Joe. "I'm gonna go inside, see what's up."

Lynne patted his shoulder. "You go, Joe. Bob and I'll wait." Lynne was dealing with her own grief but intuitively knew my demeanor was indeed concealing deep pain and confusion.

Joe, like me, had been raised Catholic and, once inside, expected the mortuary to be abuzz with people flitting about. But the place was, well, dead. He wandered back and found the large room where Andy's service would be held. At the front of the room sat a casket on a stand, its lid cocked open. Even though he assumed it would actually contain something, Joe still was surprised when he saw a body within, resting, its arms folded. It appeared to be Andy. Joe walked over and looked down at the waxen likeness, the head shaved, the features terminally peaceful.

This moment had come upon us so quickly we weren't really sure how to behave. Joe had known Andy for years, but the notion that such a bright light could be snuffed out was not yet completely within the realm of possibility for him. He truly believed that Andy was still with us, and why not? Andy was the greatest practical joker the world had ever known, the Houdini of jokesters, the Elvis of put-on artists. This could be his biggest stunt ever.

"Andy," he murmured to the prone form, anticipating that he might now be let in on Andy's greatest prank. "Hey Andy, I'm here and we're all alone, so c'mon man, you can tell me . . . this is a big fucking joke, isn't it?" No reaction. Joe realized Andy wasn't going to give this up easily. Stepping close and leaning over, Joe looked for a sign — a slight heave of the chest, a flicker of an eyelid, the tiny quiver of flesh over an artery — since this "dead" man was apparently not going to betray the gag without a fight.

"Andy?" he repeated softly, this time prodding the chest slightly. It didn't seem to be wax, but then again he wasn't sure. "Andy? It's Joe. Open your eyes."

Joe's necktie brushed the hand of the "corpse." Joe recoiled out of reflex, sensing Andy was about to grab the tie and pull Joe down, at which time Andy would furiously whisper, *Don't blow this for me, understand?* But Andy didn't move. Joe stepped back, suspiciously eyeing the still form. Andy was good, *really* good, and Joe knew he was certainly capable of this. *Wax or not?* he wondered, then turned away.

The front doors parted a moment later as Joe returned to us, looking slightly confused. Our eyes met. "So," I said, forcing a smile, "was it Andy or Memorex?"

Joe's perplexed expression gave way to seriousness. "If anybody can pull this off, Zmuda, it's you and Kaufman."

1
Opening Act

I guess the beginning of Andy's professional career started when he was about nine years old. He was in business for himself. He actually put an ad in the local paper advertising his services as a party entertainer. He got paid five dollars for two hours. I was at one of the birthday parties that he did — for my best friend, Mindy. He was wonderful.

CAROL KAUFMAN-KERMAN

It was the summer of '62 and life seemed pretty innocent. *Wagon Train* was television's top-rated show and Bobby Vinton was number one on the charts with "Roses Are Red (My Love)." The Cuban missile crisis was still a month or so away, and it wouldn't be until October that James Meredith would have to be escorted by federal marshals just so he could register at the University of Mississippi. The summer of my twelfth year would mark the end of an era for me, and maybe for the country.

A huge amusement park called Riverview was an attraction for Chicagoans, and during the summer when it was in full swing, tens of thousands of people of all colors and creeds would brave the swelter to mingle in harmony, enjoying the rides and sights of an old-time midway. One of the attractions was an honest-to-God freak show, the kind long since banned for its exploitation of the freakish and bizarre. The dirty, faded oil posters on the side of the tent vividly proclaimed the lurid visions inside, while the barker sized up the crowd and focused on the fascinated and the gullible. I was mesmerized by his stable: the World's Greatest Magician, capable of "spectacular feats" of legerdemain; the Rock Lady, portrayed by her billboard as an enormous rock with two eyes; the Amazing Two-Headed Calf, a genetic monstrosity billed as sharing one stomach with its two hideous heads; and then, of course, Turko the Half Man. Turko's poster advertised a man who appeared somewhat normal except that he couldn't wear a belt because he had no waist around which to put it. The poor mutant in the picture ended where his belly button would have been. Incredible.

"That's complete bullshit," said my dad wryly, having noticed my eyes bulge at the sight of the semiperson. "They're just tryin' to get you in the tent. It's a con. Nobody's made of rock and no guy's only half there. Total bullshit."

My father is a hard-working man who approaches life with a certain skepticism, but he was wise enough to know that my wide-eyed curiosity wouldn't be satisfied until I'd put my hands in the wounds. As the barker crowed the tantalizing details of what lay beyond the flap of the tent, my old man handed me a buck for an important life lesson.

After paying fifty cents I was ushered into a dark, airless canvas room to stand with about a dozen others waiting for the show to begin, the sights promising to amaze. The barker emerged from the back, now dressed as the World's Greatest Magician. As the man went through some lame routines, I began to get the sinking feeling that my father had been right. How come things can't be as great as they appear? I'd already seen this guy, so the sense of mystery was totally deflated. When the Rock Lady was introduced I cringed at the sight of the poor old woman inflicted with what looked like really wicked psoriasis. Then the curtain was drawn to reveal the Amazing Two-Headed Calf, and my hopes crashed — it was actually the Amazing *nonliving* Two-Headed Calf. Fooled again, I was mad I'd gotten my expectations up by praying I'd get to see the two heads fighting over some food. Not only that, but it looked like the taxidermist had been in a rush to get to his lunch hour as he attached the second head.

Dad, as usual, had been right. I, along with the other earnest audience members, had been screwed. The barker, having dropped out of his World's Greatest Magician persona, sized up the small, crestfallen group and made us an offer.

"I see by your faces you want more, so more is what you shall have," he projected in stentorian tones. "Behind this curtain," he said as he gestured, "is yet another sight. It is our greatest attraction. So unusual, so wonderful . . . so *completely strange*," he said, lowering his voice to a pungent whisper, "that I hesitate to show this to all my audiences."

The individuals in that stifling, musty little compartment brightened with interest, but we also had that fresh feeling of having been taken. The barker was ahead of us.

"I know what you're thinking," he said confidently. "'Oh, sure, we've heard this before.' Well, ladies and gentlemen, I'll put my mouth where your money is. For another fifty cents I will take you behind that curtain to witness the most disturbing sight of your young lives. And I will promise you this: if you do not think Turko the Half Man is stranger than strange, weirder than weird, I will not only give you back your fifty cents, I will refund your entire entrance fee — that's a dollar each — if you are not completely satisfied."

Well, having been gypped out of fifty cents already, the idea that I couldn't lose appealed to me. Everyone else, too, agreed to take the offer. After forking over our change we were directed into a room where the muffled sounds of the midway outside seemed a thousand miles away. This room was smaller and darker than the other and featured a lone pedestal table with a Coke bottle sitting directly in the middle. It took a moment to get accustomed to the low light. When the barker felt we were ready, he gave a flourish. "Ladies and gentlemen, the Ninth Wonder of the World, unique to all humanity, I give you Turko the Half Man!"

Suddenly the canvas parted across the room, and something seeming to be a huge bat flew toward us. We recoiled in terror as the flying menace buzzed us, then stopped and jerked back toward the table. It came at us with such frenetic motion none of us had time to react or, for that matter, even completely see what it was. In a few seconds, after the shock wore off, my eyes took in the strangest thing I have ever seen. This was truly half a man.

He had a haggard middle-aged face but a body that ended where the rest of us have a stomach. The base of his truncated torso was attached to what looked like a quarter of a car tire, which he used to hop and rock on. His arms were massive, their corded muscles more like legs. From the perspective of this hideous yet wonderful little 50 percent man, we were a dozen strangers gaping in amazement.

Turko wheeled about the room for a moment to build the effect, his movements like that of a wild animal, his powerful arms flinging a body weighing a fraction of a normal frame. Then he made a massive leap and, impossibly, landed squarely on top of the unopened Coke bottle, balancing perfectly. Miraculously maintaining his equilibrium without touching the table, he began an odd shuddering motion that slowly rotated him around the bottle top. Then he launched into a stunningly touching rendition of "Beautiful Dreamer."

My jaw was on the floor, and I knew the others in the room were just as stupefied by what we were seeing. When he completed a full revolution of the bottle, which coincided perfectly with the finish of his song, Turko flipped off onto the table and in one fluid motion grabbed the bottle, popped the cap with his teeth, and drained the Coke in a few gulps. He then spun around so fast that none of us could follow the blur, did another leap and a pirouette, and vanished behind the curtain.

Speechless for a moment, we eventually composed ourselves and slowly, numbly exited. Outside, my dad stood waiting, arms crossed patiently, expecting me to have gotten my life lesson. I had — it just wasn't the one he thought it would be.

"What did I tell you? Bullshit, huh?" I didn't say anything. How could I? I was still in a stupor over having just seen the greatest act of my life. As we walked away, my mind whirled over the implications of it all. That was like no entertainment I'd ever seen, no sight I'd ever laid eyes on. Ed Sullivan sure as hell never had anything like Turko. It was repulsive and unbelievably compelling at the same time. I never told my dad what that dollar really bought, but it changed my life. It showed me what power there was in getting people off balance, throwing them a curve, entertaining them by making them *uncomfortable*. It was wonderful.

Later that summer, a thousand miles away in Times Square, a thirteen-year-old kid named Andy, whom I would meet ten years later, went with his Grandma Pearl to see the sideshow at a storefront freak show called Hubert's Museum. He saw Turko.

From that sideshow he emerged with his life's mission.

*   *   *

Looking back, 1968 was the greatest year of my life for many reasons, but mainly because it was when I opened my eyes for the first time. The three men I have to thank for that, because of a little confrontation between them that summer, were Jerry Rubin and Abbie Hoffman on the left, and Mayor Richard Daley way over to the right. After my encounter with Turko, it was the next life-changing event in my life.

Jerry and Abbie and their Youth International Party, or Yippies, had a mission to overturn the evil capitalistic government of the United States of America by deprogramming the youth from the twisted values of previous generations, those comprising fully vested members of the Establishment. Their approach, more or less, was to shitcan every social convention that had been chartered in the previous one hundred ninety-some years of the Republic and start all over. Their goal was enlightenment by awakening the youth of America through the chaos of revolutionary thought, and their tools were sex, drugs, and rock and roll. By sending out their army of flower children to plaster my middle-class Chicago neighborhood with flyers, they announced a "love-in" in Lincoln Park.

What the hell was a "love-in"? my friends and I wondered. We were "greasers." John Travolta may have played one in the movie *Grease*, but we lived it. Clad in skintight sharkskin pants, three-inch Cuban heels, and enough Vitalis to lubricate a fleet of Cadillac Biarritzes, we may have looked tough, but we embodied the middle-class and lower-middle-class ideals passed on by our parents. Graduate high school, maybe go on to college, then pick a trade or profession, get married, have kids, and "settle down." That's what we knew, that's what we were.

So when a group of us saw the flyers, adorned with drawings of blissful-looking hippie chicks, we would have ignored them had they not featured one eye-grabbing item: the hippie girls with the flowers in their hair and the diamond-shaped dark glasses seemed to have forgotten to wear their tops. Love-ins we didn't know from, but tits we did. We decided to go. When we arrived, the park was teeming with thousands and thousands of people, stoned, drunk, having sex in public, and, of course, lots and lots of titties. It was a mini-Woodstock. For the first time in my life I smoked pot. Stoned out of my gourd, I must have made out with half a dozen different girls. It was heaven. That night when my buddies and I wandered home we vowed to return.

The next day I arrived in jeans, barefoot and shirtless. A girl gave me some "love beads" and I put them on. Overnight, the Fonz had become Dennis Hopper. After briefly coming into possession of a few joints I was at one with the cosmos. I found a group of people chanting and sat down next to an older guy with a beard who seemed to be leading the chorus of oms. Even though the crowd was not hung up on affectations like names, the bearded guy introduced himself as Allen. Allen Ginsberg. As I shook his hand someone mentioned that Allen was a writer. *Cool,* I thought. *I'm stoned and hanging out with writers and girls without tops.*

After a few peaceful hours of grooving to the vibes and the music and the sweet smell of dope drifting on the night air, Abbie Hoffman climbed onto a wall and announced to the multitude that we had been commanded by the Chicago police to clear the park because it was closing. Now, I had relatives on the force and also knew that Chicago parks never closed, so I smelled a rat. Then a cop blared through a bullhorn that we had to disperse immediately or be arrested. As soon as his announcement ended you could hear the whooshing sound of about three thousand simultaneous tokes. And nobody moved. We were thinking there was no way they could arrest us all. We figured it was a hollow threat if we sat still, with safety in numbers being our salvation. We were wrong.

The "Honorable" Richard Daley, dictator of Chi-town, was jumpy because of the proximity of our love-in to the Democrats' big convention, so he decided we were not so much Illinois's sons and daughters as crazed radicals bent on the destruction of all that he and his held holy. He took action. A midwestern Napoleon, he let slip his dogs of war, then set upon us his police, bristling with clubs and tear gas. In moments, our love-in became a scene from *Doctor Zhivago.* Surrounded by hundreds of panicked revelers, I fled, my new girlfriend in tow, smoke and gas and pandemonium reigning as we avoided the swinging billies and advancing walls of grimly determined storm troopers. Thinking we were safe, we rounded a street corner only to run smack into a phalanx of horse cops. My girlfriend slammed into the flank of an equine. She took a nightstick to the face, which knocked her senseless, and then was hauled off by several cops. I managed to push away to escape down an alley, running for my life.

Just that balmy summer weekend forced me, along with thousands of other good, law-abiding, conservative kids, to deal with the shattered myth that the government was looking out for our best interests. Suddenly the words of Abbie and Jerry and Huey and Stokely were starting to ring true. Was the government the enemy? I'd seen it firsthand.

My thinking changed. I started hanging out in the old town area, a bastion of radical thought, and eventually, for all practical purposes, moved in. My new friends weren't greasers but rather members of Students for a Democratic Society (SDS). I gave up drive-ins for coffeehouses, and though I still smoked dope I began to trade ideas, *philosophies*, with my new comrades. Though we were all middle-class kids we had just discovered that "that man behind the curtain" was not benevolent but instead was pretty scary. I joined a radical guerilla theater group. I traded my sharkskins for bell-bottoms and grew my hair long. I started saying "far-out" and "outtasight." I swore off Vitalis for good.

Every weekend, I would sneak into Second City, the famed satirical improv troupe, to catch their latest biting political shots. As time passed, the scales fell from my eyes and I began to realize that this was my country and it had to be saved from the conservative, corrupt fat cats who had sent us into a war merely to profit the "military industrial complex." It was those men who had subverted the "system" to satisfy their own cravings for power, and, worse, it was those people who had given orders to someone who had whacked my girlfriend-for-the-day across the kisser.

I was pissed. Mayor Daley had created not a "programmed" good kid in a short-sleeved white shirt with a pocket protector and a slide rule, ready to become a "productive" citizen, but rather a warrior, a radical commando, prepared to topple a system that had become irreparably corrupt. But in my case, instead of a gun or a bomb, my weapon was between my ears: my wits and a rapidly developing sense of humor. And I was ready for war.

Andy Kaufman, meanwhile, had become a drunk. Falling into a spiral of party after party in his hometown of Great Neck, New York, a small upscale town on Long Island just over the border from northeast Queens, in Nassau County, Andy spent more time in the local park than at home. Getting hammered day and night with some of the less desirable residents of Great Neck, Andy would often be cajoled into doing his Elvis Presley impression, which he labored to perfect despite the disorientation of his lifestyle. Andy had been doing a dead-on impression of his hero many years before it was hip.

Around this time he took a job as an errand boy and found himself making deliveries for the local butcher shop to comedian Alan King's luxurious home. Andy would occasionally corner King in his house and do five minutes of his routine. Though King admired Andy's tenacity, the day he discovered Andy taking an unauthorized dip in his pool he asked the butcher to send a different delivery boy. What impressed Andy most about King's lifestyle was his fully equipped bar featuring a functioning beer tap. The link between King's career in entertainment and the fact that he had his own beer dispenser made a huge impression on Andy. He soon began to inform people that he would one day have his own draft-beer delivery system.

Eventually Andy's constant partying led to a pregnancy. The girl's parents put the child, a girl, up for adoption. That event gave Andy pause, and he abandoned the parties in the park for the coffeehouses in Greenwich Village, an environment that stimulated his wildly active mind. Soon he was writing poetry and attending read-ins at the various hangouts where post-beat-generation devotees flocked. He grew a beard and let his hair grow, adopting the look of his clique. More important, Andy found the inspiration to begin serious contemplation of his future, the role he might play in the drama of life. With Alan King's beer tap in mind, as well as the attendant modus vivendi that came from a big-time career in showbiz, Andy decided television was going to be his road to riches.

With high school grades indicating he was barely above a moron, a powerhouse university was not in Andy's cards. But Grahm Junior College, in Boston, was. Possessed of a modest television department and sympathetic to Andy's less-than-sterling high school scholastic record, Grahm welcomed him with open arms. It was during this time that two things changed Andy's course of life permanently. The first was his introduction to transcendental meditation.

Founded in 1957 by His Holiness Maharishi Mahesh Yogi, transcendental meditation, or TM, was a movement that was sweeping the country. Represented by practitioners as the way to unlock the extraordinary powers within oneself through deep meditation, those in the know liken its effects on the mind and body to drawing a bow: pull back the arrow two feet, and it will fly two hundred yards. Supposedly able to bring one enhanced mental powers in addition to a well-being exceeding the effects of half a dozen draft beers, it was perfect for Andy. He jumped in with both feet and soon embraced the life of a devotee: no more booze or drugs, and two hours a day given over to alpha bliss.

It has been said that chance favors the prepared mind, so perhaps TM had a large role in what happened next. One day Andy was approached by a fellow Grahm student and asked to perform in the campus talent show. Andy had performed as a child in his own room in front of an imaginary camera, putting on lavish specials with famous guests while surrounded by spectacular sets. His shows set records for audiences worldwide. Of course the audiences were only in his mind. His experience with real audiences started around the time he was nine with little shows for neighborhood kids, always with the condition that adults were expressly forbidden to attend.

Now he was being asked to do his thing in front of an audience over whom he had no control. His knee-jerk reaction was to decline, but TM had been altering his thought processes, allaying his fears and shyness, showing him that his concerns about others' scrutiny of him were groundless. His mental placidity gave him a new confidence he had never before experienced. He agreed to do it.

Using his TM discipline to wash away the terror and jittery nerves, Andy charged himself with a million volts of electricity and went before that audience at Grahm Junior College and performed some of the same routines he had done for his friends as a child. The juxtaposition of his children's material with an adult audience was lightning in a bottle uncorked. The crowd's extraordinary reaction, coupled with his new mind-set from TM, proved to Andy that his fears were no longer part of his luggage, so he set them down and never looked back.

Perhaps he had been working up to that point of demarcation all his life. He had always lived in his own mind, but his meditation somehow allowed him to turn inside out and see outside reality as no more dangerous than had been his make-believe world as a child. Andy Kaufman had reinvented himself. It was mid-1969 and he was now ready to take the next step. Emboldened by his formal debut as an entertainer, Andy knew his next move was a necessity for his ascendancy as a performer to the great heights he envisioned. If that was to be his path, his direction in life, he required an audience with the most influential person he knew of. But meeting this person would be harder than getting to the Pope or the president, mainly because this person was bigger than either of them. Andy didn't know how he was going to do it, but he knew he had to.

He had to meet Elvis.

Andy had written a book about Elvis. Having authored several other unfinished manuscripts, Andy felt his work in progress about Elvis was worthy of passing on to the King for approval. Somewhere around two hundred pages in length, the book was more a hand-scrawled tribute than a biography, and Andy felt it was a perfect calling card for an audience with this great man. Andy's daily forays into meditation had given him the courage and resolve to meet Elvis. Almost completely broke and without a car, Andy visualized the gulf between himself and the King and saw them meeting. Now he just needed to, as they say, *actualize* the whole thing.

At this point in his career, Elvis was in the throes of a comeback. Overwhelmed by his success in the late '50s and early '60s, Elvis had lost some of his bearings and had become to many almost a parody of his former self. One of his strategies to pull himself out of his tailspin was to return to live entertaining, and Las Vegas was the Mecca for live performing. Having already failed once at a comeback, this time Elvis took notice of the successes of Tom Jones and Engelbert Humperdinck and created a power-packed, glitzy show with capes and flair and flash. Thus re-armed, he rode back in triumph as the "new Elvis," now transformed into the white-clad, sequined, high-collared stage denizen with whom we are so familiar through myriad emulators.

Andy discovered that Elvis was to do a series of shows at the Las Vegas Hilton, then the flagship of the chain and one of the biggest houses in Vegas. Having formulated the outline of a plan, and inspired by Jack Kerouac's classic, *On the Road*, Andy gathered up his looseleaf Elvis opus and hit the asphalt. On foot. From Great Neck, Long Island, twenty-year-old Andy Kaufman began hitchhiking the twenty-five-hundred-some miles to his destiny with the greatest entertainer in the history of the world. Within a week he was entering the outskirts of America's Gomorrah. By that time, Andy didn't even have money for food, let alone a ticket to Elvis's show. So he improvised.

The Vegas Hilton was a huge scurrying anthill, and within a few hours of arriving, Andy had ingratiated himself with the staff and determined that Elvis was indeed going to perform that evening, and that when he did he would pass through the kitchen on the way to the stage. A service elevator that opened directly to Elvis's penthouse came down to the kitchen, and by using it he would avoid his fans and achieve the quickest access to the stage.

Andy found a small, rarely used walk-in storage cupboard and decided it would be his command center. After scrounging a few leftovers and an empty coffee can for disposal of his bodily excretions, he slipped into the closet and left the door cracked just enough to spot Elvis, or at least to hear any commotion. Like a wild animal burrowing into a den to await its prey, Andy hunkered down and mentally prepared himself for his close encounter. More than eight hours would pass while Andy sat patiently, the Book of Elvis clutched to his chest, his eyes wide in expectation.

Finally it happened. Across the vast kitchen Andy was jarred from a transcendental reverie by an event: Elvis had left the penthouse . . . and was entering the kitchen. Andy leaped to his feet and prepared himself like a trap-door spider. Peering through the cracked door, suddenly he saw him, in the flesh: the man, the god, that son of Mississippi, Elvis Aaron Presley. Despite his TM discipline, Andy's heart raced as Elvis advanced on his position, flanked by the preeminent members of the Memphis Mafia, his bodyguards Red and Sonny, the burly West brothers.

Just as E and his coterie reached ground zero, the cupboard door flew open, and this wild-eyed, bush-haired kid popped out, thrusting what looked like a very thick subpoena at Elvis. Red and Sonny instinctively moved to shield their monarch and overwhelm the threat, but something about Andy caused Elvis to stop them.

"Whoa, whoa, boys," E said, staying any mayhem to the kid — after all, he looked harmless, and this was before stalkers turned pro . . . and psychotic.

His manuscript held out in supplication, Andy summoned the guts to speak to his bespangled deity. "Elvis, I'm your biggest fan. I wrote this book about you."

Elvis nodded approvingly. "That's good, that's very good."

As he now seemed to have Elvis's attention, however fleeting, Andy was pumped up enough to impart to Elvis the sentence he had traveled across the country to utter. "I'm going to be famous, too," he said confidently.

The King paused to regard him for a second, then uttered the blessing Andy so desperately sought: "I'm sure you will." And with that, Elvis reached out and gently patted Andy on the shoulder.

Then E continued on, a great white shark surrounded by pilot fish. The encounter had lasted all of twenty seconds, but for Andy it was timeless. Though it was over, he just stood there, still in the grip of its implications, his eyes wide, his feet unmoving. Elvis had already ascended the stage before Andy shuffled away, his book undelivered. But that was unimportant. Andy had received The Blessing. All other considerations were secondary. The moment had been perfect, with Andy saying exactly what he wanted to say, and with the King responding exactly as Andy had imagined he would. It was a defining moment for Andy, perhaps the single most motivating one of his life. He was now ready to become something, and though he wasn't sure what, it didn't matter: the King had looked into his eyes and acknowledged him and had transferred a seed of greatness to Andy. Now Andy needed only to cultivate it.

While Andy began developing his stage presentation back in New York, I enrolled at Chicago's Northeastern Illinois University. Imbued with the defiance I had inherited through experiences with fellow radicals and battles with the police, my scholastic career was oriented toward learning and protest, with the accent on the latter. While taking a literature test one day, I borrowed from my encounter with Abbie Hoffman and adapted a quote I had gleaned from his book *Steal This Book*. In keeping with the spirit of Abbie's command, I had actually stolen the book and then proceeded to read and practice his writings. When the professor innocently asked the question "What is art?" I audaciously penned, "Art is anything you can get away with, for example, 'fuck you' is art if I say it is."

My cynicism and zeal to emulate Mr. Hoffman, coupled with previous antisocial offenses, gave me two choices: leave the school permanently, or volunteer for a work-study program in the bosom of Appalachia. Quitting would have been a cop-out, so with the blessing of my school I journeyed to Pikeville, Kentucky.

Dubbed the All-American city by the local chamber of commerce, Pikeville was a sleepy little town surrounded by even sleepier little towns such as Raccoon, Hi-Hat, and Beaver. A stronghold for "Christian" values, it was a place where men called each other "neighbor" and women often referred to their cousins as "my husband." Pikeville had not yet made it into the '60s, even though it was almost 1970, and when I arrived at Pikeville College, to my horror I was told that when a few professors had protested "the war" the students had had them bodily removed. I had entered a place where the mind-set was One thought fits all. . . . Stepford with inbreeding.

I settled into life in Pikeville, and, for a while, all went well. I submerged the rebel and searched for my inner Barney Fife. Though my volunteer work at the college was only tolerable, I received new inspiration when I met a beautiful brunette, a fellow volunteer named Brenda Oyer, and we began dating. I took a part-time job at a local radio station, and Brenda and I started discussing a future together, outside Pikeville. Our best options were to head back to Chicago or to go on to Brenda's hometown of Pittsburgh, but Brenda was unsure when we should actually leave Pikeville. I'd determined that Pikeville was no longer in my game plan, so I hatched a plot to hasten her decision.

Christmas was just around the corner, and the people at the local radio station had dropped their guard and begun letting me do live spots. I had created a character named Winny the elf who, in consort with my blustering Santa Claus, exhorted children to patronize the local toy store. But I became sick of constantly deceiving the children of Pikeville in order to induce them to mindlessly line the pockets of our sponsor. So one day I arrived ready to free Winny, Santa, and the youth of eastern Kentucky from the shackles of rampant consumerism. I opened my microphone and, instead of sweetly heralding the arrival of Santa, Winny the elf shrieked, "Boys and girls, bad news! This is terrible! Santa's dead!" I was halfway out the door as the switchboard lit up like a Christmas tree.

Later that day, on the way to Chicago, I proposed to Brenda.

In Chicago I went back to school. After a year or so, Brenda and I decided to head to Pittsburgh. Once we settled in, Brenda's sister Janet sized up my subversive attitude and suggested an outlet for my energy: the drama department at Carnegie-Mellon University, one of the most prestigious acting schools in the country. I auditioned, was accepted, and soon the acting bug had seriously infected me. Rubbing elbows with fellow students Ted Danson and Judith Light, I thoroughly enjoyed the experience and began visualizing an acting career. Responding to a bulletin-board flyer announcing a summer-stock gig in Mansfield, Pennsylvania, I auditioned for and got the part of the villain in *The Drunkard*.

After a particularly artistic rendering one evening, another cast member, a guy I didn't know all that well named Chris Albrecht, approached me with the tip that a very cute girl in the audience had been particularly taken with my performance. Despite the fact that I was married, I was an *actor* first and foremost, so I approached her at the after-show party, empowered with the knowledge that I was doing my duty to my public. When she vigorously blew me off I knew I'd been had. Given the choice between punching Albrecht's lights out and laughing with him, I chose the latter. It was a good decision, as we became very close friends.

Chris and I talked a lot about acting. Eventually the subject all *real* actors discuss in their careers came up: when do we move to New York? Brenda would not endure the chaos of the Big Apple, so she and I parted, at least temporarily. It was a tough decision, but I knew that my destiny lay in New York, so I reluctantly said good-bye and rendezvoused with Chris in New York to assault the acting world.

By late 1972, Andy had become the cause célèbre of the New York comedy-club scene as the vanguard of new comics arrived. The year before, Andy's uncle Sam Denoff, a very successful television writer and producer, had introduced Andy to Carl Reiner. Thoroughly impressed, Reiner recommended Andy to his nephew and manager, George Shapiro. George saw Andy's potential and helped him gain a foothold in the burgeoning world of club comedy. Though the clubs didn't pay back then, they were great places to receive exposure if one hoped to move up to paying gigs or even television. Every night, Andy would borrow his dad's car and shuttle between the two main venues, Budd Friedman's the Improv and Rick Newman's Catch a Rising Star. Andy's act was impossible to categorize. Though agents and managers all desperately wanted him, they just didn't know what to do with him. Imagine a man coming out on stage, eating a bowl of potatoes, then climbing into a sleeping bag and snoozing while an alarm clock ticks down. No one had ever seen such an act, and incredulous audiences laughed constantly for the twenty minutes until the bell rang.

Some described Andy's presentations as performance art before the genre even existed. Some were reminded of the late comic genius Ernie Kovacs, but, still, Andy was too edgy, too unusual to permit definition. Despite the local acclaim, Andy could not even afford to buy his own beers, let alone his dream beer-tap system. But the growing perception of him as a comic "artist" was compensation enough.

Andy came to be known as a comedian, a categorization he would grow to hate, as he felt it didn't begin to express the depth of his talents or the breadth of his vision as an artist. Though

Andy would have accepted "con man" or even "bullshit artist" over "comedian," he preferred to think of himself as a song-and-dance man. But the young "comic's" evolving act encompassed a blend of the real and the unreal, often woven into a demonstration where some or all of what the audience witnessed did not occur. While the other stand-ups were simply telling jokes, Andy created a whole world for his audience — a world they were frequently unsure of. Andy was honing the birth of what I call Kaufmanism, his original interpretation of smoke and mirrors.

Unfortunately for the acting team of Albrecht and Zmuda, the light of stardom did not shine in time to save us from squandering our savings as well as from losing our apartment. Soon we were starving and homeless, which was the real, unglamourous introduction to the entertainment business that most people don't talk about. Luckily, Chris and I weren't on the streets for long, as a kingly gentleman named Dick Scanga offered us a tiny salary and lodging in the back of his Upper East Side theater. Dick was not only best friends with actor Chuck Grodin but also the proprietor of the Little Hippodrome, New York City's first dinner theater.

Dick's notion was that since Broadway shows were expensive and usually preceded by dinner, a thrifty combo would be just the ticket for budget-minded seekers of live culture. Unfortunately for Dick, New York theatergoers considered themselves far too sophisticated for such "packaged entertainment," and his big experiment was Hoovering up his life savings at an alarming rate. But Dick's financial dilemma was the furthest thing from our minds, ensconced as we were in his actors' dressing rooms in exchange for light duties around the place such as cooking, cleaning, and table waiting. Dick's only stipulation was that we have our sleeping bags out of the way by the time his thespians arrived at 7 P.M.

The clockwork torture of every audition becoming another personal rejection was beginning to take its toll on us. One night after getting bumped from our rooms by Dick's slightly less starving actors, Chris and I went separate ways to find a little solace from the lowest-rung-on-the-food-chain existence that had become our lives. Dazed and feeling sorry for myself, I took a left on 44th Street instead of my usual right. A moment later I was staring at the facade of the Improvisation, or the Improv, as it would become shorthanded, the first comedy club in America. I had a couple of bucks in my pocket (thanks to Dick), so I paid the two-drink minimum and went inside. I didn't know it at the time, but my entry into that club was no less significant than had I been riding into Virginia City, Nevada, in 1849, at the start of the gold rush. But now it was 1973, and within the next few years a comedy rush would take place, with the Improvisation as Main Street, Virginia City.

2

A Foreign Man

It wasn't an act, it was a happening.
CARL REINER

As I cozied up to my vodka that night, I watched an array of young, talented unknowns named Jay Leno, Richard Lewis, Elayne Boosler, Joe Piscopo, Richard Belzer, and Larry David take the Improv's stage. (Larry would later co-create, write, and produce a little show called *Seinfeld*.) During breaks between acts, a shaggy-haired young foreigner could be heard from the back of the room begging, then demanding, that Budd Friedman let him on the stage. The strange young man with the odd accent got the attention of everyone in the packed house as he and Friedman went back and forth about his being permitted on-stage. I didn't know Budd Friedman, but I thought he was being overly patient with this sad loser.

Finally, near the end of the evening, after numerous noisy discussions between Friedman and the weirdo, the club owner threw up his hands and relented. Taking the microphone, he announced, "Ladies and gentlemen, please put your hands together and welcome a visitor from afar, Mr. Andy Kaufman."

I didn't know much about comedy clubs, but I did know that going last was an honor. Still, this kook with the thick, unplaced accent had begged his way on as the closing act. The volleys between Budd Friedman and this guy were themselves worth the price of admission. I also remembered the law of the street for comedians and aspiring actors: pushiness works. I, along with the rest of the audience, sat back and waited for the schnook to bomb.

It didn't take long. Walking out into the spotlight, this goofy guy with eyes wider than the Hudson began with a few extremely lame impressions, or "emetations," as he called them. He started with Archie Bunker, slid into Ed Sullivan, and finished with our president, Tricky Dick Nixon. Even though each "emetation" was worse than the previous one, he emitted a rough charisma that began to grow on me. But despite that, the guy's sorry impressions, exacerbated by his indefinable accent, made me figure Friedman would be reaching for the hook in about two seconds. To my surprise, he didn't, and the man continued with his hopelessly amateurish act, a routine I was beginning to think he'd practiced only slightly in the cabarets of Budapest or Prague.

As his "act" painfully continued, some of the audience could not contain themselves and began snorting. They were not laughing with him, they were laughing at him. Some of the more sensitive shot the laughers disapproving glances, embarrassed by the discomfort this poor yutz had visited on himself and now the congregation. When he announced he was going to do "de Elbis Presley" there was a collective groan from the house. Given this was 1973, years before Elvis impersonations would be in vogue, nobody gave a rat's ass about Elvis. I looked to Budd Friedman in the back, expecting him to rush forward to put this bonehead out of our misery, but he just stood there, arms crossed, calmly awaiting the train wreck.

This poor Iron Curtain comedian then fumbled around in a tired little valise, found a comb, and began raking his hair into an Elvis coif. He reached back in and pulled out some props. He combed his hair again. I had been trying to suppress a laugh, for fear of hurting his feelings, but now I couldn't help it: amazingly, this guy was making the act of combing his hair *funny*. I started to pull for him at this point, excited that he'd managed to get the audience laughing *with* him. Suddenly the house lights went down and a single follow-spot illuminated the man on stage. The organized theatrics of that one light instantly indicated that perhaps all was not what it appeared to be.

After a few more hair combs — just enough to whip the crowd into a laughing frenzy — this weird young foreigner began an amazing transformation. Accompanied by the strains of Strauss's famous opening from the movie *2001: A Space Odyssey*, he donned a spangled jacket, popped up the generous collar, hefted an acoustic guitar, and I was damned if he wasn't starting to really look like Elvis. Then he curled his lip in that perfect Elvisian arc, and the crowd screamed.

I was asking myself, *Who the fuck is this guy?* when I sensed that we all may have been had. The classical music segued into a rock 'n' roll riff and he launched into a stage strut in that patented Elvis prowl. It seemed as if the very act of stalking back and forth and bowing repeatedly in such brilliant mimicry was actually conjuring some sort of "Elvis life force" out of the ether. After a few circuits across the stage, arms flourishing in some air karate and those commanding eyes leveled on us, he grabbed the microphone and spoke. But this time, the poor foreign soul, the cringing little man we had admired and mocked for having the guts to stand before us, was gone. The voice was now rich, sultry . . . and from the Deep South, as in America.

"Thank yeh verra much . . . you can just stare at me while ah catch mah breath."

My jaw dropped. This was no impression, this *was* Elvis. Then, as the trademark lip twitch went out of control, he deadpanned, "There's somethin' wrong with mah lip." That brought a big laugh, partly because it was funny, but probably more so because we were all still in shock. I was satisfied that this was pretty impressive — that his tribute to Elvis was good even if he wasn't *really* going to sing — so what happened next blew my mind.

Suddenly lights began to flash, and he launched into "Treat Me Like a Fool." He was actually singing instead of lip-synching, and he was great. He followed that first number with a killer rendition of "Jailhouse Rock" that brought the house down. At the end of the act, this person, whoever or whatever he was — I still wasn't sure — nodded politely, eyes agog, and said, "Dank you veddy much."

He walked off the stage, and everyone else in the place went nuts. Budd Friedman leaped to the stage and proudly announced, "That was Andy Kaufman, ladies and gentlemen, Andy Kaufman!" I just sat there, stunned, unable to clap, blink, or even close my mouth. I had just seen Andy Kaufman for the first time, and the experience was dizzying. Taking my drink, I moved to the back to see if I could get another glimpse of this man. He eventually appeared from the back room and I overheard him speaking to Budd Friedman in — you got it — that foreign accent. By now I was really curious and confused: Was that foreign accent for real? I followed him outside and watched as he started loading props into his car. He noticed me and stopped.

"Please," he said in that accent, "my beck is very hurting. Ken you help me?"

I walked over and noticed that he had a pile of items, apparently from another show. "This is it?"

"No," he said, "there is a bit more. Inside."

I followed him backstage and was confronted by a mountain of props: a 16-millimeter projector and screen, a record player, two huge congas and their stands, a set of cymbals, and assorted suitcases bursting with props and costumes. I quickly realized that whether or not this guy was from Bucharest, he obviously hadn't started doing this last week. "Man, you sure have a shitload of stuff," I noted.

He looked at me quizzically. "Shipload? I came on ship, yes."

"No . . . oh, forget it," I said, giving up, still unsure of him.

"You help?" he asked again.

I picked up the congas and groaned, "Yeah, I'll help."

About twenty minutes later I had moved everything into his car, and he hadn't touched a thing. He had rubbed his back the entire time while complaining about the enormous pain he was suffering. My back hurt now, yet he went to the driver's door without even a handshake. He smiled blankly. "Dank you veddy much."

"You're welcome," I said, rubbing my sore back.

Then his face changed completely, as if he had become another person altogether, and he said gruffly with a sneer, sans accent, "Sucker!" as he proceeded to leap into the car and drive away. The exhaust fumes boiled around me. I couldn't believe this asshole. I was shocked and absolutely pissed . . . for about five seconds. Then I started laughing. I laughed all the way back to my dinner theater/homeless-actor's shelter. I sat down with Chris and looked him in the eye. "Forget acting. I've seen the future, and it is comedy."

I spent the next hour telling him about my encounter with the very, very strange, very wonderful Andy Kaufman. After we talked all that evening and into the wee hours of the morning, Chris and I decided to abandon our careers as actors and embark on a new direction as comedians. We were excited, and we were ready to go. The only drawback was a large one, but we were young and it didn't seem insurmountable: we had no act. Details, details. We'd start in the morning.

Despite being foreigners to comedy, I wrote an act and we began to rehearse it. We scammed a photo session and had some eight-by-ten-inch glossies printed with the proclamation: "Albrecht & Zmuda, Comedy from A to Z." It was a pretty bold claim given we might have had A and B; unfortunately C through Z were not yet in our repertoire. But we were as motivated as we were broke, spurred by the notion that other comedians were getting their own shows left and right. Freddie Prinze had just made the deal for *Chico and the Man*, Jimmie Walker had made one for *Good Times*, and Gabe Kaplan was only a year away from anchoring *Welcome Back, Kotter*. All of them would go to the majors by way of that farm club called the Improv.

Chris and I figured Freddie Prinze was young: How much time could he have put in before he made it? His deadpan delivery and shtick as a "Hunga-rican" was funny, but we absolutely *knew* we could do just as well. What we needed now, almost more than an act, was exposure. And we knew there was only one place to get it. Getting in there would require cunning, perfect timing, and above all, masterful deception.

Budd Friedman had heard of our dinner theater, and we knew he'd expressed interest in getting into off-Broadway productions, as a backup in case his comedy venture failed. At that time he didn't know what he had. But given Budd's aspirations to branch out, we thought he might be interested in getting to know some guys who might be able to "help him" get into staging productions. Meanwhile, Dick owed us some money, so we threw a scheme at Dick in return for settling our wages, and he went for it.

The next day, Chris and I went to the Improvisation and casually approached Budd Friedman to invite him, as "a fellow club owner," for dinner at our little establishment. Budd readily accepted, and a few nights later we hosted him at "our club." Win-ing and dining him as an equal was a change from most evenings, when we'd be busing that table. We so impressed him with our wit and style that he had become our new best friend by the time the after-dinner drinks came. We toasted, and as I swirled the liqueur in my glass, almost as an afterthought I spoke the sentence the entire evening had really been centered on. "You know, Chris and I have an act."

"Really?" said Budd. "What do you do?"

"Oh, it's just a little comedy thing. But it's pretty good," said Chris demurely.

"No kidding," said Budd. "Well, I'd love to see it. Why don't we book you some night?"

Chris and I looked at each other and shrugged. Attempting to look cool, *almost* uninterested, I nearly snapped the stem off my glass. "Sure, okay, why not?" I replied.

We apparently did a hell of a job on Budd, as we were immediately given a top spot in the club's lineup, sight unseen. Experienced comics can tailor their act to fit a bill, but the foundation of working stand-ups is what is called their tight twenty, twenty minutes of their best stuff, relentlessly honed material guaranteed to level any audience. "Albrecht & Zmuda, Comedy from A to Z" consisted of a tight twenty all right — twenty seconds. And it took Budd about that long to figure out we were masters of bullshit, not stage comedy. But instead of banishing us for our deceit, he admired our pluck and craftiness and welcomed us into the Improv family. Budd was becoming more and more involved in opening the Improv West in Los Angeles and soon made Chris the New York club's night manager while I continued to cook, clean, and schlepp at the Little Hippodrome.

Finally, poor Dick Scanga's dream of bringing dining and acting to New Yorkers in one package failed, and, though I still had shelter, I was out of work. Meanwhile, Chris had made many contacts at the club.

"I've got a job for you," he said. "You're not going to believe this, but it's true. This job is unbelievable."

"You know what they say: If it sounds too good to be true . . ." I said.

Chris shook his head. "I know, I know, but this job, this is for real."

What I am about to tell you may initially appear to be a sidetrack to my story about Andy Kaufman, but the nature of the man you are about to meet, and the events that transpired around him, not only had a direct bearing on bringing me and Andy together, but also had a strong influence on much of the comedy we would go on to create. I must warn you that I will refer to this man only as, let's say, Mr. X or simply X. I have a strong motivation to do so: I believe that Mr. X is still alive, and, even now, more than twenty-five years later, I continue to be terrified of him. If I were to use his real name he might come after me. Why? Because he is — without exaggeration — *completely fucking insane.*

"This gig pays two thousand bucks a week," Chris said matter-of-factly, "and you'll be working with one of the top screenwriters in the world, this guy has Academy Awards."

My reality was *thirty* dollars a week, so my hearing stopped functioning after the word "week." "Two thousand?" I repeated, thinking Albrecht had gone over the top in his cruelty. I searched his eyes for evidence of deception.

"I'm not shitting you, Zmuda. This guy needs an assistant. That's where you come in. You'll learn how to write movies while making two grand a week."

"You're making this up, you're fucking with me."

"No, I'm not," he insisted. "This is one hundred percent on the level. The guy's name is Mr. X."

Chris then rattled off a partial filmography of my savior that included only big movies. I was beginning to believe him. But then again, that's when you sink the knife with a good put-on.

"Is this legal?" I asked, assuming this was the deal killer.

"Totally. He'll be at the Improv tomorrow afternoon. I want you to come down and meet him. He's a little eccentric, but you'll be fine with him."

That last sentence should have been a red flag, but I was so dazzled by the prospect of making two thousand dollars a week that I couldn't think straight. In those days you could buy a brand-new luxury car for less than ten thousand, so this was big money. Especially for a guy who had been putting thirty clams in his pocket every week.

The next day, a Wednesday, I nervously arrived at the Improv a few minutes before my two o'clock appointment. The main room was closed, but the bar was open. A few patrons were having cocktails and some employees were shuffling around getting ready for the evening crowd. I saw no one that looked like the guy who was going to lay out two large a week for "assistance."

A couple perched nearby chattered away, and off in the corner sat some poor homeless guy. I checked out the shabby old man because I was surprised Budd let him in, let alone gave him a drink. He was garbed in faded, filthy military-officer's attire, his hair was matted like foul dark moss, and his feet were naked and appeared to have been spray painted with black Rustoleum. I stole glances at this man, for he alternately fascinated and frightened me.

The bar clock was typically fast, but even taking that into account, by two-thirty I figured Mr. X was a no-show and that Albrecht had nailed me. Guerrilla comedy was wonderful but I was in no mood for it. Just as I was about to leave, Albrecht arrived. I assumed that cold son of a bitch was there to gloat over his latest coup.

"So, what do you think?" he asked innocently.

"I think you fucked me over," I responded bitterly. "Your guy never showed."

Chris looked genuinely perplexed. "What do you mean? That's him sitting right over there." He pointed at the homeless man with the Al Jolson feet. He ushered me over and the unsanitary man glanced up. At close range he looked even more soiled than from a distance. Then I noticed the solid-gold Rolex on his wrist. How could this be? This was the guy who was going to pull me out of the starving-artist funk? I reflexively extended my hand, despite being afraid to touch him. At this proximity I could smell him.

"Uh, hi. Mr. X? Hi, my name is —"

"Shut *the fuck up*, idiot! If you want this job you're going to have to learn to keep your fucking mouth *shut* for five fucking minutes! You think you can keep your fucking mouth shut for five fucking *minutes?* Do you think you could do that? That's number one."

His gravel voice assaulted me with the speed and force of lead from an Uzi. I detected Brooklyn but also some New England during his verbal onslaught. He was probably in his early fifties, but his egregious personal habits had added hard years to him. But also at this range I could see through the tarnish to the glint of brilliance in his eyes. He studied his expensive timepiece as I shut up, knowing that a word uttered here would end my chances with this madman.

After five minutes, Mr. X looked up at me. "What nationality are you?"

I decided a smart-ass answer like "American" wouldn't fly, but I figured the real answer would somehow lose me the gig as well. I gritted my teeth and told the truth. "Polish."

"You're Polish? You're hired. I always felt the reason the Nazis wanted to destroy the Poles is because the Poles were developing extraordinary powers of ESP."

Huh? I should have known what I was in for with that one sentence, but I didn't flee. Instead we walked out and climbed into a limo that had been idling at the curb all this time. X settled into the seat. "You're hired. Two thousand dollars a week, off the books, cold cash. You're paid at the end of each week. You'll assist me, and in the process I'll teach you how to write great screenplays."

Our first stop after leaving the Improv was a low-budget walk-up apartment. Mr. X and I went to the door and knocked. A peephole allowed the inhabitant to identify his visitors, and a second later we heard furniture being pushed against the door, as if to ward off vampires. "Go away, you fucking maniac!" came a frantic, muffled voice from within. "Leave me alone. I'll call the cops!" The man in the apartment and X argued through the door for a few moments, then we left. Two weeks passed before I found out that the terrorized man behind the door had been X's previous assistant.

As I got to know Mr. X, I noticed that he would often stutter during his staccato delivery, as if his mind's thesaurus were trying and rejecting words, as if when one word didn't carry enough bile or venom it would be discarded and replaced with the right combination of invective.

Mr. X was truly a great screenwriter with considerable accomplishments, but there was a secret to his success. As any writer can tell you, conflict is the essence of any good story. Though most writers create conflict either solely through their imaginations or by drawing upon and adapting actual life experiences, Mr. X went them one better. He would venture out daily to manufacture and electronically document real conflict and then immediately adapt the experience to whatever project he was writing. This sounds relatively safe until you discover that most of Mr. X's characters were in constant mortal danger. Ergo, Mr. X and, by default, I, his assistant, would be in that same danger of losing our lives.

My travels with Mr. X would begin in the morning (unless we drove around in marathon three- or four-day sessions, which did occur), when we would commute via limo to a luggage store. There I would purchase a cheap valise every day. Same store, same case. Every morning.

Then we moved on to the bank where we would withdraw somewhere between twenty and fifty *thousand* dollars in cash. The cash went into the valise. Same bank. Every day. Then it was on to the electronics store where I would buy three Panasonic battery-powered tape recorders. Same store, same three recorders, fresh batteries. Every day.

Into the three recorders I would place three tapes. One tape was of the music du jour, often Sousa or some march, sometimes rock, depending on X's mood. The next tape was blank, and I placed it into one of the recorders and punched the "record" button. The use of the third tape, containing the previous day's audio record, was the strangest. Mr. X required me to play it back, perfectly synchronized, to allow us to hear what had happened exactly twenty-four hours prior. He outfitted me with a complex array of watches, all set to different times, with which to keep track of the twenty-four-hour tape as well as when to change the other tapes. Once I dared ask, "Mr. X, why are we playing back what happened exactly twenty-four hours ago?"

X narrowed his eyes and shook his head as if dealing with the biggest dipshit in creation. "Because I want to know if my mind has grown in the last twenty-four hours, asshole." *If my mind has grown?* I knew then that I had fallen through the looking glass.

Thus would begin our days. With recorders slung over me as

if I were an overzealous street rapper, we would patrol the streets in the limo looking for excitement. And if we didn't find any, we created it. Often in our sorties, X would flag our driver to stop. X would then leap out and either urinate right in the street or rummage through a Dumpster for some discarded food, which he would then wolf down. His breath could have been classified a toxic weapon, and his body odor would have sent camels in retreat, but two grand bought a lot of patience from me, and I did my best to ignore the stench.

The end of our day would see us at the banks of either the East or Hudson Rivers — whichever was closer — whereupon I would remove the tapes from the machines for safekeeping, climb out of the limo, and hurl the recorders and empty money-carrying case into the water. Occasionally we would give the items to kids on the street, but usually they would become reef fill. Early on I asked, "X, why do we throw these away? They're perfectly good recorders. And the cases, too."

He would look at me with wild eyes and lower his voice, cognizant of an enormously dark fact to which he was about to make me privy. "Because you cannot tell if the CIA might be taping us, monitoring us through the equipment. I need to know it's virgin, that the government hasn't touched it." Tapping his temple with a finger, he added with a knowing nod, "With that stuff they could find out everything we're doing."

"But what about the cases? Why do we get new ones every day?" I said, hoping to save us from one of our errands. "Couldn't we at least stick with one?"

Mr. X leaned forward shaking his head and whispered, "Fingerprints."

I thought, *Yeah, sure, why didn't I think of that?* I kept visualizing that $2K a week in my hands. *I can do this, I can do this . . .*

X and I obtained the large volumes of cash every morning for two reasons. One was strictly out of necessity. He offended so many people that I was constantly being commanded "Zmuda, the case," whereupon I would pop open the money case and either X or I would then dole out varying amounts to salve the injuries we'd caused. But more on that in a moment.

The second reason was more complex. Mr. X was a brilliant writer, in demand not only for his original screenplays but also for his "script-doctoring" abilities. A script doctor is a Hollywood phenomenon, a writer who gets paid more than any real doctor to polish, punch up, or rework screenplays. The job is far more lucrative than the job of physician because there's far more on the line than mere human life — big bucks are at stake. Though he had not won an Oscar as Chris had claimed, he'd been nominated and was considered one of the best. Mr. X was highly sought after because his dialogue had that stunningly edgy taste of reality.

Well, no shit — he had suckers like me recording it.

But Mr. X had problems with his chosen career. He hated it. Here was a man who literally ate garbage, had seen neither a comb nor deodorant in eons, and loathed spinning off the words that made him millions. Consequently, he needed incentive. Many could find it in the huge paychecks alone, but X needed more of an edge, needed to risk oblivion, needed to keep himself off balance. That's why he spent money as fast as or faster than he made it, to give himself a very powerful reason to want to make more. As I said, the man was unquestionably nuts.

In addition to being the keeper of the recorders, I carried in my right breast pocket a tape, which Mr. X had given me explicit instructions on using. I also carried a manila envelope that was never to be separated from the tape. In the event of his arrest or impending arrest he planned to yell, "Catch-22, Zmuda!" and I was to carefully remove the tape from my pocket, insert it in the music machine, play it at high volume, and then follow its instructions. Mr. X was very serious about the catch-22 tape and frequently asked me if it was safe. I was dying to know what the tape and the envelope contained.

A few days into my new job, Mr. X and I were cruising the streets of a particularly tough upper-Manhattan neighborhood. Though the temperature was probably about fifteen degrees, the high humidity made it seem like fifteen below. X liked to hear the sounds of the streets, so he rolled our windows down. In about two minutes the light snowfall had dusted the interior of the limo like a powdered donut, and I had frost on my face and could no longer feel my hands. We used a limo service and thus often had different drivers. Mr. X noticed that our driver — a newcomer to *mondo* X who was shut off from us by the protective partition — had his windows up and the heater on. "Hey," X barked though the glass, "open your fucking windows! I am paying, man, and I want those windows *open!*"

The driver timidly looked in his rearview mirror at Mr. X. "Sir, I don't want to get cold. It's way below freezing."

X gestured to me. "Zmuda! Open the case!"

I had been through this routine a few times and knew what to do. I twirled the small case on my lap to face Mr. X, snapped it open, and exposed the stacks of cash. He reached in and pulled out some bills. "Open the glass," he commanded, *"and shut that heater off!"*

The guy noticed the cash and went for the button. The glass slid down a few inches. X tossed a couple of hundreds forward. The driver saw them but still protested. "But sir, really, it's awful cold out." He wasn't negotiating, rather just voicing his thoughts, not knowing what, or whom, he was up against. X tossed a few more hundreds over the seat and directed, "Open your windows all the way."

The guy looked at those four or five portraits of Ben Franklin staring back at him from the seat and dutifully rolled down his windows. And so it was with Mr. X. He was an insane, mobile Monty Hall, and I was Jay, always ready with a prop or cash, prepared to show enraged citizens what was behind door number two before they could kill us.

One day Mr. X spotted an art gallery in the Village and ordered us to a halt. He was far less interested in the art than he was in the young lady in the window attending the gallery. She was eighteen or nineteen and very pretty. One thing I haven't yet mentioned was that Mr. X's libido was almost as powerful as his madness. Many hours of our day were spent pursuing women for Mr. X or visiting the haunts of various streetwalkers or prostitutes. But this young gallery attendant was as pure as driven snow, and Mr. X reveled in that.

"I want some artwork," he announced as we walked in. He pointed. "That one, that one, and that one." The pretty young thing's eyes widened as Mr. X turned and gestured at another wall. "And those, too." Like most of our victims, the girl was taken aback by what fairly appeared to be a disturbed mendicant in a tattered uniform of obscure origin, so X snapped his fingers. "Zmuda! The case!"

Money doesn't talk, it screams.

I stepped forward and flipped open the money bag. "How much?" I asked.

The girl totaled the damages and couldn't believe the adding-machine tape. "Uh, the whole thing comes to, uh, fifteen thousand dollars," she said, dumbfounded by circumstances. I was thinking that a good day for her would have been two or three hundred, so this kid had hit the jackpot. I counted out the money. X then looked at me to make sure I was in recorder range and sidled up to her.

"Okay, honey, this one last thing," he said, as I braced for impact. "I want you to suck my cock now."

The girl went bleach white. "What?"

"Come on," he said. "All these struggling artists here? I've just spent fifteen thousand dollars on this shit, and I want you to suck my cock as a gratuity."

"But I . . . ," said the deer in the headlights.

"Look, honey," he rasped, "you think people are gonna buy this shit? Nobody is gonna buy this shit. I will buy it, I am paying you fifteen thousand dollars, but I need you to suck my cock, and now."

"Get out of here, right now!" she screamed. "Or I'll call the police!"

Now the girl was in tears and reaching for the phone, but X pressed his case. "You are a fucking idiot," he railed. "Do you know how hard these fucking artists worked to create this shit, and you are too selfish to help them out? All you had to do was take my fucking old cock and put it in your mouth and that's it."

The girl was now conversing with the police, so I closed the money case. Without further ado we quietly retreated to the limo.

Many of our encounters were like that: someone was pushed to the breaking point, I opened the case, and the money healed all wounds. Sometimes. The art gallery was one of the few times it didn't work. Another time happened a few days later. This incident almost got us killed, and all the money in the world wasn't going to save us.

We cruised down to Little Italy, which, as the name implies, is a bastion of the Italian-American community. It is also the favored haunt of many of those particular Italians who find the legal structure of our country an intolerance. X apparently had a plan that day, because we went directly to a small, neighborhood Italian restaurant that, despite a Closed sign in the window, had a crowd inside and people arriving in the parking lot. It was a birthday party for some Mafia capo's elderly mother. How X found this out I do not know, but as we prepared to go in he handed me a case in addition to the money case, this one containing miscellaneous oddities such as tabloid newspapers, pornographic magazines, and sexual devices like dildos and rotating butt-plugs. You know, the usual.

Mr. X and I went to the door, where a big goombah stopped us. "We're invited," said X brusquely. That was good enough for the doorman, and we entered. Spotting the guest of honor, a frail little lady obviously celebrating something north of her eightieth birthday, we approached just as she blew out the conflagration on her cake.

Mafia guys are often fat bastards, but they pride themselves on their appearance, particularly their hair. That's probably why all eyes turned to us as we walked up to Grandma Corleone. Mr. X's hair looked like something that had accumulated during a manufacturing process, and I was conspicuous with three tape recorders slung from my neck and shoulders. X reached into the variety case and pulled out a tear sheet from a tabloid, which featured several photos and a lurid headline. The photos included autopsy shots of Jack Kennedy, a frame from the Zapruder film of Kennedy taking a hit, and a group of beefy Mafia guys milling around. The headline declared: "Mafia Assassinates JFK!"

In the split second that I glimpsed the headline, I knew X was committing suicide and was taking me with him. Before I could do anything, he thrust the clipping in the face of the poor old Mob matriarch and screeched, "Hey, ma, look what your son has been doing!" Well, needless to say, she burst into tears, and we were hastily shown to the back room by a dozen raging Cosa Nostra hoods whose only concern at this point was who would get the pleasure of whacking us.

With four or five guns trained on our heads, one of the guys confronted Mr. X. "Are you fucking nuts, you fuckin' asshole? Insulting my mother? On her fucking birthday?" He made a gesture, and his henchmen knelt us down. I did the only thing that came naturally at that point: I started crying. And I thought fast . . . real fast.

"This guy's crazy. He wants to die," I said, whimpering. "His mother died yesterday and he wants you to kill him. He's so sick with grief he wants you to just kill him. That's why he came here!" Sizing up the desperation of the situation, I felt it was the only explanation that might get us any sympathy. It did. After a moment or two of deliberation, those fat bastards with the impeccable hair shoved us out the back door. We went to the limo, my hands shaking as if I had palsy. In contrast to my near-death shock, Mr. X was as cool as a cucumber. "You fucked up, Zmuda," he said. "You should have let it go on some more. We were getting great stuff on tape!"

I had never talked back to the man, but two weeks of this was getting to me. "If I hadn't said anything, we'd be dead right now."

"Maybe you're right," he agreed. "Maybe so." There was an almost calm look to this lunatic that told me this had likely been a trial run at suicide.

As far as the actual value of our commando missions, Mr. X would send the recorded tapes to a transcription service that would return them three days later, neatly typed up. He would then take that material and work it into whatever script he was writing at that time. It was a form of method writing that was apparently effective, but it was offering the very real possibility of shortening my life. I had been receiving the two grand a week as promised, but given the extreme element of danger involved, coupled with the nearly limitless stashes of cash in my hands every day, I began to make unauthorized withdrawals for hazard pay. Even though my compensation was reaching, or exceeding, four g's a week, you can't spend it if you're dead. I started to plan the moment of my resignation.

During the three weeks of "My Travels with Mr. X," I experienced the thrill of having guns and knives pulled on me and had my life threatened by everyone from bartenders, club owners, shopkeepers, and motorists, to men, women, and children. I had been deprived of sleep for days at a time as we cruised endlessly, looking for material for Mr. X, and I had been in a constant state of dire tension, like a soldier in combat, from the moment I had met him. I had reached the breaking point a few times, but on every occasion I had been able to reel it in and hold it together. Our trip to JFK airport would end that streak of tolerance.

Mr. X had decided that we would fly out of town on the spur of the moment, so we limoed out to lower Queens to catch a plane. The American Airlines ticket counter was packed with hundreds of people milling in half a dozen lines. Of course X went right to the head of one line and accosted a reservations agent.

"I want two first-class tickets to Minneapolis," he demanded. Why Minneapolis? Why not?

"Sir," said the woman behind the counter, "you'll have to wait your turn. Please get in line."

X tried for a moment to bully her, but it wouldn't work. He finally gave up, and we went back to wait with the multitude. Nervous that Mr. X had acquiesced too easily, I felt like a meteorologist who sees a tornado on his screen and just waits for someone to report it. I knew something bad was about to happen. I didn't have to wait long.

"I gotta take a shit," was X's simple declaration. Assuming that he had said that so I would hold our place, I turned after a moment to see that he had merely stepped out of line a few feet and had dropped his pants and squatted. I had seen pretty much everything in the previous three weeks, but this caused my mouth to fall open. There is a form of social denial in crowds when a person begins to act antisocially or in a very strange way: people tend to look the other way or stare impassively. Even when a woman is being raped or a man is having a heart attack, a sort of paralysis often overcomes people. They watch but do nothing.

So when this seedy, odoriferous psychopath hunkered down and began to void his bowels people looked on but pretended it wasn't really happening. I was absolutely stunned. Since Mr. X was constantly eating garbage, drinking to excess, and generally treating his system like a Nuclear Superfund Site, his waste material was not only foul, it was unholy. As if he were the Bhopal disaster, people in line began to flee his poisonous emanations, yet it was a child who finally said something, exactly as in "The Emperor's New Clothes." "Mommy," said the little girl, who had eyes bigger than the kids on one of those black velvet paintings, "that man is going poo-poo!"

Indeed he was. And as that sickening spray of noxious, loose stool issued forth, a woman screamed. Then another. My recorder recorded. Mr. X grunted. I winced.

Then the police arrived.

Realizing his compromised position, X screamed to me as he struggled to fend off two NYPD transit officers while hoisting his drawers back into position. "Zmuda, catch-22! Catch-22!"

Like a missile technician in a silo, I methodically removed the tape from my pocket and replaced the music tape with the catch-22 tape in the Sousa machine. Meanwhile, the officers were escorting Mr. X out the door, past the pool of putrefaction on the terrazzo, past the line of dumbstruck travelers. Once outside, I punched "play" and jacked up the volume.

"Officers, if you are listening to this tape, the man you are arresting is Mr. X, an Academy Award–nominated screenwriter and personal friend of mine. My name is . . ."

Well, I can't say whom the voice on the tape belonged to because it would give away who Mr. X really is. Or was. As I said, I'm not completely sure if he's dead or alive, so I'm not taking any chances. But suffice it to say, the voice on the tape commanded instant respect from the two law-enforcement officers. They paused to listen to the message.

"Assistant, please open the envelope . . ." As I quickly opened the manila envelope, the significance of the generic nature of the term "assistant" made me realize that X's turnover in help must be appalling.

". . . and take out the photo."

I removed a five-by-seven. It was a photo of Mr. X with his arm around the shoulder of the man on the tape. As did the two cops, I recognized him.

"Assistant, take out the article."

I pulled out a yellowed newspaper clipping showing Mr. X's photo and the headline announcing that he'd been nominated for an Oscar. Now that we'd established that he was who the tape claimed, the voice continued.

"Officers, you know me. I would consider it a personal favor if you do not arrest this man, my friend Mr. X."

As the cops pondered this, X waved at me. "Zmuda, the case!"

Now a seasoned commando, I whipped open the case and began distributing cash to the men, one, two, three, four hundred. . . . I counted out two or three grand each, and within seconds they not only were *not* mad they were joking with us and actually offering to escort us back inside. That was it. I cracked. As the cops walked off, I handed Mr. X his case of payoff dough, unslung my recorders, and, to his screaming protests, walked away. I was punchy from lack of sleep and feared either a nervous breakdown or a knife in my ribs. Hardly short of cash, I took a cab all the way back to Manhattan and went into hiding. And for the next month or two, I was the guy with the furniture piled up against the door.

3

A Guy Named Tony

*Andy was strangely psychological. He liked to lead you one way, then suddenly
turn the tables around and make you angry.*

DICK VAN DYKE

My exploits with Mr. X got around the Improv. It turns out I
have Mr. X to thank for my relationship with Andy Kaufman.
Though Andy was a huge hit at the Improv, he was so painfully
shy offstage that he had become a loner, speaking only to Budd
and sometimes the waitresses. He generally spoke to no one else,
not patrons, not fellow stand-ups, no one. But since Mr. X was a
regular at the club, stories of his exploits had gotten around. If
Andy wasn't outside, sitting in his dad's car and meditating, he
would sometimes sit alone at the end of the bar and eavesdrop as
people told Mr. X stories. The stories were all generally second-
hand or thirdhand unless I was talking.

Andy became increasingly fascinated by the tales of this
strange man and would pump the waitresses for tidbits. They all
told him to talk to me, because having survived Mr. X for three
weeks, I had become a sort of club legend. One night he approached me.

"Hey," he said. "Wanna do me a favor?"

"No. My back hurts," I deadpanned.

He laughed. "Sorry about that. No, I need to go over to Jersey to a club. I'm trying out a new character, and I need an audience plant."

We hopped in Andy's car. It became clear five minutes after
we left that he asked me along because he wanted to hear all

about Mr. X. It had been a few months since I'd quit, and as my fear of death by Mr. X had slightly diminished, I was starting to relish telling stories of my deranged former employer. Andy was transfixed, so much so that he missed his exit off the Jersey turnpike. He didn't care. We kept going. He had found his new role model: Mr. X.

Andy had experimented with controlling an audience through offbeat and even unpleasant routines, but for Andy, Mr. X took psychodrama to a new level, risking injury, even death. Andy was enthralled that such a man existed. And survived. Constantly pushing the envelope, always striving to break new ground, Andy's childhood fears had given way to the adult Andy's mastery of those trepidations. He had preserved the child, but he had taken his fears, which could hold him back, and corralled them, yet he kept the best of what that child had been. In many ways, Andy never grew up.

That night as we roamed Jersey looking for that club, Andy learned a lot about who I was, my guerrilla theater experiences, my days as a radical, even my flight from Pikeville, Kentucky, after proclaiming the demise of Santa. And with that, Andy began to understand how I'd managed to survive three weeks with Mr. X.

"What's your best Mr. X story?" he asked.

"I dunno, I think they're all good," I said.

"Well, yeah, I mean the story that really sums him up. But you've probably told me all of 'em, haven't you?" I could tell Andy had gotten hooked on the Mr. X stories. I also saw he was trying to understand Mr. X, to figure out what made him tick, so that maybe he could invest some of Mr. X in his own characters.

"I got one you haven't heard," I offered.

"What? What?" he said, sounding just like a little kid.

"The glazed-donut story. I tell you that one?"

"The glazed-donut story? No, no, tell me, I want to hear it."

"How close are we to this club?"

Andy shook his head. "Doesn't matter, we can be late. Besides, it's better to keep an audience waiting. Go on, tell me the glazed-donut story."

I sat back and looked out the window at the lights flitting by and pictured that day: sunny, a few puffy clouds, a generally nice day. Mr. X and I had picked up our cash that morning, nearly fifty grand. It was afternoon, and, as we hadn't even spent a dime yet, X was getting restless.

"We rolled over to Jersey one afternoon, midday maybe," I began.

"Like here? Somewhere around here?" Andy asked, trying to place the story.

"No, I think it was like North Bergen, Seacaucus maybe," I answered.

At this point in my story, Kaufman did something that was very unusual. Over the years I would see him do it hundreds of times, but this was the first. He was recording me, not on tape like Mr. X did, but in his mind. Possessing a truly photographic memory, his eyes would take on a wide, distant look, and then the tips of his fingers would twitch lightly as if he were typing on an invisible keyboard. Years later I would witness him memorizing entire *Taxi* scripts at one sitting using this technique. Not only committing his own lines to memory, but all the other characters' lines along with stage directions and page numbers. It was just like Dustin Hoffman's character, Raymond, in *Rain Man*. Oddly, Andy was somewhat embarrassed by this extraordinary ability and never flaunted it. I asked him once how he did it, thinking it was something he had learned in a TM course. Slightly flustered, he admitted that the ability came to him suddenly one day after a particularly bad LSD trip. He told me that he had also seen the future on that same trip. When I commented that that was great, he objected strongly, saying we're not supposed to see the future.

I continued with my tale. "Anyway, so we're in Jersey, drivin' along in the limo, and Mr. X sees this bakery, says, 'Driver, stop over here, I want a glazed donut.' So the driver pulls over, and we go inside for a glazed donut. Okay, so inside, it's midday and there's a few people in line, so X just blurts out, 'I want a glazed donut.' Well, everybody turns, there's some ladies shopping, and they look at him and then ignore him, so he goes, '*I want a glazed donut*,' real loud, like they're all just hard of hearing, and this woman behind the counter, her name badge said 'Flo' . . ."

"You're joking . . ." said Andy.

"No shit, 'Flo.' Anyway, Flo is matronly, an older woman, you know, kind of stern . . . so she says, 'Sir, you'll have to take a number like everyone else.'"

"You don't talk to him like that," added Andy, knowing enough about Mr. X.

"Exactly," I concurred. "But oddly, X doesn't say a word. He takes a ticket and quietly goes to the back of the line."

"Uh-oh," said Andy as he pulled the car over, readying for the story to go into overdrive.

"Yeah, 'uh-oh,'" I agreed and then continued. "So Mr. X waits, and finally he gets to Flo, and she says, 'Okay, now you want a glazed donut?' and X shakes his head. 'No, I've changed my mind. I want this here. And I want those, and that. And those over there, and all of that. Oh, and while you're at it I want those racks of bread back there. All of them.' And Flo narrows her eyes and says, 'Sir, please don't joke around. We're a business here.' And Mr. X yells, 'Zmuda? The case!' and I step forward and pop it open . . ."

"Like usual," Andy added, having heard Mr. X's "Zmuda, the case" line in other stories.

"Yeah, so I say, 'Madam, this man is Mr. X, a famous writer, he's written a number of major motion pictures, and he's a millionaire, he's very eccentric, and I can assure you he's completely serious. This case?' I point into the case, which is open showing all the cash. 'It has over fifty thousand dollars in it, and Mr. X is ready to pay for anything he wants, so please help him.' Well, Flo realizes this is probably for real, so even though she already hates him she starts ringing stuff up, and now the manager comes out of the back to see what the hell's going on. So Mr. X introduces himself while I'm lugging boxes of rolls and bread and shit out to the limo. We fill the limo, so X goes, 'Get on the phone and get a truck over here to pick up my baked goods.'"

"You hired a truck?" Andy said, his face going slack in amazement. "What? You just called a trucking company and said, 'Come over and pick up our donuts'?"

"Exactly. And they came, a full-size fucking delivery truck. Meanwhile, Mr. X's bought so much stuff we have to send for *an-other* truck. It's the Marx Brothers. We've hung out the Closed sign and cleaned out the whole front of the store. Now Mr. X goes into the back room. He starts buying all their back stock as well as shit coming out of the oven — it's still hot — not to mention all their butter and flour and salt and sugar, everything. Meanwhile, the owner, he's at his calculator, and he's in fuckin' hog heaven, he can't believe this guy, buying his place to the walls, damn near.

"So now Mr. X goes to work on the employees. First the bakers, there's like three older guys in white outfits, and he says to one of them, 'You must be pretty hot in that, it's hot back here. I'll tell you what, take off your clothes down to your underwear and I'll give you five hundred bucks. Zmuda, the case!' So I hand over the cash and the old guy strips down to his skivvies. Mr. X checks him out and says, 'Listen, for another five hundred, take off your underwear.' So the old guy drops his boxers, and he's bare-ass naked. So Mr. X turns to the others and says, 'I'll give you each a thousand if you do the same,' so two minutes later the bakers are nude, and X turns to the ladies who were working the counter and are now watching the old guys strut around naked but a thousand bucks richer. X says to them, 'Take off your clothes, only down to your underwear, and I'll give you a thousand each.' Well, they're in their underwear, bras and girdles, in about three seconds, and I'm handing them money. All of them except Flo, she's the holdout. Mr. X can't break her. She hates him. A test of wills. Flo versus Mr. X.

"Mr. X takes the challenge, he says, 'C'mon, Flo, just take off your blouse, leave your bra and girdle on, but take off the blouse. I'll give you two thousand dollars.' She says, 'I can't do that,' and X says, 'I'll make it three thousand,' and the other ladies are saying, 'Flo, do it, it's fine, it's just your blouse, it's okay,' 'cause they're standing in their girdles and bras and they're one grand richer. Mr. X ups the ante to four, then five. Now Flo's sweatin', the manager is yelling at her to drop her top, and her girlfriends are saying she's nuts. Mr. X keeps going until he finally says, 'Flo, lemme ask you this, what does your husband make in a year?' Flo won't answer, but one of the other ladies says Flo's husband, Alex, drives a delivery truck and makes about nineteen grand. So Mr. X says, 'Flo, take off your top only, leave your bra and girdle on, and I will give you nineteen thousand dollars. It's as much as Alex, your beloved husband, makes in a year. Think of his face when you bring home that cash.'

"Well, the scene is now insane. Here's the truck drivers load-ing our bread, the manager's delirious, looking for anything else to sell, here's three old men, nude, three or four older ladies in their underwear, and everyone is yelling at Flo to do it. Flo is in tears, but she stands firm. So Mr. X gets bored trying to break her and heads into the cooler, where he finds a wedding cake. 'I want this,' he says, and the manager goes white and says, 'Sorry, Mr. X, but that's a wedding cake, it's custom made, and I have to deliver it in a few hours, and they're a lovely couple.' And X says, 'I don't give a fuck, I want it. Zmuda? The case!' and I count out another three thousand, and it's ours now. Meanwhile, the bakers are still nude, and they're partying with the counter ladies on some beer we had delivered, and the manager is now about thirty thousand bucks heavier in the wallet, and he's on the phone to the wedding couple to tell them about the tragic accident on the freeway where their cake got ruined. And speaking of ruined, Flo is destroyed, her life could have changed, but she wouldn't cave in to the will of Mr. X. I say to him, 'What are we going to do with all the food?' and he says, 'Fuck it, let it rot,' so I get on the phone before we leave and have the truckers take it over to a food bank. So now we're done. X goes out and gets in the limo, and I make a final pass to survey the wreckage, the party is going full swing, and the place looks like it was looted by rats, not an edible thing left in sight, like it was never a working bakery. So I walk out the front, and as I do . . . that's when I see it. All by itself in the front display case, not even a crumb to keep it company, sits one . . . solitary . . . glazed donut."

Andy was totally mesmerized. "He's a genius," he pronounced finally, without irony.

In a very strange, upside-down universe, Andy might have been exactly right. Andy quietly started the car and pulled back out onto the road, still absorbing the impact of Mr. X's hostile takeover of the donut shop. It was Mr. X's totally sociopathic be-havior that transfixed him. Andy was fascinated by darkness, and Mr. X qualified to be if not the Prince, then at least the Duke of Darkness. He asked a few questions as we drove, but I could see that he had been deeply affected by the depth of depravity and the will it took to make such a commitment on the volition of one delayed donut. But we both understood that it wasn't the donut itself, it was the randomness of Mr. X's attack, touched off, like a drive-by shooting, by a wrong glance or a misunderstood gesture; spawned from inconsequence, it became epic because Mr. X willed it that way. We were like two Hamas terrorists who had never done anything bigger than a mailbox bombing discussing a guy who took down city blocks with hardly a thought.

We finally found the joint, and Andy parked about a block away.

"Why did you park so far off?" I asked.

Instead of answering he reached in the back seat and pulled forward a bag. "Look the other way," he said.

I turned and heard him assembling a costume. After a few minutes he spoke again. "Okay," he said, "you can turn around."

I looked at him, and Andy was gone. In his place was an apparition from the worst lounge on the lowest level of hell: he wore a really bad wig, sunglasses, and a mustache that Pancho Villa would have approved of. "What's your name?" the character asked sternly. The voice that came forth was most definitely *not* Andy Kaufman's.

"Bob," I answered, playing along, but impressed with the transformation.

"Bob? Bob? Bob, what's your last name?"

"Zmuda."

"Zmu-what?"

"Zmuda," I said patiently.

"Zmuda? What the hell kind of name is that?"

"Polish."

"Polish? Polish? Well, just 'cause you're Polish, don't think you're funny."

Still in character, he gave me instructions. "Go in the club and don't let on you know me. Understand, you stupid Polack? By the way, your name's Gorsky."

"Yeah, I understand. What about after the show? We meet back here?"

"Andy'll drive you home. You don't know me, understand?"

"Yeah, okay. So if Andy'll drive me home, who are you?"

He got out of the car and tossed me the keys. "I'm Tony Clifton, ass-wipe."

And with that, he walked off toward the club.

*　　*　　*

To my surprise, the club was not a comedy venue but rather a cozy Italian eatery with a small stage where a combo of middle-aged musicians played soft standards. I ordered a glass of Chianti and some garlic bread and prepared to wait. It didn't take long. No sooner had my bread arrived than a voice from offstage announced, "Ladies and gentlemen, tonight we are lucky to have the international singing sensation Tony Clifton in our midst." The voice was Andy, doing his best impression of a bad MC. "Folks, put your hands together and give Mr. Tony Clifton a warm welcome!"

The patrons set down their forks, wine glasses, and pizza slices and applauded softly. Tony Clifton took the stage. I had never seen Andy smoke cigarettes, yet Tony Clifton didn't have that inhibition. Lit butt in one hand, microphone in the other, Tony swaggered out, took a pull off the cigarette, then broke into an enthusiastic and marginally credible rendition of "Volare." Every once in a while he'd stop to take a drag and lose his place. I looked around and could see people starting to look up at him, and not in a good way. Finally, he lost track of the song completely, and his musical accompanists petered out.

"The hell with it," he said, taking a long pull off his smoke. "How you people doin'?"

One thing Tony Clifton demanded from the get-go was respect. When only a few polite murmurs were heard in response, he narrowed his eyes belligerently and bellowed in his thick, streetwise Brooklyn accent, *"I said, 'How the hell you all doin'?'"*

This approach brought slightly louder responses. There were probably sixty people in the house, and all eyes were suddenly riveted on Tony. He flipped cigarette ashes onto the floor and sized up the joint. "Let's get one thing straight, people. I don't need this. You know why? You wanna know why? 'Cause I'm used to playin' the big room in Vegas, not shitholes like this, you hear me? So here's the deal. You can be one of two things, a good audience or a bad audience. If you're a good audience, I'll work my tail off for you. If you're a bad audience, I'll walk right out of here, and you can have a strip show, for all I care."

Sixty-some pairs of eyes, including the owner's, his wife's, and their entire staff's, were wide open in shock. This was a nice little family place, and everyone had expected a pleasant, not-half-bad has-been to sing a few standards while they enjoyed their meals and discussed their humdrum little lives. What they got was a wolf in lizard's clothing — they got Tony Clifton.

He singled out an older man sitting within striking distance with his wife and another couple. "Whatsamatter?" he sneered. "You ain't never seen a real entertainer? Close your mouth, pal, you're attracting flies. Better yet, keep it open, there's so many they need somewhere to go."

He moved down the line, summarily executing diners with his words. I had never seen Andy like this. His Foreign Man was so sweet and gentle, a magical creation, yet Tony Clifton's unredeeming cruelty had a power all its own. Suddenly it hit me: Tony was the bastard son of Mr. X. But make no mistake, this was pure Andy. He had only borrowed elements of Mr. X to create Tony, kind of like using a corpse's arms and legs to craft a Frankenstein monster. The heart — the dark heart — was pure Andy.

He went on for a while and I felt the crowd turning against him. *What the hell kind of an act was this?* He blew smoke in people's faces and verbally abused them. It was inspiring. The place was now murmuring, and it wasn't because the diners were having a good time. Then Tony reached me.

"You. You havin' a good time?" he asked, innocently enough.

"Yeah," I said.

"What's your name?"

"Bob."

"Bob what?"

It was the routine from the car.

"Gorsky."

"Gorsky? Gorsky? What's that? Chinese? Russian? What?"

"Polish."

"*Polish?*" he roared, then sized me up. "Polish, huh? You think 'cause you're Polish you're funny?"

"I don't know," I said, trying to sound browbeaten.

"Well, are you funny?" he demanded.

"Yeah, I guess so."

"Well, mister funny Polack, you think this is funny?"

And with that he poured my full glass of Chianti over my

head. I looked as shocked as Sissy Spacek did in *Carrie* when Travolta dropped the blood on her. After my initial shock I burst into tears, leaped up, and ran into the men's room. Of course, my "tears" resulted from trying to contain my laughter. A big bruiser followed me into the can and offered to kick Clifton's ass. I pleaded with him to not do it, as I was a "pacifist," a technical label people were well aware of back then. I excused myself and went quickly to the car to wait for Kaufman. About two minutes later Andy came running at full tilt down the road toward me. Out of breath, he tossed his bag in, jumped behind the wheel, and, laughing hysterically, yelled, "Give me the keys! Let's get the hell out of here!"

I gave him a puzzled look and held up my hands. "Keys? I don't have 'em. You have 'em."

For about one and a half seconds, the look on Andy's face revealed as much shock as he'd ever showed in his life. It was priceless. Then I handed him the keys. "Gotcha."

He fired up the engine, slammed it into gear, and we dug out. Safely down the road he looked over. "You're as crazy as me, aren't you?"

I nodded. "Yup."

That night, Tony Clifton was born, and our lifetime friendship was cemented. Andy was my new best buddy from that point on. I was impressed with his total originality, and he saw that I had a deep subversive streak much like his own. Having a close friend was a new experience for Andy since he'd always been a confirmed loner.

Chris got me a job bartending at the Improv, and when Andy went on stage I'd break away to catch his act. I got to see much of his experimental stuff and finally discovered the purpose of that heavy 16-millimeter projector. Andy would come on stage in an uncharacteristically serious demeanor and announce that he had rare footage of the assassination of Abraham Lincoln. He would explain that filmmaking was in its infancy back then, but it just so happened that a man named Frederick Astor had one of the first experimental cameras set up at Ford's Theatre to record the play the very night that John Wilkes Booth changed the course of history. How Kaufman got his hands on such a rare artifact was beyond me. The footage is quite shocking and sad.

When Andy would conclude the screening by offering up, in a breaking voice, a group prayer to Lincoln, there were few dry eyes in the house.

Years later, Andy admitted that movies did not exist in 1865 and that he had lifted the footage from D. W. Griffith's 1915 *Birth of a Nation*, also known as *The Clansman*. The whole thing was a hoax, but he presented it with such commitment and solemnity that everyone believed it. One never questioned its authenticity, for who would lie about such a sacred event? As the audience was crying their eyes out over the film and the prayer, Andy was offstage laughing.

After his performances we'd get together, and he'd invariably ask what I thought. He appreciated my always being straight with him. He often used my suggestions, and I was gratified when they worked.

Brenda and I had been in touch, but our marriage was strained by our separation as well as by different life paths. She finally came to visit, claiming she would give New York a shot and see if she could live there with me. We didn't last long. Within a week she decided that the city was far too big and chaotic, and we parted, now with the understanding that, despite being married, we could go our separate ways since our lives weren't exactly going to remain tightly joined. I was sorry to see her go back to Pittsburgh, but I knew that she wouldn't be happy in my town and I wouldn't be happy in hers.

Most nights after Andy's sets, we'd get together and I'd tell him his favorite Mr. X stories, and we'd talk about how we could create some chaos of our own. Andy was mesmerized by Mr. X's commitment to anarchy and professional sociopathy. He became so obsessed with Mr. X's methodology and dedication to creating and then channeling mayhem that Andy persuaded me to help manufacture incidents on the street while he recorded them with his little handheld tape recorder. Later we'd listen to the results, which would provide the jumping-off point for dialing in his material.

We made trial runs at "street comedy" by going to Coney Island on off nights, enjoying the rides and the roller coasters. One of our favorite gags was to ride the "Rotor," a huge spinning wheel attached to a hydraulic lift. A couple dozen riders would stand inside with their backs against the inner wall of the huge hoop; the device would start to spin, and soon the floor would drop out, but the riders would be held in place by centrifugal force. The thing spun pretty fast, and sometimes people would get nauseous. For our bit, one of us would fill his mouth with water before the ride started, while the other — once we got going — would begin to feign sounds of impending vomitus. When the "sound-effects" man let go, the "water bearer" would spit the water, sending a spray over our fellow riders. Of course, no one could see the puker, and the effect was nauseating on its own.

Another act of fakery occurred on the roller coaster. We'd board the machine, and at the end of the ride one of us would pretend to be crying like crazy, scared shitless, just like a little kid. Then we'd pay again and swap roles. During one of the circuits, Andy turned to me. "Someday I'm going to be famous, and when I am, I'm going to make you my writer."

As the coaster plunged to the bottom, my eyes teared up, not because of the wind, but because someone, Andy Kaufman, believed in me.

During this time something happened to me that was so embarrassing I told only Andy. To this day, he is one of but a handful of people to whom I ever revealed this ugly secret. Andy always thought I had done it as a prank, despite my swearing I didn't. He proclaimed it wildly subversive and later cited it as an inspiration for our particular form of lunacy. After he'd told others the story many times, I eventually gave up trying to disabuse him of the notion that it had been accidental.

A friend named Barbara worked as an usher at a big theater on Broadway. Barbara would call from time to time with an offer to sneak me in. It was an opportunity for me to see a ridiculously expensive Broadway show for free. Despite the usually packed houses, she always tried to give me at least an hour's notice before show time. One Saturday morning a little before noon, I got a call from her. "Can you get down here around two?"

Unfortunately, I had been up all night and felt like warmed-over dogshit. "Richard Burton is doing *Equus*," she continued.

"It's a great show. I can get you in if you get here a little before two. Whaddya think?"

Fuck it, I thought, *it's Richard Burton in the hottest show in town. The man hasn't done Broadway since* Hamlet. "Thanks. I'll be there," I said, excited I could participate in a little bit of history.

At the theater, Barbara met me at a back door and cautiously spirited me in, showing me to a seat right in front. I was thrilled by my unequaled view of the stage. *Equus* is staged as a courtroom drama, and to fill the jury, audience members are selected. The seat I occupied happened to be one of those seats, so just before the play began I was ushered onto the stage and my terrific seat suddenly became a whole lot better. Then Richard Burton took the stage. It was very impressive to see him working at that range. I was in the first row of the jury box, so I was about as front row as you could get. Unfortunately.

The toll of probably thirty or more hours without sleep began to overtake me, and after about an hour of listening to the marvelously lilting voice of the Welsh artist, it began to have a tragically relaxing effect on me — I completely zonked out.

Now, the only thing worse than falling asleep on stage was awakening myself with my own snoring. And the only thing worse than awakening myself by snoring in the middle of Richard Burton's performance was to open my eyes to find Richard Burton inches from my face, his own countenance fire-engine red in nearly uncontrolled fury.

I had single-handedly (or single-nosedly) stopped Richard Burton dead in his tracks on a Broadway stage. Unbelievably disturbing as this was, I arose in abject mortification and looked to the master thespian for his forgiveness. "Sorry, Mr. Burton, I haven't slept in two days."

As Burton's eyes flared angrily, I turned to the audience and, raising my voice, inadvertently took control of the house. "Sorry, I haven't slept in a couple of days. Sorry."

I then walked off the stage, down the center aisle past a stunned audience, and out the front door. So shaken, I went home and couldn't sleep.

*   *   *

One evening Andy dropped by my place. "Wanna see a show?" he asked.

"A movie?" I assumed.

"No. Theater. Live stuff."

"What, like a musical?"

"No." He shook his head. "Great drama. Classical Greek."

I figured it was another Andy put-on and that we'd end up seeing a movie, probably *Night of the Living Dead*, which he loved, and which we'd seen six times. But he seemed serious. Then again, that's when he was really setting you up. We caught a cab across town, and when we arrived in front of the huge marquee, I knew I'd been had — it read: TONIGHT: PROFESSIONAL WRESTLING. The card listed Bruno Sammartino versus some Indian chief. I looked at Andy. "Classical Greek drama, my ass."

He was indignant. "You're wrong. Wrestling is the basis of all drama. It dates back to the ancient Greeks."

He said it with such conviction that I knew he wasn't kidding. Years later, I would realize wrestling so appealed to Andy because of the black-and-white nature of its conflict: it was good versus bad, pure and simple. This would emerge as a theme of Andy's: righteousness versus evil, Andy versus Tony, pure versus profane, star versus has-been, Andy versus women, success versus failure, and, finally, life versus death. Though the conflict that night occurred in the ring, Andy saw it as both a metaphor and as its most powerful, basest term: winner versus loser.

Watching that rowdy crowd cheer on their heroes, I didn't realize what he was actually seeing. Andy saw the future, his own career, his destiny as an artist. He had been going in that direction for some time, but I know now that the energy in that room thrilled him with the possibilities. The wrestling was actually a show, with preselected winners and losers, and in a way, the audience was in on it. No one could watch and truly believe that men that big and strong could pummel each other that long and hard and survive, let alone thrive. Andy studied the dynamic between the crowd and the wrestlers and saw a childhood game: *You be the cowboy, I'll be the Indian, and I'll shoot you. Next time, you be the cowboy.* It was a mutually agreed-upon fantasy between the participants and the viewers: we'll pretend to hurt each other, and you'll pretend to believe it.

One time Andy showed me his high school yearbook. Under his photo, next to the legend "career goal," was written "kids' performer." That was how he saw himself; that the kids had grown up was of no consequence to him whatsoever. Andy was always playing, no matter what his character or routine. The first time you saw Andy, you didn't know what to make of him. After that, you knew he was playing with you. Sometimes even seasoned Kaufman audiences got a surprise: Andy would make them think they knew what was coming, then purposely self-destruct in front of them just to show them who was in control.

During those early years Andy developed what he called his bombing routine. This was Andy at his darkest, when he would go onstage and cause to happen what every comic who's ever lived fears most: the complete failure to get a laugh. There is an unwritten rule between comedians and audiences: the comedian is supposed to make the audience laugh. Andy had been mislabeled a comedian because he got his start in comedy clubs, so audiences were often perplexed and even irritated when he did not come through with the laughs. But Andy would thrive on that conflict he created, feeling the tension rise in a room and feeding off it like some comic-book superhero who ate negative energy. This was payback for calling him a comic. *You think I'm funny? I'll show you* . . .

Andy's fame had spread, and he got a gig opening for Sonny and Cher, superstars even then, at a club called Bachelors Three. The club manager was an asshole and immediately rubbed Andy the wrong way. I don't even remember what the altercation was about, but when the guy walked away, Andy muttered, "Okay, if that's how you want it . . ."

That evening, Andy went on before a packed house and started in with his usual Foreign Man routine. At the turning point in the act, when he'd become Elvis, Andy kept going — as Foreign Man. The bad impressions and jokes eventually got the audience mumbling angrily, and finally, because he wouldn't change direction to please the house, they brought the curtain down right in the middle of his act.

Andy said nothing, he just walked over and began gathering his props. I knew it was a very good booking for him, and to blow it out of the water took either insanity or real courage.

Andy's two homes were the Improv and Catch, and venturing outside them took him beyond his familiar bounds. That he had settled into those two clubs was comforting to him, but at the same time he knew if he was to grow as a performer he needed to leave the nest. He may have seen the Bachelors Three gig as a warm-up to that severing of ties. He also may have felt the early tugs of rebellion that grew almost exponentially as his career blossomed. Catch and the Improv not only were home turf but also allowed him great flexibility as Andy Kaufman *the artist*. Bachelors Three was just a job and made him feel like Andy Kaufman, the assembly-line comedian. His reaction that night was probably twofold: one, *You can't talk to me like that so take this job and shove it*; and two, *You think I'm funny? Well, I'll show you.*

In the early months of 1975, two men, NBC's director of late-night television, Dick Ebersol, and Lorne Michaels, a twenty-nine-year-old Canadian who had been producing shows for Lily Tomlin, were charged with the task of filling the network's void on Saturday evenings while seizing that potentially lucrative youth market. *Saturday Night Live* was their solution to the problem. They assembled a cast of talented unknowns, such as John Belushi, Gilda Radner, Jane Curtin, Dan Aykroyd, and Chevy Chase. The show's sketch format was subversive, but only in comparison with the safe shows of the time. In reality it seemed radical only because it was fresh, with the first season exuding an edgy sensibility that was funnier than it was risky. The *National Lampoon Radio Hour*, one of the progenitors of *SNL*, was far more vicious and acid than *SNL* ever was. But *SNL* was television, not radio, and offered something no one had ever *seen*. It soon found a berth in the viewing habits of that new, young demographic. And Andy figured prominently in its early success.

In the summer before *SNL* went on the air, Dick Ebersol caught Andy's act. Ironically, though Andy had cut his teeth at New York's Improv, where Ebersol's show was going to be produced, Andy came to Ebersol's attention at the Los Angeles version of Budd's club. Budd had recently opened the Improv on Melrose Avenue in West Hollywood and needed some horsepower on stage, so he brought Andy out — one of his top acts from New York — to help build a following.

Ebersol went back to NBC's headquarters at Thirty Rocke-feller Plaza and told Lorne Michaels about this strange and won-derful talent he had seen, and soon Andy was invited to appear on the debut episode of NBC's new late-night, youth-oriented variety show. As the "live" aspect of the name implied, the show was to hark back to the early days of television with a live broad-cast (at least to the eastern time zone) and was to offer hip, cutting-edge comedy, a hot guest host, and musical guests at the forefront of their industry.

On October 11, 1975, at 11:30 P.M., eastern standard time, from the ninth-floor studio at Thirty Rock, *Saturday Night Live* went out over the airwaves helmed by guest host George Carlin, a slyly sharp observational comedian who had elevated drug humor to thought-provoking existential musings. Following the opening sketches, Andy stepped out into a lone spotlight, smiled, set the tone arm of a small phonograph onto a record, and a scratchy rendition of the theme song from the *Mighty Mouse* car-toon series began. Saying nothing, he bobbed along to the music until the refrain *"Here I come to save the day!"* which, while flour-ishing his hands, he lip-synched. He then fell mute until it ap-peared again. When the song finished, he removed the tone arm and bowed. 'Nuff said. It brought down the house.

It was by no accident that Andy selected "Mighty Mouse" as a way to introduce himself to *Saturday Night Live*'s audience. After all, "Mighty Mouse" had been Andy's opener for years in his nightclub act. It worked on so many levels. It was highly original, yet at the same time childlike. But more important, it told us ab-solutely nothing about the person performing it, as Andy didn't utter one sound, but merely lip-synched to a child's record.

Of that performance, Lorne Michaels observed, years later, "It wasn't that he was lip-synching to 'Mighty Mouse.' It was that he was only doing one part in it. It was the standing and waiting beside the record player for his cue that was such an original move. There was something so . . . confident . . . in the comedy."

Andy was invited to return to the show, so two weeks later, on October 25, he did a reprise of his lip-synching routine, this time with "Pop Goes the Weasel." It was the same act he'd done as a twelve-year-old, the same act he'd been doing at Catch and at the Improv, and it killed on national television. People were now talking about *Saturday Night Live*, but many were saying, "And did you see the guy who sang 'Mighty Mouse'? What was that all about?" Andy Kaufman was becoming a television star.

Though I was not on the writing staff of the show, I was Andy's writer and frequently hung out with him at *SNL*. One day, a few months into the first season, while passing through the nearly deserted ninth-floor lobby, Andy and I ran into Gilda Radner. She looked like a fragile little China doll in pigtails, and she shared with Andy a childlike sense of wonderment. She had taken a liking to him and rushed over and gave him a big hug. Then softly, so only he could hear (though I overheard), like an eight-year-old girl on a playground talking to one of her play-mates, she said, "Can you believe it? We're becoming famous." They reveled in that awe for a moment, as only they could experience it and begin to understand it. It was a precious moment, for indeed they were becoming famous, yet they were still very sweetly naive.

As Andy's star began ascending, I continued schlepping at the Improv. I needed to eat, and though Andy was a guest on *SNL* every few weeks, he was still doing his club act and neither needed new material nor made enough money to justify paying me. So when he told me in early 1976 that he was moving to Hollywood, I was both excited and terrified. I knew Hollywood offered unfathomable opportunities to him and that he'd be an idiot not to explore them. But I feared his ship pulling out of the harbor and never coming back to pluck me off the island of my dismal existence.

"Look, you're still going to be my writer," he reiterated. "But I just need to go out and get settled in. Once I've got the place figured out, you'll come out."

"How long?" I wondered out loud.

Andy shrugged. "I don't know. A few weeks, a month or two maybe. I'm not sure."

This open-ended situation left me uneasy, but I had no choice. Andy was the point man, the guy who was taking the chance, and I was the rear guard.

"Well, then, knock 'em dead, Kaufman," I said cheerfully.

Andy's move to Hollywood was long overdue, as was his recent stardom. He had been a hit for years on the New York nightclub stage, and the who's who of New York's chic artistic community knew him well, even if middle America was just learning his name. In Andy's head, this new interest in him only magnified the fact that he had been passed over for so long. That his act was so far above those of his peers, and that most of his compatriots were already on the West Coast doing their second or third Carson shots, only pushed him harder to make the move. Besides, patience was never one of Andy's virtues. Hadn't he told Elvis years before that he was going to be famous? What was taking so long?

I always had the feeling that he was reliving his career, as if it were some extended déjà vu. Andy had taught me a meditation technique of projecting one's wants into the future. While in a relaxed state, one visualizes something one wants to achieve and then locks it in as if it has already happened. The fact that Andy practiced this technique religiously for more than twelve years could account for much of his frustration with the concept of time as we know it. His predictions of what was to come were often uncanny.

My relationship with him, both personal and professional, mirrored this technique. Andy and I were very seldom in the moment. Our times together were often lived in sheer fantasy. Together we played out hundreds of television and movie scenarios, casting ourselves as various characters and then performing the roles. Andy was no longer alone in his room with an imaginary friend — that imaginary friend was now real. The only problem was that Andy was moving his room to the West Coast without me. And just when I was really getting to know him.

Once out in Hollywood, Andy quickly got attention through the efforts of his managers, George Shapiro and Howard West of Shapiro/West and Associates. They were admired within the industry not only as top handlers of talent but also for their rebelliousness. George and Howard, with their exodus from the William Morris Agency, had spawned the defections of Michael Ovitz and some other young agents who left to found the legendary Creative Artists Agency, or CAA. George and Howard's function was to advise their clients, make introductions, and weigh all career (and sometimes personal) decisions performers must make to obtain and secure their position.

With his heat as a talent building, Andy acquired an agent, the Agency for the Performing Arts, or APA. Now with his team of spirit guides in place, he was ready to take on the exceptionally complex task of becoming a star. In addition to his performances at the Improv and junkets to New York for an occasional *SNL* stint, Andy's managers and agents started getting him more television time in Hollywood. He made appearances on Monty Hall's *Variety Hour* and did whatever could get him exposure.

Andy got his first series, a role on comedian Dick Van Dyke's show, a variety/comedy show that first aired on NBC on September 20, 1976. He did about ten shows. On December 30, 1976, *Van Dyke and Company* aired for the last time. But by then Andy had made an impression not only with the youth market of *SNL* but also with the mainstream.

Andy made acquaintances in his new town. One of them was Steve Allen. Andy did his first *Tonight Show* in late '76 with guest host Allen, who took a liking to the young entertainer. Andy had always appreciated Steve Allen, a multifaceted talent who had carved a niche for himself as a sort of Renaissance Man of Hollywood. Andy admired Steve for his many accomplishments, which included being the original host of *The Tonight Show* as well as the first guy in television to take a camera out on the street to pull pranks. So when Steve invited Andy to his home for dinner one night, Andy leaped at the opportunity. Upon arriving at the Allen residence, Andy was met at the door by Steve, who whisked him inside, then promptly lowered his voice.

"Jayne," he said, referring to his wife, actress Jayne Meadows, "has had a long day and got home and didn't know you were coming."

Andy was confused. "Should I leave?"

"No, no," said Steve, "it's just that she took off her makeup, and she doesn't ever let anyone see her without it."

Now Andy was really confused. "And . . . ?"

"And so when we eat," Steve continued, "I'm going to seat you so you can't see her. She'll be sitting sort of behind you. Okay?"

Andy nodded. "Sure, okay." This was quite weird, even for Andy Kaufman.

Steve and Andy chatted before dinner, and when the time finally came, sure enough, Andy was positioned at the table so he couldn't see Jayne, who was sitting somewhere behind him. Like the warning to Lot's wife, Steve's instruction to Andy was not to look back. During dinner Andy and Jayne conversed, but Andy had to fight the urge to turn, and Steve's eyes would occasionally widen to remind Andy of the warning. Andy was uncomfortable the entire evening. As time wore on, he began to fear the consequences of looking at Jayne/Medusa. When he finally left, he drove quickly away and never returned.

Two weeks before the *Van Dyke* show tanked, Andy as Foreign Man (though introduced as Andy Kaufman) performed on Dinah Shore's daytime variety show. On the bill that day were Marvin Hamlisch, Bob Hope, and Sammy Davis Jr. The camera kept cutting to the old pros, who were perplexed and obviously struggling to understand how this yokel had gotten on the show. But when Andy metamorphosed into Elvis, he brought down the house and received instant respect from the legends watching him from one side of the stage.

Another big break came with a second invitation to *The Tonight Show*, this time for a meeting with the King of Late-Night Television, Johnny Carson. Though Andy had done *The Tonight Show* with Steve Allen, it wasn't quite the same as having Johnny laughing at you. On January 21, 1977, Andy was introduced by Johnny himself and proceeded to charm people with his stories of his native "Caspiar," a country "somewhere" in the Mediterranean. Though some knew Foreign Man by now, after a little more than a year of *SNL*, even those who did not still loved this googly-eyed little immigrant and his silly "emetations."

Andy read from *Dick and Jane* to demonstrate his facility with English, and Johnny "helped" him through the tough parts. Carson was clearly charmed by Andy, despite knowing the act was a put-on. Then Andy sang a harvest song from Caspiar in his native tongue — carefully contrived gibberish — that had the audience dazzled and in stitches, with most probably thinking he was for real. The other guest, Florence Henderson, didn't seem so sure. Johnny loved Andy because Andy stayed in character, which gave Carson myriad opportunities to make his trademark mugging asides to the camera. Andy's pop-eyed, innocent Foreign Man was a hit, not only with Johnny but also with the audience. From New York, I watched my friend steal *The Tonight Show* and thought about his promise to take me along on the ride.

On March 3, 1977, Andy was invited back to *The Tonight Show*. This time he started out as Foreign Man and then did his centerpiece act, Elvis. The Foreign-Man-becomes-Elvis-becomes-Foreign-Man transformation was still his showstopper, but Andy knew he needed more material for the mainstream to consume. His childhood act was a hit, but he was secretly concerned he was going to become a one-note performer. Andy's portfolio of material was pretty eclectic and wildly inventive, but the national television market wanted Foreign Man, and that was that. He could see his characters becoming co-opted and didn't know how to stop it. Andy was a growing television presence, not yet a star but getting there, yet he knew that his television history and the gilded cage that had pigeonholed acts like Pat Harrington's Guido Panzini and Bill Dana's José Jimenez were closing on Foreign Man, and it worried him.

Five months later Andy returned to *The Tonight Show*, but on that night he did Foreign Man, told a story, did Elvis, and then took a step that killed his chances with Carson for the future — he dropped out of character. The real Andy Kaufman just chatted with Johnny, but it wasn't as much fun for the master host. Andy did make another appearance on *The Tonight Show*, but it was with guest host Steve Martin, never again with Carson.

I was always excited to see Andy in his appearances, but each time I felt us getting further and further apart. I was still working the Improv, but my wages kept me trapped in New York, barely ahead of the wolves each month. I wanted to get out to Hollywood to be with Andy, to get in on some of what he had going, but I was stuck. Then one day the gods smiled upon me. I was living in the Village, and as I walked home I saw a guy sitting inside a car at a red light and throwing a complete fit — punching the visor and the ceiling, screaming, the whole nine yards. I honestly thought he was going to have a heart attack, so I walked over and tapped on the window. "You okay?" I asked.

"Okay? Okay?" he repeated rhetorically as he punched the dash repeatedly. "Am I okay? I've been trying for two fucking hours to find a fucking parking place for this piece of shit and I've fucking had it! I'd sell this shitheap for fifty bucks if I could!"

Half thinking he was kidding, I quickly looked the car over and said, "Sold!"

"I'm not kidding," he said. "It's yours. You got the fifty?"

I lived two blocks away. He drove me there, I got my money, paid him, and he climbed out. "It's all yours." He signed over the pink slip and shook my hand. "One last thing. Do you mind?" he asked, pointing at his enemy of late.

Seeing that I'd paid fifty bucks, I didn't care. "Knock yourself out," I offered.

For the next few minutes he proceeded to kick the car a few dozen times. When he'd finished, one side of the car featured a kind of accordion texture to the sheet metal, and most of the nameplate had fallen off. He took a deep breath. "Whew, thanks, I needed that!" And he walked away. My new prize was a '67 Rambler Rebel 550, a vehicle that was considered junk fresh off the assembly line, yet this one had significant body cancer through and through due to its road-salt intolerance.

I used the car to perform a magic trick for friends. I'd climb up on its top and lay a handkerchief on the roof. With the aid of a broom, I'd pass the handkerchief through the rotten metal, into the interior, and then down through the decayed floorboards to the asphalt. "Handkerchief Through Car," I'd proclaim. I parked the fifty-dollar car a half hour away and would go visit it from time to time and sometimes actually drive it. But now I had a car. I could escape.

I also had a girlfriend, a cute Jewish girl named Shelly, who also worked at the club. We began to plan our escape. Realizing we were too broke to leave New York at that time, we worked extra hours, pooled our savings, and soon had enough for our cross-country odyssey. I planned to heed the words of John Babsone Lane Soule that appeared in 1851 in the *Terre Haute (Indiana) Express:* "Go west, young man." That's where it was happening, the West. Shelly and I bade good-bye to our friends and hit the road with abandon. No jobs, no responsibilities, no plan, just a general direction and a lot of hope. I was truckin' down Route 66 with my "old lady," gettin' high and crashing with friends along the way. It was right out of a song. I was absolutely certain the results, when we got wherever we were going, would be just as promising, just as romantic.

I had no idea of the patience that I was going to need.

4

Go West, Young Man

You just never knew what Andy Kaufman was going to do.
RICK NEWMAN

In the back of my mind I knew that the road west would eventually take us to California, but Shelly and I stopped off in Chicago before moving on. This was home, and we needed a little grounding before jumping into the next frying pan. While staying at the apartment of my good friend Joe Troiani, Shelly and I gathered a little more money and prepared for the road ahead. Joe was heading out to San Diego for military training and invited us to join him there. After resting up for a few months (we needed it after being pummeled in the Big Apple for four years), we jumped in the beater and pointed the hood ornament toward the Golden State. *California, here we come . . .*

For me, trucking across the face of America is one of the great experiences of life. It awakens in me a sense of what the pioneers encountered as well as a feeling of patriotism, a feeling of country. Three weeks after departing Chicago, we looped over the north end of the Bay Area and headed down into the heart of San Francisco to that wellspring of free love, the Haight-Ashbury district. When we arrived at the intersection of those namesake streets, I got out of the Rambler and just stood and stared at the crossed street markers. Far more than just two street signs that had spawned the name of a community, it represented a way of life that was now gone but had altered, in however small a way, the course of human culture. Though the evidence of madras plaids and love beads and patchouli wafting on the air was fading, we had been out of Vietnam more than a year, and the notion that love could conquer hate had made its impression on more than a few. The free-love movement had served its purpose, and society had moved on, the better for it, one hopes.

Shelly and I spent just a few days in Haight-Ashbury. I had been headed to Hollywood all along, I just didn't know it. I had rolled Andy's words around in my head about a million times, but, given his increasing visibility on television and my decreasing finances, I kept hearing the little devil on my shoulder whispering in my ear, *Give it up, he'll never call.* I didn't want to believe it, so we struck out on Highway 1, down the coast to Sodom.

Since our money was running low, we pitched our tent along the ocean and took our time getting to Los Angeles. The coastline was stunning to a Midwest boy who had never seen such magnificence. When we finally rolled into La La Land, we made the requisite detour from the coast highway and headed the twenty miles over to Hollywood. The actual section of Los Angeles called Hollywood can come as a bit of a shock to anyone who has never been there. It covers a very large area, and the unsuspecting find that it is not glamorous but rather aging and somewhat run-down. Even in 1976 it was shabby. Today crews are working to gentrify Hollywood, but it is still frayed around the edges.

Still, as we passed through those streets, every time I'd glimpse one of the famous Hollywood soundstages looming in the distance I'd get depressed because I wasn't a part of it. I didn't even drop down to Melrose to visit the Improv, for fear of running into someone I knew who would see how down on my luck I was. As we made our way back to the freeway, Shelly sensed my despair.

"You should call him," she said.

"Call who?" I replied, playing dumb.

"Andy. Who did you think?"

"Why?" I said, wanting to hear her rationale; maybe it was more hopeful than what I was imagining.

"Because he's your friend and he said he wanted you as his writer," she said simply. But it was too easy. Andy hadn't called me. It was his move, he was the big star. "Call him," she said. "It's about your career, it's important."

"He's forgotten all about that by now," I said bitterly.

"No, he hasn't, he's just busy. He's not like that."

She was so naive, I thought. What did she know?

"Fuck Hollywood!" I said, my voice rising in rage. "Fuck my career! Fuck the phoniness!"

We drove in silence for a while, and as we left Hollywood I had a deep sense of dread. I hadn't been there an hour and I hated the place. It was ugly and cruel and run-down and I so desperately wanted to be part of it I could taste it. I pointed the car south to San Diego.

"They said Californy is the place you oughtta be, so we loaded up our truck and we moved to . . . Diego. San Diego, that is . . ."

We settled into a well-known hippie enclave called Ocean Beach, or O.B. to locals. It was a funky, eclectic community that ran the social gamut from people on welfare to those whose second car was a Bentley, but our particular area featured a well-insulated collective of free spirits. Many of our group were into crystals and auras way before most people knew dick about their chakras. O.B. was a laid-back but partying little place on the southwest corner of Mission Bay and the Pacific Ocean. Shelly and I rented a small bungalow two blocks from the beach and settled into Bohemianism. Shelly got a job at the People's Food Co-op, which, in keeping with the anticapitalistic credo of our adopted class, didn't pay a salary. But they did offer her carte blanche on all the organic fruits and vegetables we could eat, so out of necessity we became vegetarians.

On weekends I would go over to Balboa Park, by the zoo, and work as a street performer, doing the same magic act I'd done as a kid. Eventually I took a job as a short-order cook at one of the nearby hotel restaurants. After a few weeks an accounting indicated I was averaging precisely ninety dollars a week. This reality caused me to up my consumption of marijuana to carry me away from thoughts of a career that had never gotten going and the broken promises of a former friend that could have changed my life. The more dope I smoked the less I worried about my station in life, which was one of slinging hotcakes and eggs to people who could buy or sell me with the spare change in their pockets.

I had tried to become a radical, a social commando bent on changing the system by becoming an important part of it, but now I was at the lowest rung of the ladder, powerless, and my dreams went up in sweet smoke every night. Shelly and I had no phone or television, lest they bring tidings of someone we had known in our previous lives, "good" news that someone else had "made it." I was terrified of television, for it promised at every turn of the dial to slap me in the face with the success of my former associates at the Improv.

I slipped into my routine of rising at five-thirty to be at work at six to dish up fried animal products to the ruling class. Shelly and I were living a marginal yet pleasant existence, so finally, like an emergency-room doctor who's been beating a dying patient's chest too long, I just gave up. Why didn't I pick up the phone and call Andy? I guess my pride wouldn't allow it. He was in the driver's seat. If he didn't call me, then calling him wouldn't make any difference. Feeling a lot of self-pity, I figured the parade had not only passed me by but also run me over.

I have never been a believer in psychic phenomena, but something happened to me during this time that deeply rattled my skepticism. I still have a hard time accepting what transpired because I absolutely cannot explain it, but I have a number of friends who witnessed it and will verify its occurrence.

One morning around eight, I was at work dishing up breakfasts from my griddle when I heard a voice. It wasn't like someone speaking next to me, but more like one in my head. (I warned you.) It was unsettling because it was so clear, so arresting. *"Take off your apron, immediately, walk off this job, go home, and wait for further instructions . . . for your life is about to change,"* said the voice. The voice was so strong, so compelling, that I set down my spatula, undid my apron, and handed it to my stunned boss on the way out.

"Where you going?" he asked.

"I just quit. Nothing personal. See ya," I said, and walked out.

I went out and climbed into my rusted Rambler Rebel and drove home, where Shelly was getting ready for work.

"What's wrong? What are you doing home so early?" she asked.

I told her the story and she was cosmic enough to accept its possibility, so she kissed me good-bye, wished me luck, and left. I sat down, fired up a joint, and awaited my instructions from the other world. The day passed and I waited patiently, knowing something was going to happen.

That night Shelly asked to hear the story again. As I retold it, her enthusiasm renewed mine. We went to bed with the certainty that the next day would bring me my new destiny. The day came and went, and by the end of the third day I was beginning to doubt my sanity. Shelly and our friends were becoming concerned about my mental state, and I discussed with them the possibility of seeing a psychologist at the local free clinic.

The next day I got up, still jobless, kissed Shelly as she exited the door for her job, and sat down to mope about my fragile mental and financial condition. Sometime around midafternoon there was a knock at the door. I thought it was a well-meaning neighbor coming over to "counsel" me, but to my surprise it was a delivery man.

"You Bob Zmuda?"

"Yeah," I said warily, as if my bad luck had manifested some forgotten misstep from my previous life.

"I gotta telegram. Sign here," he said, thrusting his clipboard at me. I signed, and he handed me a sealed telegram. I went inside and looked at it for a moment, scared that it might be bad news, but also filled with excitement from the promise of my "voice." I opened it.

BOB — CALL MY MANAGER GEORGE SHAPIRO IMMEDIATELY. SIGNED, ANDY

I stared at the message in my hand for a moment or two, almost disbelieving it. Andy was becoming a big star, he wanted me, and the "voice" had told the truth. The phone number was in Los Angeles. Hollywood. It was two-thirty on a Wednesday afternoon, and I ran in my bathrobe, screaming in glee, to a phone booth down the block. I got an operator who instructed me to drop some coins in. I was still dropping in coins when George Shapiro's assistant, Diane, answered.

"Good afternoon, Shapiro/West," she said.

"Uh, yes, may I speak to Mr. Shapiro?"

The sounds of the coins coupled with the naïveté in my voice caused her to shortstop me. "Mr. Shapiro is not in. May I take a message?" she said with the slightest touch of derision. I was crushed.

"Well, when will he be back?" I asked, still hopeful, but taken down a notch.

"Later. May I take a number?"

"Sir, you'll have to insert another seventy-five cents," said the operator.

Now Diane was really wondering, and when I said, "Sorry, I don't have a number," she dismissed me.

"I'll tell him you called. Your name?"

"Bob Zmuda," I said as I shoved my last three quarters in the slot, trying to keep the connection. Suddenly all hell broke loose.

"Bob Zmuda!?" she screeched. "You're Bob Zmuda? George, George! It's him," she screamed to Shapiro. "It's Bob Zmuda! We found him!"

The quality of life in Hollywood is determined by who takes your calls. I'd arrived. George Shapiro got on the phone, out of breath at the prospect of talking to the elusive Bob Zmuda.

"Zmuda? Bob Zmuda?" he asked, almost shrieking.

"Yeah, I'm Bob Zmuda. I got Andy's telegram."

"Where the hell are you? Andy's been looking for you for weeks! What are you doing?"

"I'm in San Diego, working as a short-order cook."

Shapiro turned to whoever was in the room. "He's in San Diego! He's a dishwasher!"

I don't know how Shapiro got dishwasher from short-order cook, but to this day that's my occupation when he tells the story. *George, repeat after me: short-order cook.* Shapiro returned to me and said, "Well, kid, your ship just came in. Andy told me you're the greatest writer in the world and he wants you to fly to Hollywood to write his next show, a ninety-minute special he's doing for ABC. I guess you'll just drive up, huh?"

I couldn't believe what I was hearing. The "voice" had been dead-on. "Yeah, I'll drive. When do you want me there?"

"How about yesterday," cracked Shapiro.

"I'm already there," I said.

That telegram would change my life forever. But what about the voice? How did it know and whose voice was it? Back in Los

Angeles, Andy's phone was ringing. George was calling to let him know that they had found me. Andy, in a deep meditative trance, was oblivious to the noisy phone. Besides, he already knew.

Shelly and I packed up the Rambler and headed north. This time the squalid streets of Hollywood looked like they were paved with gold. That evening I saw Andy for the first time in months.

The first thing out of his mouth was, "I'll bet you thought I forgot about you."

I lied through my teeth. "I knew you'd call."

Andy and I enthusiastically went back to work and were soon writing his special. One of the guests on the show, Cindy Williams, was also starring in *Laverne and Shirley*. Cindy loved the way Andy and I worked together and approached me one day. "You want to write for me?" she asked. "I mean keep writing for Andy of course, but I need some ideas for a movie I want to do."

I was taken aback. "Yeah, I'd love to, but you'll have to ask Andy if it's okay."

"Oh sure, absolutely," she said. "I'll ask him this afternoon."

Cindy asked Andy, who thought it was a great opportunity for me, so suddenly I was writing for Andy *and* Cindy Williams. During that time Andy introduced me to Rodney Dangerfield, a supporter since Andy's early days. One day Andy came in the door of our office. "Want to work for Rodney Dangerfield?" he asked. "He needs some help on his special. I said you'd love to. You got the time . . . whaddya think?"

I was stunned. I took it. In the course of about a month I had gone from fry cook at ninety bucks a week to Hollywood writer making five *thousand* a week. At the end of the day I thought perhaps I had judged Hollywood too harshly. We started eating meat again, a choice brought on by our financial bounty, and possibly also a metaphor for our new existence. Radicalism was for saps; I was now a pillar of the system and I loved it.

George Shapiro couldn't have been happier that I was in town, for now there was someone else to hold Andy's hand. And Andy Kaufman needed a lot of hand-holding. Eccentric to the point of compulsion, Andy was a slave to routine. He would rise around 11 A.M. and do his bathroom routine, which would take an exceedingly long time. (Andy had a bizarre habit of using a different toothbrush for every day of the week except Sunday, when he skipped brushing altogether.) By twelve-thirty he'd begin his ninety minutes of yoga and meditation. By two o'clock Andy would be ready for breakfast. When we'd finished eating and returned to the office it would be three-thirty, maybe four o'clock before we wrote word one.

Writing with Andy was never dull. Andy accepted adult responsibilities, but whenever those duties required the drudgery of what appeared to be *work* he would shut down. Don't get me wrong, Andy was one of the hardest-working human beings I've ever seen, constantly in motion, but if it seemed like work, not play, then he resisted. So we didn't *work* when we wrote, we *played*. Andy was a staunch believer that creativity wasn't summoned like a quivering servant, but rather was spawned from the muse; when pressures on the mind and body were suspended, creativity then just bubbled to the surface from the deepest recesses of the subconscious.

Our "writing" sessions consisted of sitting down with legal pads and pens in front of us and then talking about everything but the special we were to write for ABC. We spent days just jabbering away, but once in a while, when we least expected it, we'd be hit by inspiration and an idea would be committed to paper. Typically we would sit around for hours, and the ideas came almost like afterthoughts. Andy hated pressure, and when we were feeling pressured — that the weight of the entire special was on our shoulders — Andy would get on the phone and order in some strippers. When the strippers arrived we would forget our task and spend the rest of the afternoon and evening entertaining and being entertained by our "guests." After one of the stripper sessions we were driving home in my Rambler, laughing about how we'd blown the whole day without writing a word and had partied with two strippers. Then it hit us: that was how we'd open the special.

When we got over to Andy's place we really went to work, this time thinking solely about the show. We decided to have him confess to having blown all of ABC's money on strippers instead of sets and costumes. Then we decided Foreign Man should not only open but host, but because the strippers wouldn't work with Foreign Man's naive mystique we cut them out and had him just confess to blowing all the money. That's how the special eventually opened: Foreign Man, all alone with one camera, telling on himself. It was hilarious.

Andy had his own form of beta-testing material: like Mr. X, Andy and I would draw from real life, or manipulate real life, then adapt the material for his use on stage. We would draw on various events, examining their value and how Andy might use them onstage. Once, years before I met him, Andy was accosted on the streets of New York by toughs who demanded his money. Foreign Man was instantly invented as a fast-thinking Andy haltingly pleaded ignorance and poverty with a thick accent, causing the thugs to abandon the pathetic little immigrant for more worthy prey. On another occasion, Andy witnessed the worst act in Las Vegas and Tony Clifton was born.

Often Andy tested material live and, occasionally, even on national television audiences. This was, to most professional entertainers, insane. When most comedians, even brilliant "extemporaneous" comics such as Robin Williams, are riffing, it is usually very carefully planned — it just looks brilliantly improvised. Going out on stage with a "concept" was terrifying at best, but that was how Andy often sought to discover what was behind the curtain, what the mystery was all about, by pushing that envelope far past his comfort level. To walk out in front of a large group of people with a carefully mapped game plan, then change it, was potential professional suicide, but Andy loved the danger and fluidity of the situation. He was not unlike a sort of behavioral scientist who would step out on stage and begin pushing buttons just to see what would happen. Though Andy was supposed to be the performer, the audience didn't know it but Andy was really watching *them* from the stage.

As a new arrival in Hollywood Andy wanted to remain as grounded as possible and not be subject to the glittering temptations that he'd heard so much about. He rented a room in a Hollywood Hills home owned by a man named Richard and his girlfriend, who were fellow practitioners of TM. Richard was a pleasant guy who dabbled in his basement creating works of art — sculptures and whatnot. One day while Richard was out I commented to Andy about one of his pieces, a sculpture of a plastic baby, bleeding as it popped through the shattered screen of a derelict television. Andy's off-the-cuff comment, "Oh, that's probably just a metaphor for his life," didn't mean anything to me and I didn't pursue it, but it would come to have a lot of meaning soon enough.

Andy's obsession with studying failure — its progression, its mechanics, even its chemistry — caused him to begin formulating what he dubbed the "Has-Been Corner." Inspired by what he saw as the caprices of fame and inevitable decline as he got the lay of Hollywood, Andy felt bringing a has-been on stage with him would be an interesting element to incorporate into his act, a subversive thought given most performers' desperate need to keep the limelight to themselves. In what he pictured as a showcase for the once-famous, the has-beens would be sent out to flounder in front of an audience like fish in the bottom of a boat, in an attempt to regain some of their vanished fame.

Andy saw the Has-Been Corner as celebrating the entropics of a showbiz career, a decay that intrigued him more and more as he flew closer to stardom. He was fascinated by the *ideatum* of the inevitable divestment of dignity one must accept after thrusting oneself in the public eye and accepting that praise and adulation. He wanted to re-create the moment when the big karmic wheel spun around and, on the bottom of its arc, squashed the former famous person just as he or she tried to relight that torch of celebrity. Andy wanted to observe that moment. He was beginning to see the mean-spiritedness that came with fame, the quick investiture and equally quick dethronement, and he wanted, like a little kid screwing around with his chemistry set, to watch what happened when certain ingredients were mixed together. He was gripped by the state of being a has-been because, as he put it, "If it could happen to others it can happen to me."

While we were discussing the more nihilistic aspects of the Has-Been Corner, Andy remarked offhandedly, "You know Richard's a has-been."

I pictured his roommate, the artist. "From what?" I inquired.

"Remember *West Side Story?*" he asked.

"Yeah . . ."

"He played Tony."

"What? Like on Broadway? Or some high school production?" I said.

"No, no, he was Tony in the movie, the major motion picture with Natalie Wood."

My face fell. I was stunned. I'd seen the movie, more than once as a matter of fact, and I hadn't recognized Richard as Richard *Beymer*.

"He had a good career going out here in Hollywood," Andy continued, "then the bottom fell out. *West Side Story* was this huge Broadway hit, and when they decided to do the movie, instead of using the Broadway stars they cast the leads with two movie actors, Natalie Wood and Richard. When they shot the movie they lip-synched the singing, and because of that they took a rash of unkind press, especially back east. Anyway, when the dust settled, Natalie Wood survived, Richard didn't."

It was a sad, ugly story but Richard was not bitter, though he would caution Andy from time to time with advice like, "Watch out, Andy. Once they have no use for you they'll discard you like an old washrag. I know. It happened to me." Years later Richard would be cast in David Lynch's gothic soap opera *Twin Peaks*, but until that happened his acting career was effectively over. Andy convinced Richard that he should be the first participant in the Has-Been Corner. He may have been a has-been, but Richard was also a good sport.

The West Coast Improv became Andy's new home, and just like back in New York, Budd gave Andy free rein to experiment with an audience anytime he chose. And we did, often. Any wacky idea we had, Budd let us do it. As a run-through before working the Has-Been Corner into our television special, Andy booked Richard some stage time at the Improv. Andy came out and told a packed house he wanted to give a former star another chance, then Richard took the stage. Describing his early successes, then his last big gig as Tony in *West Side Story*, Richard held the crowd rapt as he detailed his fall from grace. "If I'd only been allowed to sing 'Maria' in my own voice, I would have been a star even today," he said, wistfully.

"Richard," prompted Andy gently from the side of the stage, "why don't you sing it for us? Sing 'Maria.'"

Richard seemed to demur and the crowd erupted into polite but encouraging applause. Finally acquiescing, Richard wrested the microphone from its stand as the lights went down and a single spot illuminated his face. A hush fell over the house as the familiar Leonard Bernstein/Stephen Sondheim musical strains began. "The most beautiful sound I ever heard . . ." Richard sang, "Mah-ree-ah . . ." Then it happened. Richard hit a clinker note, but continued gamely. "I just met a girl named Mah-ree-ah!" and another clinker. And another. The audience cringed. Richard sensed their discomfort but plunged on. Now he was dying and it was only getting worse. The crowd sat in horrified silence as the has-been proved why he was just that. Now they all knew why he'd been overdubbed in *West Side Story*.

Suddenly, Richard stopped in mid-refrain. The music ground to a halt. "You're right, Andy," said Richard shakily through his tears, "you're right. I am a has-been!" And with that he dropped the microphone and rushed offstage and out the door, faster than if he'd just insulted Richard Burton. The audience was stunned and embarrassed for him. Andy quietly thanked them and exited.

Outside, Andy *and* Richard shared a good laugh: the put-on had worked. Richard had died on purpose. In fact, Richard had a pretty fair singing voice and could have impressed if not wowed the club. But that wouldn't have been fitting for a has-been. Andy was so impressed with the disturbing dynamic of Richard's Has-Been Corner presentation that he enthusiastically pressed Richard to take the act on national television, a feat Andy could arrange through his special. In spite of his good nature, Richard could not be persuaded. A few hundred people at the Improv was one thing, but proclaiming your lameness in front of the entire country? That stretched even Richard's sense of humor. He declined.

By July of 1977 we were ready to begin taping the special. Despite the opening joke about blowing the entire budget, there was sufficient money for Andy to fulfill two of his childhood dreams. The first was to hire Bill Bellew, Elvis Presley's favorite costume designer. (Elvis was still with us at that point. He didn't turn up dead in his bathroom until August 16, 1977.) Bellew crafted two Elvis outfits for Andy, identical copies of those worn by the King. Bellew even had a jarful of buttons he used on Andy's costumes that had once been on E's outfits but had popped off. Andy was constantly hounding Bill about what it was like to work for Elvis and one day Bill told us the secret of how he'd managed to stay costumer to a vain man whose weight varied like an overseas cargo container.

"I never measure him," confessed Bellew. "He loves to eat, among a lot of other things, Monte Cristo sandwiches. Other costumers did their job but when it was time to check his girth, they'd get fired — you know, shoot the messenger. So I caught on fast. After every concert I get hold of his pants and let 'em out a little. I know he knows it isn't true but we both keep up the charade his pants still have a thirty-two-inch waist. In reality, I think they're probably closer to fifty-two."

Despite the slam on the King, Andy loved the story and had Bill repeat it from time to time. Some months after Elvis was gone, Andy ran into Bellew and asked a curious question. "You think he faked his death?"

Bill Bellew didn't hesitate. "No. He's dead, no question about it. Nobody could eat that many Monte Cristos and live." Case closed. That must have ignited in Andy some fears of overconsumption, for soon after, he took me aside and, looking slightly alarmed, said, "You think I eat too much chocolate?"

Andy did consume an extraordinary amount of chocolate — lots of chocolate during the day topped off by a bowl of chocolate ice cream after every dinner — but I didn't think it was harmful because he didn't seem to show any effects, unlike Elvis. "No, I don't think so. Why, you think you eat too much?"

"Apparently not." He shrugged and that was the end of it. He never ceased his prodigious chocolate ingestion, but the cautionary nature of Bellew's story must have remained in the back of his mind. Years later, when he lay dying in his hospital bed at Cedars-Sinai Hospital, he looked at me and summed it up. "Chocolate has killed me."

The second childhood dream Andy saw come true through his ABC special was being able to work with Howdy Doody. In December 1947, a thirty-year-old guy who had changed his name from Robert Schmidt to Buffalo Bob Smith went on the air with television's first children's show and made entertainment as well as cultural history. Though there were only twenty thousand television sets nationwide when the show began, *Howdy Doody* would go on to enchant that generation of baby boomers, and would eventually build an audience of more than ten million loyal fans per week.

Andy, of course, was one of them, but his identification with the little wooden sideman of Bob's, the puppet that became known as Howdy Doody, was more than just that of an ardent fan: Andy truly believed that Howdy possessed a life of his own. So when Andy had the power to put nearly anyone he pleased on his ABC special, it was somehow fitting that the first choice of the man who was still a kid was not even a flesh-and-blood person but rather an animated figment from the dawn of television and the dawn of Andy's cognizance of the art of entertainment.

Booking Howdy Doody on his show was a dream come true for Andy. "He was the first real star of television," Andy said to me, the reverence in his voice and on his face no sham, so honestly in awe was he of getting the little wooden man as his guest. As a lonely kid in Great Neck, while the other kids played outdoors, Andy would sit in front of the television accompanied by his imaginary friends, transfixed by the interplay between Buffalo Bob and Howdy. When Howdy spoke Andy felt it was to him and him alone. Andy even appeared on *Howdy Doody* as a member of the Peanut Gallery. *Howdy Doody* would become the spiritual foundation for many of our future productions, including that ABC special.

Once the edict from Andy went out that we would have Howdy Doody on the show, the first miracle to be performed was finding him and Buffalo Bob. *Howdy Doody* had ended its run in 1960, and though Smith and the producers engineered a kitsch resurgence of Howdy appearances on college campuses in the early seventies — along with a short-lived revival on the airwaves — Howdy and Bob had more or less disappeared.

Andy had a friend named Burt Dubrow from their days together in Grahm College's television department, and Andy recalled Burt once telling him that from the time he was about ten years old he had known Buffalo Bob. Andy called Burt, and with his help we found Bob and arranged to have him, Howdy, and the puppeteer fly out to Hollywood to tape the show. Andy wanted only Howdy on camera with him, so the plan was for Bob to lay down Howdy's voice track, and for the puppeteer to provide the action.

When Howdy (in his box) and the puppeteer, Pady Blackwood, arrived at the studio, we cleared the soundstage of all personnel. This was going to be a big moment for Andy and he wanted privacy. After Pady had unboxed Howdy and propped him up for the meeting, I went to get Andy, who was holed up in his dressing room, waiting nervously for the big moment.

"Is he there?" he asked me, shaking. I knew that he hadn't slept the night before, so anxious was he over the prospect of facing his entire childhood in the form of a small, wooden marionette.

"Yeah, he's there. Howdy's ready to meet you," I said.

Andy wrung his hands expectantly and slowly rose. His trembling was no joke. He looked at me with a slightly stricken expression. "What if he doesn't like me?"

As surreal as that question was, I resisted the temptation to make a crack, for I realized this meeting was possibly bigger for Andy than his brush with Elvis. "Andy," I said gently, "he'll love you. You're making him a star again."

That convinced Andy that it would be all right, so he ventured out into the hallway and headed toward the big stage door. The cast and crew were assembled outside as Andy slowly swung back the door and entered the lighted studio in a scene not unlike that when Richard Dreyfuss enters the alien vessel in *Close Encounters*. I closed the door and waited for the historic meeting to begin. Not twenty seconds had passed when the silence was shattered by a blood-chilling scream and Andy burst through the door, headed for the security of his dressing room. "That's not Howdy Doody! That's an impostor!" he yelled in a rage.

I followed him to his door, but it was locked. "Andy, what's wrong?"

"That's not Howdy, that's the impostor, Photo Doody!" He spat the words angrily.

I went into the studio and found Pady Blackwood, who was quite shaken by the incident. I pointed at the alleged Howdy Doody. "Is this the real Howdy Doody?"

"Yes, of course it is," he said. "It's the same marionette we've been using for years."

I looked him straight in the eye. "You can honestly guarantee that this is the *original* Howdy Doody? What's Photo Doody?"

The guy paused for a moment as if considering his next words. "Well, actually, this *is* Photo Doody. He's just like the other marionette only he's used for still photographs and so on. He's got better cosmetics than the original and no strings to get in the way. The other puppet I brought for the taping is the same only with strings. Hardly anybody can tell the difference between these two and the original."

Andy Kaufman could. I went back to Andy's room and, when he finally calmed down, explained the situation. After a short meeting we decided that the real Howdy would be brought to Hollywood immediately.

On the day of the taping, Andy walked out onto the stage toward the original Howdy, who was propped up, patiently waiting for him. Andy had apparently done a lot of meditation over this moment, for when he first saw Howdy it was magical. Before we got the take used in the special, we could see Andy in the monitors gazing lovingly at Howdy in crystal-clear sincerity, the man-child revealing the true depth of his feelings for this small wooden man, probably his only real friend as a child. Andy was actually choked up. After he recovered his emotions, we brought in Pady the puppeteer, and the scene went perfectly.

A few days before we got around to shooting that precious moment, Buffalo Bob arrived to lay down Howdy's audio track. Andy had anticipated a charismatic and delightful older man, clad in his frontiersman outfit, dispensing sage advice to all the "girls and boys" on the set. What he got was an old guy wearing a rumpled leisure suit, sucking up cigarettes, and apparently hungover. Andy was startled by Bob's appearance, but the coup de grâce came two minutes after they met when Bob launched into a barrage of foulmouthed "pussy" jokes. I could see Andy's face noticeably flush. Had Tony Clifton been around, he and Bob would have gotten along famously, but Andy couldn't wait to get away from the guy. During the taping Bob broke into an uncontrollable hacking cough that infused the recording booth with the foul odor of cigarette residue and the booze still in his system. Once he had the cough under control he looked at Andy, shaking his head. "I hate that fucking Howdy voice. It kills my throat." Once the voice tracks were done Andy left and did not speak to Bob again.

An even less fortunate has-been was poor Gail Slobodkin. Andy was friends with the young, struggling actress and offered her a part in the ABC special. A cute, perky honey-blonde, Gail had once played in *The Sound of Music* on Broadway but enjoyed little success afterward. Thus credited, we bestowed upon Gail the honor of being the first candidate for our nationally televised debut of the Has-Been Corner. The tape rolled just as she was about to perform her segment, and to create believability that she was truly a has-been, Andy asked her something on-camera that he never would have said even in private: "When was the first time you realized you'd never make it?"

Seemingly taken aback, Gail was nevertheless pleasant despite Andy's cold-blooded question. Andy, undeterred, pressed on. "Gail," he asked, "what's it like being a has-been?" The sweet girl was gut-shot by his remarks but cheerfully defended herself and her decision to return to showbiz. Andy summed it up, "Well, I hope you make it . . . but I don't think you will." And with that rousing introduction Gail sang a selection from *The Sound of Music*, the charming "Lonely Goatherd." As Gail gamely belted out her song, Andy was in the background conducting an "angry" discussion with the floor director, me. When he'd notice the camera on him he'd shove me away and let Gail continue. We did this twice, then Gail finished.

During the taping Gail was obviously hurt by Andy's mean comments and reacted by giving him a gentle slap. It was done more out of her own pain than to inflict pain on Andy. She kept her chin up, did the show, and left the building. Three days later a distraught Gail checked into a low-rent Hollywood motel, took a hot bath, ratcheted open a can of Van Camp's pork and beans, shoveled the cold beans down her throat with a plastic spoon, then cut that throat with the jagged can lid. Her body was discovered by the housekeeper the next morning. Her suicide note blamed Andy for his cold-hearted mockery of her on national television. The LAPD finally passed the note on to Andy, who kept it by his framed picture of the Maharishi. Only once did I summon the courage to ask him about his feelings surrounding Gail's death.

He never answered because it never happened.

You've just been had. Gail Slobodkin not only is still alive but is living happily in southern California. It was all a put-on. Gail's reactions were all carefully staged and her feelings were intact. The point of the story was to demonstrate to you, the reader, the feeling of being Kaufmanized. This was the same emotion Andy and I sought to evoke not only in audiences but often when we were out in public, just the two of us. A mass Kaufmanization of an audience was fun, but the process itself was the rush, and to befuddle just one person was often just as thrilling.

The Gail Slobodkin story is an example of the tomfoolery Andy and I attempted to perpetrate with our special, but the executives at ABC were reluctant to become victims of Kaufmanization and resisted many of our suggestions about elements of the special. For instance, psychological games were one thing, but fucking around with the God-given technology of our medium? Well, it was unthinkable. When Andy told the network brass that we wanted to cause the picture to roll at one point during the telecast so people would think that their sets needed adjusting or that there was some interference from beyond their living rooms, the TV execs wet themselves. Andy told them he wanted the rolling to endure for as long as three minutes. The suits became terrified that people might switch channels to check what was wrong and not come back. They obviously had a lot of faith in the ability of our material to hold people's attention. After a lot of wrangling we finally acknowledged that three minutes might push the limits of even the most ardent Andy fan, so we limited the rolling picture to about thirty seconds — just long enough to irritate but not completely lose our viewers. It was typical Kaufman brinkmanship, not only in the picture rolling itself, but in the process of scaring the executives with the inflated estimate of the time the effect would last. We never intended the rolling to last three minutes, we just used Kaufmanization to soften them up.

Another offbeat routine that I wrote for that special was a musical interlude where Andy played the congas backed by four burly, bad-ass-looking brothers. The song? Disney's "It's a Small World after All." The juxtaposition of a children's song and tough guys as the singers was Kaufman and Zmuda at their best.

When the special was complete we proudly handed it over to ABC, sat back, and waited for a time slot in the near future. Fred Silverman, ABC's president and the man who would later go on to be recognized as the savior of NBC, scrutinized the pilot in his office with a gaggle of ass-kissing programming executives. Had Silverman been a medieval king with the power of life and death, he first would have chosen the rack for us and then chopped off our heads and put them on pikes for all the vassals of the Kingdom of Hollywood to see and fear. Since he couldn't do that, he exercised his next best option: he proclaimed that our special was "unairable" and that "people in Kansas wouldn't understand it." He promptly banned it from his network. We were crushed.

After letting the dust settle for a year, Shapiro/West took the program to NBC, but lo and behold, Fred had taken his court there, and once again we were stymied. I was deeply depressed and hurt at the time, feeling that our rejection stemmed from having gone in such a strange, unconventional direction. I was certain the fruits of our labors — of which we were very proud — would never see the light of cathode ray tubes across the country. Then, about a year after the NBC pass, Shapiro/West again knocked on ABC's door. This time the castle was in the hands of Tony Thomopoulos, who, bless his heart, loved our special.

ABC finally ran the show — on August 28, 1979, more than two years after we'd taped it — and put it up against Johnny Carson. When the Nielsen results came in, we had knocked Carson off his throne, at least for that evening, and our special was hailed by critics as genius invention, with one critic saying it was "the most innovative TV special of its type." We were finally vindicated. Even Fred Silverman was lambasted for his lack of vision and for sitting on the program. It was a sweet moment for us, but the process had taught me a fundamental fact about Hollywood: it took only one executive to shut you down.

Andy's famous penchant for wrestling had its roots around the time of his twenty-ninth birthday, in January 1978. I didn't have a clue what to get him for his birthday. Andy had enough money to buy what he wanted, but lived below his means and didn't really want much. The only thing he wanted — his own television show — I didn't have the power to grant him.

My solution was to try and fulfill one of his fantasies. Our relationship had become very close, so I started asking him what got him off. He had heard that Elvis loved watching wrestling between girls who were clad only in white cotton panties. (This was before Albert Goldman's 1981 book, *Elvis*, revealed all manner of weirdness ascribed to the King, including that pastime.) Andy too was thrilled to observe scantily clad young women grappling in a no-holds-barred scenario.

One afternoon, soon after making my inquiries about his sexual thrills, I was at his place working with him on some material. "Oh, I've gotta show you something," he said, jumping up and heading into his bedroom.

I followed. "What is it?" I asked. He closed the curtains in the room as I entered. Though this was around the time videotape recorders were first available, neither of us had one. Andy pulled out a little 8-millimeter projector.

"What's this? Porno?" I asked, feeling I was about to have my question answered regarding the nature of his titillation.

"You'll see," he said as he spooled up a film and flipped the switch.

The projector beamed to life and suddenly we were watching two bikini-clad babes wrestling. I could hear Andy's breathing rate increase despite the sharp crackle of the machine. When the grainy, three-minute featurette ended I had an idea of what would constitute Andy's dream gift. I could tell he was still aroused by the footage, so I tossed another log on the fire. "Who would you like to see wrestle?"

"What do you mean?"

"Two women, maybe even someone we know, wrestling."

His eyes lit up. "Someone we know?"

"Yeah, like, say, Marilyn and, uh, I don't know, maybe Gail," I offered.

The prospect of those two friends wrestling began playing in his mind. Marilyn Rubin was an aspiring actress in our circle whom Andy had been eyeing but had not yet made a play for. And Gail Slobodkin, Marilyn's best friend and our "has-been" actress, was also someone that Andy found attractive. They had both appeared in our ABC special, and as I explained, Gail had survived.

"Get them to wrestle?" Andy asked, hoping I wasn't kidding.

"Yeah, sure, in bikinis, just like your girls there," I said, indicating his projector.

A few days later, on the night of his birthday, we held a party at his apartment with about twenty friends. Once the evening was well under way, I cleared part of the living room and laid down a wrestling mat. I put Andy in a chair ringside and then changed into a referee outfit. Then I introduced the contestants, Marilyn and Gail, who entered from the bedroom wearing skimpy little bikinis. It was all good, clean fun, but I knew Andy pretty well, and I could tell he was dizzy from overstimulation.

That night everyone but Marilyn Rubin went home, an occurrence that would be repeated many times: girl comes over, they chat, they wrestle. To facilitate those assignations, Andy installed a mat in his bedroom and frequently wrestled his female guests before capping off the evening grappling between the sheets. That night — whether as a voyeur or as a participant — Andy had discovered the joys of live wrestling, which would soon become a large part of his act. Many people thought that the wrestling was just another put-on, that it was Andy being Andy.

In fact, it was just Andy being horny.

Andy's affair with Marilyn would be on and off for years. She confided to me that what she found so amazing about Andy was that on the outside he appeared shy and wimpy, yet in the sack he was the exact opposite. She said she was flabbergasted the first time and called him "one of the greatest lovers" she ever experienced. Secretly, I was somewhat relieved when she qualified him as *one* of the greatest lovers, as I also had a brief fling with her.

Marilyn proudly boasted that Kaufman made a point of calling her every New Year's Eve, no matter where he was. What she didn't know was that I had the opportunity to spend one of those New Year's Eves with Andy, and from noon to midnight I watched him work the phone from his little black book. It was inspirational to watch him in action, personalizing his contacts like an ace salesman, with both past lovers and potential new leads.

That was when we came up with the concept of wrestling Andy's female college fans. It was an excuse to go somewhere and it gave him the opportunity to rub against a number of different student bodies every night. Watching Gail and Marilyn thrash around was one thing, but to actually rut around with new girls, *strangers* even, was heaven for Andy. It also paid off in terms of his success with his opponents, for he not only *always* won but also had sex with at least a third of them.

The college shows were fun for Andy, but I had to find a way to make them pay for me. Going on the road was going to cost me in lost income, for when I was absent from Hollywood I was not receiving my five or six thousand a week for writing. I brought it up to Andy one day, early on, before we actually went on the first tour. "I need to get paid for this, especially if I'm doing the whole setup, producing it and all."

Andy shrugged. "Yeah, sure. Talk to George."

I made the phone call. "How's a thousand a show?" I asked Shapiro.

"Sounds fair," he said. And that was that.

We were booking sometimes three shows a week, so making three thousand was technically a loss, but it was still damn good money. And of course, surrounded by fawning coeds more than made up for any financial deficit I suffered when I was away from town. Our forays into the heartland to obtain sex partners for Mr. Kaufman came to be referred to by us as the Fan Mail Sex Tours.

Meanwhile, it was March 1978 and Andy wanted a new angle on his Great Gatsby routine. He had been reading *Gatsby* to audiences for years but wanted to take the act on *Saturday Night Live*.

Budd Friedman had let Andy do the bit on nights the club was slow, but only just before closing time. When he wanted to clear the place out he'd send Andy on stage, *The Great Gatsby* in hand. People would laugh for about fifteen minutes, but after that, exactly to plan, it became a deadly bore (with apologies to F. Scott Fitzgerald) and the place would empty almost as fast as if you'd yelled "Fire."

Lorne Michaels wisely never agreed to let Andy do the full routine, given that the show's sponsors wouldn't appreciate Andy "clearing the house." I came up with a way to keep the bit to five minutes and make it funny, thus making the transition from an experiment to test the tolerance of an audience to a part of his act that worked for all and was actually funny from start to finish. Andy went along with the alteration.

On the night he first performed the revised bit, Andy took the *SNL* stage in front of the cameras. Instead of his trademark turtleneck he was wearing an ascot. When he spoke it was in an exaggerated "English" accent — actually akin to the stilted dialect many American screen actors of the '30s and '40s adopted — and the audience knew they were in for something special.

"Tonight, I am going to read *The Great Gatsby*," he informed them. He didn't say, "I'm going to read from *The Great Gatsby*." The implication was that he was going to read *the whole thing*. Then he began reading . . . from page one. Occasional laughter erupted like sporadic gunfire, but most individuals were transfixed by a man reading a book on national television. A few minutes into the reading the audience rebelled in unison and "British Man" slammed the book shut and scolded them. Then he offered them a choice: more Fitzgerald or a record. The small record player sitting nearby, coupled with the almost cult following from Andy's lip-synching of various children's standards and the audience's boredom with the book, made the choice clear. The crowd screamed for the record and Andy, wearing the slightest of smirks, gave them what they wanted. He dropped the tone arm and the record turned out to be . . . none other than British Man reading *Gatsby*. It got a huge laugh, was a perfect out-cue for the bit, and later Andy went on and on with praise for my coming up with the idea. This was an important step in the Kaufman-Zmuda relationship. It showed Andy that even a routine he'd been doing for years could be improved.

Andy's peculiar habits saved him from much of the savaging that went on behind the scenes of *SNL*. All week during the rehearsals, and right up to actual airtime, Lorne would be making constant adjustments to people's sketches. Andy was able to avoid having his material downsized for a couple of reasons. First, since he was not a cast member, he was required to show up only a few days before the airdate to briefly run through some blocking. His other excuse stemmed from his habit of meditating up to the moment of his actual performance. For those reasons he was usually unavailable for conferences with Lorne, which, for anyone else, often meant a cut in their screen time.

Because of that scarcity of presence and since he never participated in any sketches (at least in the first few years), Andy also was not privy to all the backstabbing and claws-out infighting that went on backstage at *SNL*. Even when Andy's pieces went a little long he experienced none of the resentment that anyone else would have suffered. As a fly on the wall I began to see the cast and staff's vision of Andy: almost a holy man of comedy, pure and simple and brilliant. There was the sense that Andy was a real "artist" in their midst, and everyone treated him with sincere respect.

The late John Belushi, himself a rebel, marveled not only at Andy's onstage antics but at his offstage ones as well. In every dressing room at *SNL* there was a television monitor displaying the show — the same feed that was broadcast. Every dressing room, that is, but Andy's. He couldn't have cared less about the telecast and always had his TV switched to a wrestling match. Although a few cast members were appalled that Andy wasn't watching (and let him know it), Belushi often joined him. One time, Belushi, in his killer-bee outfit, settled in with Andy in his dressing room to watch a wrestling match. Meanwhile, as the show went out live, the talent wranglers were hysterically combing the corridors looking for Belushi, fearing he had walked out of the building.

On March 14, 1978, three days after Andy did Gatsby on *SNL*, we jumped on a plane to Columbus, Ohio, to conduct an experiment. Andy's old friend Burt Dubrow, with whom we dug up Howdy and Buffalo Bob, was there producing a children's show for Group W called *Bananaz*. Intrigued by anything to do with children's entertainment, Andy had approached Burt with the idea of his making an appearance on the show, whose format allowed for such flexibility. Burt assured Andy, as a visiting celebrity, that he could do "anything he wanted." What Andy did not immediately tell Burt was that the show was going to be a test for a concept we'd been kicking around.

One night during our writing sessions for Andy's special, we discussed an incident that had occurred on Carson's show several years earlier. Ask any freshman comic from the '60s or '70s about the unscheduled "wave-over." If Carson liked your act, at his whim you were invited to the next level, which was to cross the stage and actually sit and chat with His Excellency. If you finished your act and didn't get the wave-over, that is, if Johnny just applauded and thanked you but made no attempt to speak to you, you probably should have considered the insurance business as a new career before you even left the stage. Many comedians survived the non-wave-over, but it was a bitch to really make it without that stamp of approval from the man who'd launched the careers of probably 80 percent of all working comics.

After performing his set on the stage of *The Tonight Show*, a young comic got his big break and received the much-coveted wave-over from Johnny. This was his chance to interact with the Titan of Late-Night Comedy in a way that could get him better bookings, better-looking women, and, best of all, a shot at his own series. It sounds insanely capricious but the wave-over could indeed represent such opportunities. Unfortunately, at the same time the comic was getting his wave-over, forces were at work to unhinge his karmic fortune. Don Rickles was taping a sitcom down the hall and decided to waltz over to see what his buddy Johnny was doing. Just as the young comic was plopping his ass down for some quality time with Mr. Carson, Rickles entered stage right and the audience went bonkers. Rickles, as usual, was hilarious. Suddenly the young comic was rolled over by the wheels of the Master of Put-Down Comedy, and Rickles wasn't even aware of it. Carson was now in stitches and the young comic became wallpaper.

Andy was taken by the unfairness of show business and the small twists of fate that propel one person to great heights and cast another into the depths. In keeping with the Has-Been Corner and its cavalier dismissal of one's life work, Andy loved the notion that just as one guy's big chance presents itself, another, bigger fish just swims in and sucks him up without so much as a second thought.

For our little experiment in Columbus, our young comic was replaced by Dr. Zmudee, an expert on an arcane field of psychology called psychogenesis. Psychogenesis is an actual field of study. In laymen's terms, it is the origin of physical or psychological states, be they normal or abnormal, as seen as a product of the interaction between conscious and unconscious psychological pressures. Did I lose you? Good. That said, we went to Ohio to play out this human drama.

We met with Burt outside the production facility and told him what we planned. He balked at first but Andy reminded him of his promise to let us do what we wanted. Andy also stipulated that Burt was not to tell anyone else of our charade — or that Andy and I knew each other — particularly the host of *Bananaz*. Then I left for the studio.

Once the taping of *Bananaz* was under way, the host introduced me to his audience, comprising people ranging in age from about six to ten.

"Kids, today we have a very smart man, Dr. Zmudee, who has written a really interesting book called *Psychogenesis*. Welcome, Dr. Zmudee," he said as I entered and sat down. "So, tell us about your book."

Had the host said I was going to come out and skin a live cat the applause might have been warmer, but undaunted I proceeded to launch into a turgid description of the theory of psychogenesis and my attendant book. The real study of psychogenesis is so complex it would have taxed a room full of physicists, but to a pack of children my words instantly threw them into exquisite boredom. Meanwhile, the host, though completely lost in my gobbledygook, was trying his best to feign interest as I earnestly tried to convey the extreme importance of my life's study.

Magically, out of the wings, like the angel Gabriel sent to save the show, came the rising young television star Andy Kaufman. There was a collective sigh from the children, the host, and the crew, as if they were being delivered from a firing squad. Andy entered waving. No one of his caliber had ever guested the show. In just a few seconds the audience had been spared a death by psychogenesis and had been given the joy of having a real entertainer in their midst. In about ten minutes Andy had the crowd nuts with glee, as Dr. Zmudee sat mute and smoldering, his big chance at explaining psychogenesis trammeled by this upstart. Andy finally left to screams and cheers, and Dr. Zmudee began where he'd left off. A pall again visited the set and settled in as the good doctor rambled on about his abstruse field of interest.

Suddenly Andy appeared again, this time armed with his congas. The house went wild and he began an animated set of drumming and singing as the now quite irritated Dr. Zmudee sat uncomfortably nearby and watched as his opportunity passed. After a few minutes, Dr. Zmudee could stand it no more. He jumped to his feet and demanded of the host that the enormously rude Kaufman be made to leave so that he could finish his interview.

"Hey kids," said Andy brightly, "who do you want to see? Him . . . or me?"

The kids clamored in unison, "YOU!!!" The vote thus tallied, the steaming Dr. Zmudee had lost by a landslide.

"You're just a bunch of uneducated little brats," spat Dr. Zmudee. "You wouldn't know something of substance if it bit you on the ass!"

The gauntlet now hurled, the kids responded with angry hisses and boos as the host paled, having lost any control. Andy tapped his conga as he beat out an attack on Dr. Zmudee. "Hey, Doc, why don't you take your book and go home. Better yet, why don't you write the follow-up, *How to Put an Audience to Sleep in Two Minutes.*"

As the kids laughed him to scorn, Dr. Zmudee snapped. He leaped across the stage at the conga-playing smart-ass who had ruined his big interview. (Allow me to note that this production was going out *live* to greater Columbus.) Dr. Zmudee shoved Andy to the floor, but the plucky comedian responded by rebounding and applying a classic wrestling hold. The battle escalated to the cheers of the little Romans. A shocked Burt Dubrow made a quick decision from the control booth. Reaching over the console, he flipped a switch cutting the signal to thousands of sets across the city.

Suddenly the station's switchboard lit up like Times Square. Hundreds of incensed and distraught parents were furious over the spectacle of two men fighting on their children's show, but were probably even more pissed that the station went to black before they could ascertain a winner. Burt was summoned to his boss's office and given the ultimatum that his job was at stake if Andy and Dr. Zmudee didn't go on the five o'clock news to explain and apologize.

When the time came we faced the camera, side by side, ready to be interviewed by the two anchors. We stared blankly into the lens like a pair of zombies, seeming merely to mouth the words we'd been given. We later called this the "Viet Cong Confession."

"So Andy," said one of the chipper anchors, "you two actually know each other?"

"Yes," droned Andy, doing his best automaton, "that is true."

"Yes, right," I concurred robotically, "we know one another."

The anchors didn't know what to make of our odd behavior and continued. "And Dr. Zmudee? You're not really a doctor, is that right?"

"No," I said.

There was a second of confusion as the other anchor picked up the cue. "Is that no, you're not a doctor, or no, that's not right and in fact you are?"

"Correct," I said.

Before they could ask any more dumb questions Andy and I suddenly turned on each other and started the fight all over. They quickly cut to a commercial as we caromed off the desk and nearly destroyed their weather map. Security was called to escort us out of the facility. Separate cabs were hailed and we were sent to the airport, where we reunited in a lounge and laughed our asses off.

Burt kept his job, mostly because the station's ratings quadrupled during that five o'clock newscast. Perhaps Burt discovered something that day, for he would, years later, become a wildly rich man as co-creator and executive producer of that other un-bridled slugfest, *Jerry Springer*. Years later, Andy and I would reissue this bit, including the Viet Cong Confession, on the ABC show *Fridays* to a great deal of clamor in the press and from the public. The influences of Kaufmanism would be felt near and far for years to come.

5

Stuck in a Taxi

*It was as if all the other comedians were speaking English
and he was speaking Chinese.*
JAY LENO

From Columbus we flew to Philadelphia for Andy to do an appearance on *The Mike Douglas Show*. The interview went fine, but it was what Mike told Andy off-camera that blew his mind. Jerry Weintraub, who had been a business partner with the late Elvis Presley, was an acquaintance of Mike's and once told him that of all the Elvis impressionists, the King thought Andy was by far the best. When Mike passed that on, Andy was shocked and touched. That he had come full circle from that encounter just outside the cupboard in the Las Vegas Hilton gave him a lot to ponder.

One reason Elvis had so appreciated Andy's impression of him was that Andy did a very early version of Elvis — the period of which Elvis was most fond. Unlike most imitators, Andy didn't do the standard Vegas Elvis, but rather did the younger "Rockabilly Cat" that Elvis had evolved away from but always yearned to return to. When Andy did *The Tonight Show*, *SNL*, or any network show, he always chose some obscure Elvis song with which to lead in.

Andy's management, myself included, always argued he should go with the more mainstream, better-known Elvis numbers, but Andy was adamant about leading with a little known ditty — little known, that is, to everyone but extreme hardcore fans . . . and the King himself. The fact that Andy was actually a pretty respectable rockabilly singer has been pointed out to me a number of times over the years by some very well known musicians.

Many people have asked me about Andy's reaction to Elvis's death, and I told them all the same one word answer: none, at least publicly. Andy Kaufman had been an Elvis fan almost from day one. All the uproar put him off, as if a bunch of distant acquaintances had arrived at the funeral, and Andy, as a close family member, had had to retreat into his own private grief. Andy's relationship with Elvis was very personal to him and therefore did not require the validation of public garment-rending.

Several years later, Andy and I found ourselves in Memphis before one of Andy's infamous wrestling matches with Jerry Lawler. We decided we had to make our pilgrimage to Graceland. Inside the gates of the Temple of Elvis, some of the employees recognized Andy and whisked us out of the main tour group and into the area normally off-limits to the public. The woman showing us around took us into a room containing Elvis's collection of videotapes.

"Elvis, he was a big fan of yours," said the custodian. She pointed at a section of the tapes. "Those have you on 'em."

Andy slid a tape out and, sure enough, it was marked "Andy Kaufman." Andy's eyes teared at the notion he'd had an influence on the King. Mike Douglas telling him thirdhand was one thing, but this was putting his hands in the wounds. Andy looked at me and for the first time I'd observed, his eyes expressed both the surprise and sadness that Elvis was gone. It was almost as if Andy were mourning the loss of his chance to say, *Hey, Elvis, remember me? That crazy kid in the cupboard in Vegas?*

"I guess it's true," he said simply. "It's true what Mike Douglas said."

"Yeah," I said, "it sure is."

We were then shown upstairs to the King's bedroom. We both eyed the door to the very bathroom where The Man exited this mortal coil. I engaged our guide in some bullshit conversation while Andy made a beeline for the can before she could object. A few minutes later he reappeared, accompanied by the whooshing sound of the just-flushed commode. As we walked downstairs to see the grounds, Andy whispered to me, "I used

Elvis's throne . . . I mean *really* used it! It was amazing, absolutely amazing." Andy was discovering that celebrity had its rewards.

After our Graceland tour we drove down to Tupelo, Mississippi, to pay homage to Elvis's birthplace. As we pulled up, Andy and I stopped and looked at the humble boyhood home of Andy's hero. I decided to Kaufmanize my friend. "Hey," I urged, "you oughtta put on your Elvis outfit, the full show. Go in like that."

Andy looked at me, eyes narrowed. "Really? You think I should?"

"Oh yeah, absolutely. Elvis would have wanted that."

Andy surveyed the small home with a few people milling around. "Think it's too much?"

"Jesus, Kaufman, has that ever stopped you?"

He pondered for a moment, as if weighing the fine line between blasphemy and a heartfelt tribute. "Okay."

He got out of the car, removed the outfit from the trunk, and put it on, right there in front of the house. "How do I look?" he asked, now fully Elvisized.

"Like Elvis," I said.

"Okay, let's go," he said, like a man going into combat.

We entered the humble little home to some pretty serious stares, some not so friendly. The caretaker looked slightly irritated. As we entered Elvis's bedroom I motioned to the bed. For a moment we were alone. "Get on, I'll take a picture."

Andy looked around. "You think I should?"

"Of course, it's a natural."

Andy gingerly lay on the bed, as if the ghost of Elvis would suddenly rise from the mattress and clutch him as payback for this transgression as well as for using his crapper. I snapped a few shots. In the car as we drove away I looked over shaking my head. "I can't fucking believe you did that."

He looked at me, puzzled. "Whaddya mean? Did what?"

"Got on Elvis's bed . . . dressed as Elvis!"

"Well, shit, Zmuda, you told me to!"

I started laughing. "I know, I know, but I didn't think you would!"

Andy began laughing with me. "Those people must have thought I was crazy."

"Oh yeah, they did."

Our laughter went to the next level. As tears streamed down our faces, and I fought to control the car, Andy sputtered, "I'll get you for this, Zmuda!"

Andy had loved the experience, and that situation sort of summarized our relationship: two friends pushing each other to do things we never would have done on our own. And if they were stupid or silly things, so much the better.

One reason Andy went to Hollywood to pursue his career was that Lorne Michaels wouldn't put him on full-time at *SNL*. Lorne's excuse to Andy was that his appearing more than once every few weeks was too much given Andy's bizarre brand of humor. Lorne tried to persuade Andy to remain in New York as the darling of the chic entertainment/art set. When Andy went west, Lorne was disappointed, feeling he'd lost one of his favorite resources. Before Andy left New York Lorne cautioned that sitcoms were the lowest form of entertainment. That was before *Taxi* was even a notion in the heads of the producers. Lorne's words stayed with Andy, and despite Shapiro and West's efforts to find him a sitcom, he told me he was hesitant to take the opportunity if it arose.

Taxi was still on the drawing boards when Jim Brooks and the show's other writers and producers sat down at the Comedy Store one night in the spring of 1978 to check out Andy. Tony Clifton appeared, did an obnoxious set, and then introduced Andy, who did his usual oddball but terrific set. The producers were enamored of Foreign Man but were stunned and wholly impressed when they learned that Clifton was really Andy. Strong word of mouth coupled with that eye-opening firsthand experience was enough to persuade the producers to make an offer. Andy accepted on one condition: they had to create two contracts, one for Andy, another for Tony. It was agreed that Tony Clifton would appear in one or two episodes during the first season. Tony was also to be assigned his own parking place. Andy took the deal and signed on to star in *Taxi*.

In reality, the makers of *Taxi* were essentially buying Foreign Man. They loved the character and had in mind a variation on that theme for the show. Though it was a huge break for his career, Andy was still uneasy. Lorne's words rang in his head and he feared the co-option of weekly television and how it might affect him as an artist. At this point Andy had enough money to meet his needs and making that much more didn't really matter to him. He'd long since given up the beer-tap dreams of his youth and lived a modest existence. Though Andy lived to perform his own material, George and Howard and I convinced him that *Taxi* was part of paying his dues. Though he'd be tied to a schedule, we emphasized that the money was outrageous and the exposure, if the show stayed on more than a year, would give him solid national recognition.

Taxi was scheduled to begin production on July 5, 1978. Andy saw that date as equivalent to the date the draft board had given Elvis twenty-some years prior. Andy's recent proximity to the Elvis iconography had him fishing for parallels, and this was one that seemed to scream in similarity. He sensed the impending dissolution of his purity as an artist and decided something must be done in advance of the systemic poison called television sitcoms. Andy decided he would figuratively and literally rise above the coming onslaught. One day he made an announcement to me.

"You're what?" I said, assuming it was a typical Kaufman put-on.

"You heard me. I'm going to levitate," he said in all seriousness.

"As in 'fly'?"

"No. Levitate. It's different," he assured me. "Here, look."

He thrust a *Time* magazine article at me that reported on the recent phenomenon wherein devout practitioners of transcendental meditation were flocking to a retreat in Switzerland to become adept at the "ancient" art of levitation. The article featured a photo of several TM devotees pretzeled into lotus positions and floating two feet off their carpets.

"That's total bullshit," I said. "No way anyone can float. C'mon, Andy, there's just no way anyone can do this. These photos are doctored."

"No, they're not," he said defensively, flipping the magazine shut. "It's true." He spoke with the same defiant conviction a little kid would use in defending the existence of Santa.

"You're gonna learn to fly?"

"No, Zmuda, *levitate*. I will," he insisted. "I've talked to other TMers who've been to Switzerland. They've taken the course, it's eight weeks, and they can do it — they can levitate."

My eyes betrayed my complete skepticism.

"Listen," he continued, "that these photos were leaked to *Time* really upset everyone in the movement because now it's only a matter of time before the CIA gets hold of that ability and misuses it."

I heard an echo of Mr. X. "CIA?" I asked.

"Yeah. Of course. Don't you see? They'll close us down soon and steal the process, so I have to go before *Taxi* starts. I'll be back in two months."

"Andy?" I said, putting my hand on his shoulder. "This I gotta see."

He truly believed that he would be able to levitate when he returned from Switzerland. They say that con men themselves are the biggest saps for a con, and that was a quality that really endeared Andy to me: wickedly smart yet wildly gullible. Later I took another look at the *Time* article and had to ask myself, *Could this be true?* After all, I really did hear those voices in San Diego. The story out of Switzerland soon became the talk of the fad-embracing entertainment industry, and as time went by my mind expanded to the possibilities. As I drove Andy to the airport, I casually noted, "You know, you could have saved yourself some money on that plane ticket."

Andy looked over naively. "Yeah? How's that?"

"Well," I continued, trying to keep a straight face, "you really only needed a one-way ticket. I figured you could levitate home."

Patiently, as if instructing a child, Andy said, "Look, I know you don't believe this, but it's true, I'll be able to levitate when I get back. You'll eat your words, Zmuda. I'm serious, I guarantee it." He continued, "I'm going to ask the Maharishi for permission to use levitation at the Huntington show."

We were planning a big show late in the fall at the Huntington Hartford Theater in Hollywood. We expected a house of a few thousand people. "You're going to levitate? What, over the audience?" I asked.

"Yeah, exactly. That is, if the Maharishi lets me. It would be the first commercial application of levitation ever. It would be great for the TM movement."

Bidding Kaufman good-bye was a relief. As much as I cared for him, baby-sitting Andy had become a full-time occupation. I was beginning to see why George Shapiro had been so relieved when I came to town. As his plane taxied away from the terminal the producer in me began to fantasize over the theatrical potential of a transcendent Andy Kaufman in concert, scrunched into a lotus position, an air of total bliss over his face as he drifted like a leaf in the wind over our open-mouthed audience. I pictured the headlines in the *Los Angeles Times*, *Newsweek*, and *Variety*, then the interviews Andy would do with David Frost and Barbara Walters. I visualized a pay-per-view deal that would leave Don King jealous. I started figuring the legal exigencies of lifting the pitch line from the Superman movies: *"You will believe a man can fly."* The whole thing was a done deal in my mind before I reached the airport parking lot. Now if only the Maharishi would buy the pitch. I crossed my fingers. Then I pinched myself. *Wait a second, people can't levitate!* I realized I was hanging around Kaufman too much. Then I flashed back to my psychic "summons" in San Diego and thought, *But I'll be damned if I can explain that voice.*

No sooner had Andy left than a struggling young comedian named Steve Lubetkin planned some levitation of his own. What Steve Lubetkin did one night in West Hollywood inspired a change in the comedy business that would affect all working comedians, including Andy. Steve motored to the Hyatt on Sunset, parked his car, and rode the elevator to the fourteenth floor. From there he took the stairs to the next level, the roof, and sized up his target below. Taking a run at it, he leaped and tried to will himself to land in front of the Comedy Store. Sadly, Steve missed by a few yards, landing unceremoniously in the parking lot, but his futile gesture did not go unnoticed. A note pinned to his shattered, bloody body read: "My name is Steve Lubetkin. I used to work at the Comedy Store." That said it all.

What Steve was protesting in his stylish but rather final way became the genesis of a debate that marked the darkest days in American humor, a rising of bad blood that would come to be known as the comedy wars. The martyrdom of Steve Lubetkin served as both a rallying incident and a metaphor for the ills of working comedians everywhere. Though they were paid for television and most other appearances, up to that point comedians had never been paid for their bread-and-butter performances, those at the clubs. That 98 percent of working comics never saw a television studio or paid venue meant that most plied their trade for free. Thus the two most important clubs in the business, the Improv and the Comedy Store, became the enemy to many young comics. In no time, lines of conflict were drawn that would rival those of the Civil War in acrimony.

The top comedians of the time were involved: Robin Williams, Elayne Boosler, David Letterman, Garry Shandling, and Tom Dreesen. A young Jay Leno headed the strike committee and, to show he meant business, sported a Fidel Castro beard and menacing military fatigues. As a battle cry, "Remember Steve Lubetkin!" didn't have quite the pith of "Remember the Maine!" or "Give me liberty or give me death!" but the sentiment was the same. And when comedians chose sides Andy fell onto the side of the club owners.

Andy didn't want to get paid by either the Improv or the Comedy Store or any other club. His rationale was simple: as soon as they pay they can expect every set to be a killer. Andy loved to experiment with such esoteric routines as eating a bowl of potatoes on stage or curling up into a sleeping bag for a twenty-minute siesta while a perplexed audience looked on. If he started taking money his employers would in turn demand conventional entertainment, which could severely inhibit his style. Andy's point was valid, for getting paid would have affected his freedom to investigate the bounds of comedy (and frequently audience tolerance), which was an essential part of his career tactics. But there were uncounted struggling comedians who did not have the benefit of numerous paid bookings and the promise of a television job that would yield hundreds of thousands of dollars a year.

Fortunately, Andy never suffered retribution for his position;

he was considered an anomaly, even in a business populated by so many free-spirited rationalists. Since Andy's point of view was unique — he was seen as existing within his own bubble and not really as a working-class comic — his position allowed him tacit dispensation from the body politic of the cause. Deep inside, many comics realized they were just that, *comics*, whereas Andy was in his own league, a Copernicus of comedy who arrived on the scene spouting the outrageous concepts that the sun, not the earth, was the center of the solar system and that as a comedian one does not always need to be funny. Interesting, yes, but funny? . . . not necessarily.

The comedy-club owners eventually caved and started paying their comics, but the comedy wars ended the careers of many aspiring and worthy jokesters before they really got started. It was the intrusion of the hardest aspects of serious *business* that killed an innocence and spontaneity that had existed until then. Some of the old animosities survive to this day.

By the early '80s comedy had become a legitimate career path. The next generation of comics sprouted, bloomed, and thrived from the mulch of the Steve Lubetkins — most of them unknowingly.

Eventually Andy would begin exploration of another seditious notion, that whether or not the audience liked you was unimportant. If one were to transmute the old shopkeeper's saw, "The customer is always right," to showbiz terms and then Kaufmanize it, Andy's new apothegm would be "Fuck the customer." It's not that Andy disliked his audiences; on the contrary, he loved them, but he sought to redefine the relationship between a performer and the crowd before whom he or she stood. Andy's goal was to foster an environment where neither the audience nor the performer had any expectations from one another. That sounds impractical, if not ridiculous — entertainers *entertain* — but on many occasions I saw Andy take the stage to face a happily expectant group only to leave them irritated, confused, angry, even infuriated. But never, ever bored. Even after he broomed the Improv with the full Gatsby routine, people returned to see what Kaufman was going to do next.

*   *   *

When Andy arrived home from Switzerland I patiently awaited his proud phone call whereupon I planned to invite him over so he could levitate around my place. I fantasized him floating from room to room with me running behind screaming, "Holy shit, Kaufman, you did it! You're flying!" and he'd be correcting me on the fly, "No, Zmuda, I'm *levitating*." But his call never came. After a few days of his avoiding my calls with abrupt *"I can't talk nows,"* I went over to his house and knocked on the door. When he opened it I didn't even say hello, I just got to the point. "Can you or can you not levitate?"

He exhaled a deep sigh and stepped back, so I entered. "Well? Can you?" I persisted.

"No," he said, avoiding eye contact.

"See," I exploded, "it was a bunch of bullshit!"

"No, it really isn't," he said calmly.

"Andy, Andy, Andy, why the hell do you give those people your money?"

"Bob, listen, it's not bullshit. It's true, people can really levitate. I could levitate." What he said next stunned me because of the complete conviction with which he said it. "I could levitate, really I could, but I choose not to. It's that simple."

"Wait a second, you're telling me you now choose not to? Two months ago you flew halfway around the world to learn how to levitate and now you're saying you don't want to? I smell bullshit."

"No, look," he said, "the thing is, I could do it, but the process requires you to purify yourself for a year. I choose not to purify myself that way for a year. That's all."

"Purify yourself? How?"

"They told me that to purify myself I'd have to be celibate for more than a year."

I broke into hysterics. "Celibate!?" When I caught my breath I said, "Kaufman, you are the most gullible son of a bitch I've ever met! Celibate for a year? I can't believe that shit! That's hilarious!"

Andy shrugged, not finding the humor. "Well, it's true," he said, like a hurt little kid who needed the last word. "I just choose not to." The whole thing was pure Andy: one day he's Tony Clifton, the next day Pinocchio.

*   *   *

Now back from his flirtation with levitation in Switzerland, Andy had to prepare for that new aspect of his career, *Taxi*. After his brush with wingless flight and our antics on *Bananaz*, the prospect of doing something as controlled as a sitcom was as boring to Andy as Dr. Zmudee's theory of psychogenesis was to those kids. Despite his often childlike demeanor, Andy was almost overly purposeful and couldn't stand sitting still for any period. Consequently he had George Shapiro negotiate what amounted to an anticontract — in Hollywood terms — for his part in *Taxi*. Andy demanded the unprecedented: less participation.

In a town where people cut others' throats for an extra two minutes of screen time, Andy had George work out a deal with the *Taxi* producers, Jim Brooks and Ed Weinberger, that actually minimized his role. Andy was required to appear in only thirteen of the twenty-two episodes that first year, and he would be available only two days a week, instead of the typical five. In a business driven by egos, his behavior before the series even began was unheard of. Asking for a smaller role? *What the hell was with this Kaufman guy?* the rest of the cast wondered.

Andy was to play a sweet, naive immigrant from someplace similar to Caspiar. Foreign Man, having been acquired by the producers, was born again and rechristened Latka Gravas, now the house mechanic of the Sunshine Cab Company. But if you had gone to the set in those days, most of the time you would have seen a black man in Andy's stead, a stand-in for camera blocking. The rest of the cast, Judd Hirsch, Tony Danza, Danny DeVito, Marilu Henner, Jeff Conaway, and Randy Carver, were required to be there. Andy contracted for and devoted to *Taxi* exactly what he felt it required of him — no more, no less.

Being excused from most of what was perceived as the normal workload created some friction between Andy and the rest of the cast. But if you ask any of them today they will tell you that only one actor in the cast *never* fluffed a line: Andy Kaufman. Though he was rarely there, and when he was he often meditated off set, the moment he stepped in front of the camera he was a consummate pro. It helped having a photographic memory, a quality most never knew Andy possessed. Andy's diminished presence was not the behavior of a prima donna, but rather was based on the precise calculation of an extremely goal-driven man of how much of his time this particular project deserved. In retrospect, it's almost as if Andy somehow knew his clock was ticking down and had a lot less digits left than did most others.

He also considered the sitcom one of the most ignoble forms of entertainment perpetrated upon modern society. Taking a job on a sitcom and cashing the paychecks was not hypocritical of him because he did acknowledge the impact sitcoms seemed to have — personally, he was just uninterested in them. He valued *Taxi* because it allowed him to explore other more interesting forms of artistic expression. As far as I know, Andy never watched one episode of *Taxi*. Neither did I. He didn't hate sitcoms, he just felt they were unimportant. That *Taxi* earned enormous popular and critical acclaim was moot to him, mainly because it wasn't his baby.

Cindy Williams told Andy about the time she stormed into *Laverne and Shirley* producer Garry Marshall's office and exploded into a distraught tirade about how the scripts were silly and didn't deal with "real issues." The estimable Mr. Marshall, whose sister Penny played Laverne, was calmly practicing his putting. He patiently waited until she ran out of steam and then gently looked her in the eye.

"Cindy, it's *Laverne and Shirley*. Just take the money." Then he quietly went back to honing his green game as Cindy left, having recognized the elemental truth in his words. *It's just a sitcom*.

Cindy's career trajectory was a constant reminder to Andy of what might await him if the siren song of television took him away from his spiritual roots. Before the debut of *Laverne and Shirley* in January 1976, Cindy had been on her way toward establishing a substantial film career. She had performed in George Cukor's *Travels with My Aunt* in 1972, George Lucas's blockbuster *American Graffiti* in 1973, and Francis Ford Coppola's brilliant drama *The Conversation* in 1974, where she received billing over Robert Duvall *and* Harrison Ford. Clearly she had been headed for serious stuff, but the pull of a regular gig and the larger and larger paychecks kept her imprisoned in living rooms everywhere. She hired me and another writer to flesh out an idea that she hoped would get her back into films.

Occasionally she and I would head over to Musso & Frank, Hollywood's oldest restaurant, located right in the heart of the city, a '40s steak joint with brusque older waiters and generous, hand-rubbed wooden booths where you'd expect to see the ghosts of Raymond Chandler or Errol Flynn lounging. Cindy always insisted on taking my storm-tossed Rambler Rebel. She got the biggest kick out of cruising Hollywood Boulevard in that rattletrap. Her fame as Shirley caused her to be recognized everywhere, and yet she reveled in the incongruity of being seen in a fifty-dollar car. Cindy squealed with glee when people would see her, do a double take at the car, then look back at her and dismiss her as a look-alike nobody.

Like Andy, Cindy understood how fickle the public was and kept her feet firmly on the ground, holding few illusions about celebrity. That she could be so easily dismissed because her context was wrong — *that couldn't be Cindy Williams in that piece-of-shit car* — intrigued her. I was learning that celebrity had its downside, primarily limiting one's freedom. Celebs have far less flexibility than "civilians." I remembered a bluntly funny quote from Dustin Hoffman in *Time* magazine back in the '60s when asked what he saw as some of the drawbacks of being a celebrity. His answer: "It makes it tougher to pick up hookers on Fifth Avenue."

Unlike Mr. Hoffman, Mr. Kaufman found celebrity to be an enhancement to his sexual life by affording him hitherto unavailable opportunities to meet and date girls. Lots of girls. And as the number of his appearances on television increased, so did the number of people who recognized him and, in turn, so did the number of women who wanted to have sex with him. Once Andy had dinner with the great songwriter Sammy Cahn. Andy asked about Sammy's illustrious career, one filled with hits and Grammys and countless accolades and, of course, lots and lots of money. "Isn't that what it's all about?" Andy asked. "The work? Creating all the things you have, the accomplishments?"

"The career? It's good for one thing," said Sammy. "You know what it all gets down to? What the notoriety and the fame are all about?"

Andy leaned in to get the meaning of life from this Yoda of twentieth-century pop music. "What?" he asked.

"Pussy!" he exclaimed. "Fame gets you better pussy, kid!"

Andy was excruciatingly shy. He just wasn't equipped to make the small talk necessary to meet women on a normal basis. After briefly dating Cindy Williams, Andy concluded that spending time with another celebrity wasn't going to work because he, and he alone, had to be the center of attention. Over the years I saw a host of girlfriends come and go (if you'll forgive the pun), and generally, the most successful relationships he had were with primarily submissive women.

When Andy was around eleven or twelve his parents owned a liquor decanter in the form of a scantily clad woman striking a sexy pose. Late at night when his brother and sister and parents were asleep, Andy would remove it from its shelf and spirit it to his room, where he would slip under the bedcovers and begin furiously polishing the container with his groin. The act of sexual stimulation by rubbing against something, called frottage, was Andy's introduction to masturbation.

Years later Andy still retained a fondness for that procedure. Various women with whom Andy was intimate told me his favorite practice was to have them lie naked and completely still in bed next to him while he ground against them. One of his better-read lovers referred to the process as exhibiting all the earmarks of mild necrophilia. Also, Andy was repulsed by any form of oral sex, both giving and receiving, which was particularly odd given alter ego Tony Clifton's almost morbid fascination with it.

My reasons for encouraging his sexual achievements were twofold. On a practical level, because Andy required a great deal of attention from me, my own relationships suffered. I felt that if he was off somewhere ticking off his hours with a woman, then I would have more time for my own relationships. The other reason I promoted his sexual buffet was out of sheer voyeurism: I was continually dazzled by the number and quality of women who attached themselves to him. As Henry Kissinger once observed, "Power is the great aphrodisiac."

Women who never would have given Andy Kaufman, were he a Kinko's counterman, a second look, literally threw themselves at Andy Kaufman the celebrity. Being a hopeless romantic myself, the phenomenon often left a sour taste in my mouth and considerably reduced my respect for those ladies, but despite that, I never tired of observing the mesmerizing, ongoing socio-cultural study. Andy fully understood their motives, that they were raining their affections upon him for who he was, not what he was, so he reciprocated the exploitation. If they wanted to dabble in starfucking, Andy would give them all the help they needed — he acknowledged and respected goal orientation. As a matter of fact, Andy decided to set up an assembly line procedure to make it easier for them.

Even before the first few episodes of *Taxi* began to create a fan base for Latka Gravas, Andy had developed his own following. Andy would comb through his fan letters, discard any sent by males, and sort those sent by female admirers. If they contained photos, the images were evaluated and categorized for desirability. If the letter bore no visual evidence, Andy would send an eight-by-ten with the request, "I'm sending you a picture, perhaps you could send me one of yourself." He also casually requested their telephone numbers.

The photos poured in, and although the bowwows went into the circular file, the more promising talents got a phone call from their hero. During the call — which all were absolutely thrilled to receive — Andy would, like any good detective or insurance investigator, ask probing questions regarding their marital or boyfriend status and their availability. Wildly flattered, all would offer him a standing invitation to visit — whether they were attached or not. The pictures became sort of a "little black book" for Andy, which he would sift through for friendly local talent when he had booked an out-of-town gig.

6
Hijinks

I've seen him be booed, I've seen him with standing ovations, I've seen people hysterical, I've seen people in awe, I've seen people repulsed. I mean, he was incredible.
RICHARD BELZER

Not only was Andy's stage act on the edge, but so was his personal life, I realized as we became closer. Andy was one of the most incorrigible behavioral scientists around and it was fascinating to watch as he applied his knowledge of human motivations to his own life and relationships. For one thing, he was a freethinker who never became a prisoner of love. None of his relationships with women (with the exception of Lynne Margulies) lasted long or went very deep. With his newfound fame he discovered an access to women he once only dreamed of. Living a life that would have made Hugh Hefner proud, Andy Kaufman was a cocksman of the first order. To merely say he was oversexed would do him a disservice. A lover of life, he thoroughly enjoyed every minute, and if it hadn't been for his TM discipline I believe he would have become a total hedonist.

Yet psychologically Andy was one of the more sound people I ever met. He carried himself with a sense of great knowledge — those near him often felt that he harbored some great truth. He may well have been what Abraham Maslow referred to as the self-actualized individual. I don't want to give the impression that he was constantly at peace, for he could erupt anytime into an uncontrollable rage at even the smallest thing. But he thoroughly enjoyed himself during those eruptions. As a matter of fact, he felt tantrums were something one should experience more of, and he encouraged others to engage in them. He could have been the poster boy for primal-scream therapy.

And if Andy couldn't get an entire audience to walk out on him, he certainly could get a girlfriend to walk out, and on many occasions did, but not before he would provoke a screaming match between them. Screaming match or wrestling match, he loved them both and would have a hearty laugh when the fighting stopped. Andy thrived on confrontation. For a while, Andy dated a girl named Jennifer. He really knew how to push her buttons, which he did with relish. They had a number of fights that were monumental, a few of which ended in Andy calling the police to have Jennifer removed from his premises. He took great glee in recording those battles on audiotape and playing them back for others. More lessons from Mr. X?

Andy was a paradox. He could be the quintessential in-your-face guy one moment, then flip the switch and become the ultimate gentleman a moment later. He believed that to excel at the art of living a person should experience all aspects of behavior, good and bad. Once he got into a hypothetical but graphic discussion with me about what it would feel like to kill someone with your own hands. Not that Andy would have been capable of such a thing, even in self-defense, but he loved to imagine.

Andy couldn't wait to get out of Los Angeles because the town was beginning to remind him of one thing: his growing responsibilities, which directly translated to the insidious word "work." Just like Maynard G. Krebs from the old sitcom *The Many Loves of Dobie Gillis*, Andy's philosophy was akin to my own, that the true job in life was to have fun, and to do so required perpetual vigilance. To both of us, showbiz was nothing more than a hobby that paid well. Andy was on a sitcom that hadn't even aired yet, but all its demanding job requirements made him feel that he might as well have been actually driving a taxi. Andy barely tolerated being the star of a sitcom, and that stemmed from a combination of many things.

First of all, the idea that someone else would put words in his mouth was foreign and uncomfortable to him. To that point, I was one of a tiny group of people ever allowed that privilege. Additionally, Foreign Man's co-option began to stick in Andy's craw, as if you had sold your baby into white slavery and were suddenly having second thoughts. Though Andy loved regularity, the schedule imposed on him by *Taxi* — by other people — cramped his style.

Creating the college tours was a break from the grind of churning out a sitcom every week. Andy could go to new towns, have sex with new girls, and do his act without the pressures of directors and producers and managers and the rest of the hovering horde who were now making his life their business. To Andy it was a vacation, but for me as the writer, and now producer, it turned into a hell of a lot of work.

As the producer of our road shows I had myriad duties. Aside from getting Andy to the airport on time, which was often a full-time job itself, I checked us into hotels, organized rehearsals, dicked with props (that again), went over lighting cues, planned scene and costume changes, rehearsed the band, and then conducted any last-minute radio or television interviews if we needed to enhance ticket sales. On top of that I often had to hold the promoter's hand, and then made sure we got our check when it was all over.

Though Andy's TM regimentation strictly forbade the use of alcohol, drugs, or even coffee, he did have one major vice: the ladies. All shapes and all sizes, all the time. As his producer, I had the job of producing them too, which I did happily. Making sure Andy had fun was my paramount consideration. I can confidently guess that in Andy's short life he bedded at least a hundred times more women than the average male who lives to be seventy-five, thanks largely to the wrestling portion of the show.

The wrestling segments were advertised in advance with the offer "Win $500 if you can pin Andy Kaufman." The posters or ads always stated in bold italics that all contestants must wear loose clothing. When the time for the wrestling portion of Andy's show arrived, the band would clear the stage and the stage crew would haul out a huge wrestling mat (usually borrowed from the school's athletic department). Next, I would come out on stage dressed as a referee, holding five crisp one-hundred-dollar bills in my hand, fanned out. I wouldn't have to explain much as the prepublicity had always done its job. On average, fifteen to twenty girls would volunteer and come up on stage. To prove that the chosen girl wasn't a plant, I would have the audience select the winner by applauding loudly for their favorite. Nine times out of ten they would select both the biggest and the sexiest, one as the winner and one as the runner-up.

At that point, Andy would enter the stage dressed in his ridiculous wrestling attire, which consisted of full-length thermal underwear beneath a baggy black swimsuit and his father's robe. Sporting black socks and old gym shoes, he would taunt the audience and they would boo appropriately. If the winner of the audience selection was the big girl, Kaufman would decide to wrestle two women so he could get the beefy one out of the way, allowing him to focus on the runner-up, the sexy one. I always made sure the girls signed a release form to ensure that Andy wouldn't get sued if one of them was injured. No one ever was.

Once the show was put to bed, I had to make sure Andy got laid and then went to sleep at a reasonable hour so we could start the whole thing over the next day. Though I was technically the producer, the reality was I was there to be Andy's playmate.

One night we played a college near Chicago and, as usual, Andy offered to take on all female comers as the Intergender Wrestling Champion. That was a title we had invented, along with the elaborate title belt, and it was the shtick that gave Andy license to wrestle girls. His main foe that night was a very cute buffed blonde who exuded loads of confidence and felt she as much as had our five-hundred-dollar prize in her pocket. She and Andy approached each other in the ring and began to tangle. She was feisty, a good fighter, exactly the type of opponent he liked. She darted left, reached in, and Andy countered. They slammed to the mat. As I leaned in looking for the pin, I overheard Andy.

"Can you believe all these people are watching us do this?" he said in her ear. "Must be five thousand." As the ref, I'd heard him do this rap many times — his idea of foreplay.

"Huh?" said the foxy grappler, not yet understanding they weren't *really* antagonists.

Andy purred in her ear. "What are you doing after the show?"

The poor girl couldn't take it and flipped him over. Andy rolled her back, straddled her briefly, rubbing against her, then leaped to his feet. *"Why don't you go back to the kitchen where you belong, baby!"* he yelled for the crowd's benefit. *"I got the brains,"* he screamed, pointing at his head, *"and you're just a girl!"* Andy loved punching that hot button of vicious sexism.

Hopping mad, she leaped at him, going for the takedown. Just before they crashed to the mat I could see he was now sporting a raging woody. They rolled around for a few minutes, but unfortunately for her, Andy really knew his moves, and in a flash he spun, pinned her shoulders, and I flew to the canvas and began banging my open palm. "One! Two! Three!" I jumped up. "Kaufman *wins!*" The crowd went wild, half booing, half screaming in delight. Realizing Kaufman was pitching up quite a tent, I rushed to swaddle him in a robe lest the people in the first few rows get the true idea about the nature of the match. As the crowd roared I heard Andy make another plea to the blonde. "C'mon, meet me backstage."

"You've gotta be kidding," she spat. "Not in your dreams!"

The next morning I got up and pondered our schedule. We had a gig at another college about two hundred miles away and our plane departed at two o'clock. We were supposed to check out around noon and a limo would whisk us to O'Hare in time to make our flight. We would arrive by three so we could have a four o'clock rehearsal with a band we'd never met, then run through all the lighting and music cues for an eight o'clock show with an audience of five thousand.

Though I was too busy to check on Andy all morning, I figured he'd stroll out when he was ready, as usual. At twelve-thirty the limo arrived and no Kaufman. I went to his room and found a handwritten note taped to the door (the Do Not Disturb sign was not good enough): "Under fear of death do not disturb — I am MEDITATING." Typical Kaufman melodrama. I knew his meditation took only twenty minutes, so in case he had just put the sign out I gave him exactly that long and then returned. I knocked and then entered. (I had learned by then to secure my own key to his room.) He knew it was me, for no one else would have dared go in, given the written threat. Andy was lolling on the bed in a bathrobe, enjoying some room-service fare and watching cartoons. I heard the rush of the shower.

"We gotta go," I said. "The limo's waiting."

The whooshing water stopped and a moment later the bathroom door opened. A rush of steam heralded the entrance of a lovely young thing clad only in a towel. A blonde. The "not-in-your-dreams" blonde.

"Kelly?" Andy said between bites of Cap'n Crunch. "Zmuda. Zmuda? Kelly."

"Kelly."

"Zmuda."

Kelly casually dropped her towel and dressed as I tried to avert my eyes and Andy focused on the story line from a *Felix the Cat* episode. I was impressed with Andy's resolve. He had overcome serious objections to ultimately make the sale with Kelly. I felt pride. "Let's roll," I urged, as Kelly slid into her clothes.

Andy roused very slowly, so I applied the lash. "Ten minutes, Kaufman, I mean it. We're gonna miss the flight."

"Don't worry, I haven't missed a show yet, have I?"

I stepped into the lee of the door and paused, lowering my voice to the sternest pitch that would convey the seriousness of the situation. "I'll be waiting downstairs in the limo. Ten minutes."

I left him to dress and went to the lobby to fret about the growing likelihood of missing our plane. Sure enough, ten minutes later Andy appeared but with Kelly in tow. "We've got to drop her off," he said. It was now one-thirty, thirty minutes to departure time. Andy's chivalry was going to cost us a gig. And on top of that it had started to rain. Hard. My tension level went through the roof.

After delivering Kelly we made it to the airport — at two-thirty. I assumed we were screwed, but to my complete surprise, when we got to the gate the plane was still there. Luck was with us, as it often seemed to be when I was with Andy. Then the tables turned.

"All flights are canceled," said the sprightly young airline employee. "Rain," she said simply. And she was right. The midafternoon sun had been erased as low-flying clouds arrived and unloaded their cargo with a vengeance. According to the airline all flights were delayed until the next day. *Tomorrow!? Impossible! We have a show* tonight! I felt like Edmond O'Brien in the movie *D.O.A.* when he's been told he's already dead from the poison.

I panicked and called George Shapiro. He calmed me down and told me not to worry. "I'll take care of it. Stick by the phone, I'll call you back." Before I could tell him the airport was closed he hung up. Ten minutes later he called back.

"Get to the limo," he said. "I got a plane for you."

As we hung up again I was thinking, *Holy shit, nobody has connections like a Hollywood manager.*

The limo took us to another section of the airport. Now the rain was coming down so hard I barely made out the tiny Piper Cub with a lone man standing in front of it clutching an umbrella. The man beckoned, so we stopped and raced over to him.

"Hi," he said between the gusts of wind, "I'm Wes, your pilot. It's a pleasure to meet you, Mr. Kaufman."

Wes was allegedly a pilot and sported a uniform of indistinct origin. I thought of Mr. X's nondenominational military attire. I later discovered Wes's wife had fashioned the costume for him.

"I thought the airport was closed," I said, ever the nagging pragmatist.

"Oh, it is," said Wes confidently, "for commercials, but we're private, we can go."

I looked at his flying machine, all of fifteen hundred pounds soaking wet, and wondered about the logic of us going up in it while hundred-and-fifty-ton machines sat idle. Sometimes you just gotta say *What the fuck.* Like idiots, Kaufman and I climbed aboard.

Andy wanted to meditate, so he crawled into the back of the plane and assumed his position. I figured that was good because if we actually made it to our destination alive he would have gotten the meditation out of the way and could go right to rehearsal. The plane was so small the three of us were required to sit single file. I was directly behind Wes — close enough to put my hand on his shoulder if the need arose — as he went through his short preflight checklist.

He punched the start button, and the engine coughed a few times and then sputtered out. He made several attempts to bring our plucky little engine to life, and each time it died so did I. Finally he lit it and we taxied to the runway. Though it was not even four o'clock the heavy weather had damn near rendered the day to night. As the rain hammered the cracker-thin aluminum shell Wes began a conversation with the tower.

"Control, this is Echo Alpha five seven nine, requesting clearance for takeoff."

The tower shot back, "The airport is closed. You are *not* cleared for takeoff."

Wes knew where that dialogue was going, so he switched off the radio. I suddenly thought of Buddy Holly, the Big Bopper, and the ever-young Ritchie Valens. *Was that a rainstorm or wing icing?* I didn't have time to decide, because my concentration shifted when Wes gave us some steam and we barreled down the runway, bound for either a small Illinois college or oblivion.

The sky was now black, and startling forks of lightning stabbed around us. *If not for the courage of the fearless crew the Minnow would be lost . . . the Minnow would be lost . . .* The wind shear was so violent that Wes had the plane crawling sideways half the time. The tiny motor strained. I looked back five minutes into the flight to see Andy calmly meditating.

Fifteen minutes later the weather thickened and the wind began hurling us up and down like a roller coaster that could very easily end our lives. The four little cylinders groaned like a lawn mower encountering heavy, wet grass . . . *I think I can, I think I can . . .* We were doomed.

Wes reached up and drew a small curtain between us. This was ludicrous, as the shroud nearly touched my nose and did nothing but obscure my view of the instruments and the blackness ahead. The death grip I had on my seat was possibly the only thing holding us aloft, so I felt that my losing sight of the instruments might somehow bring us ruin. Then I heard Wes whispering to himself. Assuming he was trying to figure out how to get us out of this mess, I concentrated hard and listened in, curious about what procedures a highly trained pilot goes through at a time like this.

"Our Father who art in heaven, Hallowed be thy name. Thy kingdom come . . ."

Oh, fuck. Instantly, my terror-gripped mind spun out a newspaper, like one of those old movies, and the headline read: "Andy Kaufman, *Taxi* Star, Dies in Crash with Pilot, Other." My death would be merely a tiny footnote in the history of American popular culture. I comforted myself with the knowledge that at least Andy and I would have company to chill with up there, others with whom we could relate: Buddy, Ritchie, the Big . . . I made a mental note to kill George Shapiro in the off chance we survived.

Again I turned to check on Andy, and the son of a bitch had his eyes closed and the sweetest expression of calm I'd ever seen. I made a mental note to kill him, too. Now Wes had advanced to his Hail Marys and I lost my shit. Remember *The Mummy* with Boris Karloff? In one of its best scenes an archeologist is all alone in the tomb one night, going over some scrolls, when the Mummy comes alive. As the hapless scholar sees the undead king coming toward him he becomes so frightened he loses his marbles and begins to cackle madly and laugh uncontrollably. That was me in that plane.

Somehow, Wes managed to find the tiny airport and get us back onto terra firma. I later found that Wes had precisely forty-six hours of flight time, including the two with us, and that the FAA required forty to receive a license. Wes had also just purchased the plane and needed all the paying customers he could get to make the payments. Andy later said it was meditation that kept us in the air. Perhaps. As soon as I could find a phone I called George and bitched him out, screaming, "Never again!" After I calmed down a bit I firmly stipulated that neither Kaufman nor I would ever fly on an aircraft without a center aisle or fewer than two engines.

Our show went off without a hitch and, as a matter of fact, was one of the best we'd done to that point, probably as a result of the euphoria brought on by the "I'm alive" thrill of dodging a bullet.

Afterward, we had a pleasant surprise awaiting us at the hotel. It seems the Hilton chain had received some inside info regarding a freeway that was to pass through this little town. Following the business axiom "Build in the path of progress," Hilton jumped in and erected a lavish multimillion-dollar facility. Once complete, they flung open their doors and waited for that concrete ribbon to deliver multitudes of road-weary customers. It never happened. Somebody had gotten some bad 411 and Hilton was stuck with a white elephant. With no choice but to minimize their losses, the hotel management began offering a "fantasy weekend" to the locals (read: college students) and cut their overhead by employing but one co-ed to work the front desk.

When Andy and I arrived to check in, we were dropped into the middle of something the likes of which we had never seen. We heard a commotion, so after we schlepped our bags to the rooms, we went to the pool area to investigate. To our extreme delight, we found upward of a hundred college students, all naked. It was as if a nudist colony had convened safely within the walls of a respectable three-star hotel. What made it even better was that most of the students had just been to the only entertainment in town that night, our show, so Kaufman was like a pig in shit.

After he disrobed poolside, everyone cheered as a buck-naked Andy strutted back and forth before diving in. There's something quite primal about communal nudity, and soon we were at one with everyone present. Booze and joints passed between nude bathers, and soon the aquatic partyers were all pleasantly hammered. Normally, given the presence of dope, Andy would have fled, but this time he stayed, likely due to the influence of the dozen or so lovely ladies lavishing attention on him, making sure he went nowhere.

We were scheduled to depart the next morning to return to Chicago, but we broke plans and stayed on, unable to tear ourselves from the mass of naked college girls. Can you blame us? That night Andy finally settled on four young ladies with whom he retired to his room and had his way a number of times (that TM discipline at work). Meanwhile, I hit it off with the solitary desk clerk, Julie. Moving me to a room closer to the lobby, Julie joined me over the next days in the ingestion of blotter acid and explorations of the Kama Sutra, all deftly handled between her responsibilities at the front desk.

After two days of all-you-can-eat co-eds, leaving was one of the hardest things Andy and I ever did. But duty called and we had to get back for a big show at the Park West in Chicago. Years later I returned to that place to relive the shadow memories of those extraordinary two days, but alas, the Hilton had gone condo and no trace remained of that shining moment of heaven on earth. *Farewell, Shangri-la!!*

* * *

One of my strongest bonds with Andy was forged as I told him stories of numerous hoaxes I'd perpetrated as a kid and young actor in my college and guerrilla theater days. He loved that I was as willing as him to fabricate elaborate deceptions, and that I'd been practicing them for years before I met him. To him, that made us comedic soul mates — I was one of the very few he allowed in close. Andy was, despite his public persona and uncounted sexual liaisons, a deeply private person. You could meet him physically, but the real Andy Kaufman was a genius jokester operating his body from the bridge of his mind. The scant few who were allowed into the Captain's quarters were privileged.

Andy had a strong sense of history, a reverence for the very ground on which important events occurred and where the great had trodden — it's just that his ideas of important and great were sometimes considerably different from others'. Just as he had had to see the hallowed haunts of Elvis, when we went to Chicago he insisted we visit and revisit the locations of the tales of my childhood. Andy and I created a culture between us wherein the spoken word was elevated to almost a religion. We revered each other's stories and delighted in teaming up to create new stories that we would co-own in the future, retelling them as if they were favorite movies you watch over and over. As Andy is now gone I am sharing our stories with you.

I can't recall a time when my folks didn't pull practical jokes on us, so I come by the practice honestly. By the time my older sister Marilyn had reached puberty she had perfected the Zmuda tradition of "pulling one over" and began to experiment on me with more and more elaborate deceptions. By the time I was eight or ten, I too was an accomplished trickster. In retrospect, the jokes we all pulled on one another weren't cruel; as a matter of fact, they gave me a strong sense of self-worth and balance as they led me to understand how important it is to one's mental health to be able to laugh at oneself.

Andy particularly loved my childhood sham that I called the Séance, a fraud I honed to perfection as a kid and used at Halloween to terrify my friends — that is, at least until we all went to college. I studied Houdini's work extensively, and by the age of fifteen I had a solid repertoire of magic. I used the Séance bit for many years after that, even making some money in college when I mounted the shows. Andy delighted in the Séance story, so I took him by the home where my greatest performance of it was staged. He acted as if we were visiting the Arizona Memorial in Pearl Harbor. I loved that innocence about him.

Andy also enjoyed my other tales of practical jokes played on friends and family over the years. Another of his favorites was the Ghost Tour, the butt of that joke being my own mother. A good friend named Richard Crowe had a nice little enterprise in Chicago. He rented a bus and then charged tourists to see various lurid locations in town, such as the site of the St. Valentine's Day Massacre and John Wayne Gacy's home, where dozens of young men had entered and never come out. He called it the Ghost Tour because the main hook was seeing places where lots of people died . . . or where there was the *potential* for death. One day, I took the tour.

Noticing we were in the neighborhood of my parents' home, I seized on an idea for a put-on. My mother is a world-class pack rat, a character flaw that possibly stemmed from her childhood during the depression. That dear, sweet lady could not bring herself to discard *anything*. Bottles, sacks, rubber bands, tinfoil, you name it; it never saw the trash can in our house. As kids, my two older sisters and I were embarrassed to bring anyone home because we were ashamed of the detritus my mother had so carefully assembled over the decades. Well, now it was payback time, Mom.

I whispered to Crowe that I had a special place to visit. He introduced me as Dr. Bob Troiani, a "noted parapsychologist," and handed over the microphone. (Our friend Joe Troiani was then establishing himself as a psychologist, so in his honor we appropriated his last name.)

"Ladies and gentlemen," I said, standing at the front of the bus and solemnly addressing the thirty or so Japanese tourists. "Many years ago, a lady named Sophie Zmuda went to a séance that changed her life. During that séance, spirits contacted Sophie from beyond and told her as long as she never, *ever* threw anything away that came into her house — not a bag or a jar, belly-button lint, *nothing* — she would stay alive. But the moment she threw something out she would meet an untimely demise."

Our Nipponese visitors leaned forward on their seats, mesmerized. "Behold," I said, pointing out the window, "that very house . . . the residence of Sophie Zmuda."

Our bus stopped and the tourists piled out, cameras ready, to see the accumulation of years of paralyzing fear as well as possibly to catch any noncorporeal emanations in this obviously haunted abode. I ran up and rang the doorbell. Mom answered, and to her surprise there I was with thirty Japanese standing behind me, trigger fingers poised on their Nikons and Canons. We went through the house, and as I opened closets and drawers and rooms, I did not disappoint, as bags and bottles and crap fell out everywhere. The Japanese were fascinated by the painful story of this pitiable woman, too terrified to discard even a plastic milk jug. On leaving the house, many wished Mom well and told me it was the highlight of their trip to the United States.

Andy was knocked out by that story, deeply impressed that I not only could think so fast on my feet but also had the strength of will to use my own mother as an unwitting device for a gag.

Back in Chicago again, still aglow from our sojourn to that college-town Elysium, Andy was in an even more playful mood than usual and hatched a plan for our show the next day that deviated quite a bit from his standard set. We were booked into Chicago's Park West. As I listened to him lay out the crazy scheme, the dutiful producer in me was momentarily weighed down by my responsibilities. "I don't know, Kaufman," I said. "This isn't some college show, the Park West is pretty legit. People aren't paying to get jerked off. Just do your killer set."

One thing about Andy: you never told him what to do without consequences. That's one reason he so admired Mr. X: for his almost fatal stubbornness. "No, I'm bored with the 'killer sets.' We're doing something different," he said. "If I have to say 'dank you veddy much' one more time I'm gonna throw up."

The Park West show the next night, September 17, 1978, was a departure. This was a big week in terms of Andy's career, as five days earlier, on September 12, the first episode of *Taxi* went out over the nation's airwaves. The stakes were getting higher and I was more concerned than ever about his image. But at the same time I was painfully aware that big-time showbiz was threatening to take the fun out of what we did.

I finally persuaded him to compromise: for the first half of the show he would do his standards like "Mighty Mouse" and "The Cow Goes Moo," and Foreign Man and Elvis. The rest of the show we would allow to be, well, "interesting." Once I accepted Andy's notion of a bizarre second half, I became an eager coconspirator and began brainstorming plans.

That night on stage, at the beginning of the second stretch of the show, Andy walked out and took the microphone. "Ladies and gentlemen, last night I saw an amazing show, and I wanted to share it with you tonight. After witnessing this extraordinary act I went backstage and asked the performer if there was any limit to his abilities, and he said no, and then I said, 'Is there any limit to what you can make someone do?' and he said no. So I asked this person to come here tonight, and he agreed. So without further ado, I give you . . . the Masked Hypnotist!"

The crowd, thus intrigued, applauded loudly as a mysterious man, the Masked Hypnotist (a ski mask rendering him so) took the stage. Four volunteers, two men and two women, were selected from the audience, brought up, and the Masked Hypnotist began his magic, hypnotizing the four. Starting out innocently enough, the Masked Hypnotist induced one of the women to sing like Maurice Chevalier. It was silly, but not too embarrassing.

Then the heat was turned up. The next "hypnotee," a middle-aged man, was asked by the Svengali to dig his finger deep into his nostril and strip-mine whatever congealed snot he could extract. When he put his findings into his mouth a few women screamed and one fled the auditorium. Now there was no turning back, the gauntlet of repugnance having been cast down.

Next, the Masked Hypnotist persuaded the other woman, a prototypical prim, young schoolteacher — hair in bun, glasses, blouse buttoned to her chin — to throw her inhibitions to the wind, and, accompanied by David Rose's famous *Stripper* theme, she began to do just that. First the bun came down, then she lost the glasses and began strutting the stage like a real stripper. The transformation was incredible, and when she tossed her blouse into the audience they were simultaneously stunned and aroused. As she doffed her attire, the Masked Hypnotist told the nose picker to cease his antisocial practice and observe the denuding educator, strictly for the purpose of the nose picker's becoming sexually stimulated.

As this was unfolding, Andy was at the edge of the stage watching, like the foreman in a slaughterhouse. The audience was taken by the power the hypnotist had over his subjects, and the Masked Hypnotist himself was beginning to wallow in his amazing influence.

The fourth and last victim was a man in his thirties, a very straight businessman-type. The Masked Hypnotist focused on him, while the nose picker rubbed his crotch and the school-teacher continued to bump and grind and doff garments in the background.

"You will piss in your pants, *now!*" commanded the hypnotist to the clean-cut executive. An uncomfortable murmur rose from the crowd. They could see this originally harmless demonstration now flirting with the edge of the cliff. Andy sensed that the audience was at their breaking point and stood. "Listen," he said, "this has gone far enough. You can stop now."

The hypnotist stared Andy straight in the eyes. "You will *sit down!*"

Andy promptly dropped back into his seat, clearly no longer in control of his own actions. "Don't look into his eyes!" he exhorted the audience. "Don't look at him!"

"*Sleep!*" said the angry mind master, and Andy laid his head over and just winked out. The crowd was now becoming frightened. Their anxiety level increased a few notches as the poor executive, standing before them, arms at his sides, was commanded once more to wet himself.

"*Piss your pants!*" was the order. Suddenly his light khaki pants darkened around his crotch and urine began running down his legs to pool around his feet.

"That's disgusting!" someone yelled.

"Silence!" barked the Masked Hypnotist, and his wish was obeyed.

By now, the formerly proper young pedagogue had lost all her clothing save her panties, and the middle-aged man was aggressively massaging his crotch as she danced. The Masked Hypnotist made eye contact with the schoolmarm and waved a finger, whereupon she dropped her underwear and was now completely nude. Then the bewitcher crossed completely over the line. *"Fuck her!"* he yelled to the groin grinder. *"Fuck her!"*

The audience was now beyond uneasy, and some members were rising, anticipating having to rush the stage. The former nose picker undressed and proceeded to mount the bare schoolteacher. Meanwhile, the executive had off-loaded at least a quart of urine into his pants and onto the stage. It was a truly disgusting display.

And that is precisely when the outside stage door burst open and the police raided the party. Someone had apparently slipped out and alerted the authorities to the nascent perversity unfolding on the Park West stage. Applause filled the house as the officers covered the young lady and her zombied-out rapist and escorted them and the urinater offstage. Kaufman was awakened, and the Masked Hypnotist was cuffed and removed. Just as the police were about to arrest Andy, several audience members intervened, saying he had made an attempt to end the vile exhibition. Andy was allowed to leave, and the audience disassembled, shaken but buzzing like they'd just seen a flying saucer land in front of the White House.

Clearly, Andy had been right: this beat the shit out of "Pop Goes the Weasel." What the audience did not know was that the young woman who did the Maurice Chevalier impression was Andy's sister Carol. The man who ate his boogers and then participated in the "rape" was our close friend and psychology whiz Joe Troiani. And speaking of whiz, the man who wet himself was Andy's future brother-in-law Rick Kerman. The "urine" was actually tap water, rigged to flow from a bag attached to his waist. The "innocent" little teacher was in fact a real stripper who could look sweet when necessary. And the cops were authentic Chicago police officers, but they were off duty and also happened to be good friends of mine.

Oh, and that scoundrel, the Masked Hypnotist? Yours truly.

The Kaufmanization had been complete. To this day, there may be folks still talking about that show. Meanwhile, Andy and I went back to L.A., where he had to continue with his job on *Taxi*.

After so much fun on the road, that hamster wheel called television became more and more of a drag to Andy, a golden anchor that he needed to lighten for his own mental health. There was only one man who could save Andy from what he saw as spirit-killing drudgery: that purveyor of chaos, the one and only Tony Clifton.

Since Tony's introduction to that unsuspecting audience at the Italian restaurant years before, he had survived occasional stage appearances but had been neglected as Andy climbed the ladder of success. Now, more than ever, Andy needed Tony's callousness and lit-dynamite persona to keep him renewed.

Since he came onto the scene six years earlier, Andy's original shtick of seemingly walking in from the street with all his worldly possessions in his suitcase had evolved considerably, at least in the minds of the viewers. Back then he'd been that sweet, mixed-up émigré with a bad act that charmed, but by late 1978 he had become a very famous, sweet, mixed-up émigré with a bad act that was now seen for its brilliance. The evolution began to severely intrude upon Andy's mien. The shy little Foreign Man was now being appropriated for a weekly television series, and audiences across the country clamored for his extraordinary (but far too well known for Andy's comfort) Foreign-Man-to-Elvis-and-back transition.

When his peers trod on that sacred ground where Andy and Foreign Man came together, he reacted. Once Andy entered the Foreign Man character, he stayed there, no matter what. One night at the Improv, Jay Leno went over to Andy (while Andy was Foreign Man), and Andy wouldn't drop out of character, even when the two of them were out of earshot of anyone else.

"Andy, it's me, Jay," he said, surprised that he was being treated like a civilian.

"Do I know you?" Andy said in his Caspiar-inflected accent. "I am pleased to meet you."

Andy was not above punching anyone's buttons, even fellow stage veterans. But despite those occasional goofs, his well-known characters had been co-opted by familiarity. Andy needed an escape, and Tony Clifton represented the perfect vehicle with which to make his getaway.

Clifton Unchained

We calculated the return of Tony Clifton. The essence of the plan was not only to create a new and improved Clifton, but also to give Andy back the anonymity he so loved. Our first task was to create the look. Andy's previous model of Tony consisted of little more than a fake mustache and sunglasses. The next version of Tony had to be something quite different. The specifications of our new Tony required that he look nothing like Andy, a chore that would require some very serious preparations.

I sat down with my sketch pad and designed a whole new Tony Clifton, from head to toe. Everything would be altered: height, weight, hair, costuming, and full prosthetic headpieces that would remake his nose, chin, jowls, and even his ears. It was a fairly complex undertaking, considerably more involved than simply slapping on some greasepaint, and once Andy approved the concept we then had to somehow execute it in latex. Andy's paranoia concerning the discovery of our "creation" kept us away from any potentially gossiping Hollywood makeup experts who possessed the advanced skills to pull off the transformation. That left me.

While at Carnegie-Mellon I had taken some stage makeup courses, but the creation of Clifton was something else. I acquired every book I could on the subject and studied carefully. Once I felt confident, I obtained some modeling clay and the sculpting tools and went to work. Andy impatiently called every day, wondering when Tony would be complete.

"Soon," I said, "soon. Keep your pants on, Kaufman, I'm an artist, I need time."

He'd laugh and hang up, but sometimes he'd call back a few hours later and have me describe the latest additions to our gestating baby. It took a few days of trial and error, but when Tony's clay visage was finally complete I called Andy to come over. When he entered my place he slowly approached the clay head, his eyes wide in wonderment. "I love him," he said, "he's perfect."

And with that, Tony Clifton was born again. Next I made a mold of Andy's face and then resculptured Tony's features onto his so the prosthetic pieces would fit his face seamlessly. I made a new mold of the altered Tony face and then began the laborious process of layering the latex into it by brushing it on in liquid form, letting it dry, then applying a new layer. After several layers I had an appliance that was sturdy yet not so thick as to call attention to itself. When it was complete I placed the pieces on the original head and phoned Andy.

"Hey Kaufman, you ready to become Clifton?"

"I'm on my way."

When Andy arrived I sat him down and over the course of the afternoon carefully placed the Tony Clifton face parts over his. Then I got the patented bad hairpiece in place and attached the padding for Tony's big gut. It took a few hours of makeup to blend the prosthetics with his face and I didn't let him see it until it was finished. As soon as I had made the final adjustment I stepped back to appraise my handiwork. If I do say so myself, it was quite remarkable.

"Well?" he asked.

"Go look," I said, pointing to the bathroom.

I followed him and watched his face as he gazed into the mirror, now wholly unrecognizable as Andy Kaufman. There was a brief flicker of surprise and satisfaction, then Andy completely vanished. His body shifted and he assumed a different posture in a split second.

"Hey, not bad for a Polack," he snapped in his trademark nasal Bronx twang. "What you say your name was again?"

"Bob." I was now talking to the reborn Tony Clifton.

"Bob? Bob? I like Bugsy. What say we go meet some dames, huh, Bugsy?"

We hopped in Andy's other car, a pink Cadillac ragtop he'd rented just for Tony, and headed down to Hollywood Boulevard, where Andy, er, Tony outfitted himself with a whole new wardrobe. Tony Clifton's new duds consisted of a ridiculously bright peach brocade tuxedo, a blue ruffled shirt, and a butterfly bow tie, just like the kind Jerry Lewis wears on his telethon. The transformation was complete, so we headed to the steak joint where Cindy and I used to have lunch. As I described it earlier, Musso & Frank is a classic steak house in the middle of Hollywood where celebs are often seen wolfing down hearty filets and sirloins. We blew in, and Tony immediately started working the room, hopping from booth to booth like some glad-handing star whom no one recognized but everyone was sure was "somebody." Tony chatted with people at their tables and bought drinks all around.

From the moment he walked in he was the life of the party, the antithesis of Andy, who normally would have disappeared into the rich, polished woodwork rather than risk having to speak with anyone. The restaurant management deferred to us, given Tony's overwhelming demeanor, and we were quickly given the best seat in the place and assigned two waiters. Then Andy as Tony did something that horrified me: he ordered a glass — not a shot — of bourbon and a steak the size of a dictionary. He also asked one of our waiters to get him a pack of cigarettes.

Andy Kaufman was a confirmed vegetarian and teetotaler who would usually leave the room if anyone even hinted at lighting a cigarette. But as Tony Clifton, he sucked down the bourbon like soda pop and consumed the immense steak quicker than a condemned man. Then he lit up his Camel and smoked it like a guy who'd been doing three packs a day for years. His total commitment to his rediscovered character was very impressive, but as his friend I couldn't help but be alarmed.

"Andy?" I said, leaning over the table and whispering. "You better slow down, you're not used to drinking."

"You fuckin' asshole!" he screamed. "Don't ever call me Andy! That fuckin' creep couldn't get laid if his life depended on it! I'm Tony, Tony Clifton, and don't you ever forget it or I'll push your face right in your soup!"

Andy never swore, so this was further evidence of his surrender to the persona of Tony Clifton. I briefly reflected on the notion that maybe it was really just the cape and tights that gave Superman his powers. The latex appliances, wardrobe, and bad hairpiece had changed Andy Kaufman so utterly I wondered for a moment if they also didn't possess magic powers.

Years later a noted clinical psychologist had an opportunity to meet Andy and Tony and was convinced that Andy exhibited very strong indices of multiple personality disorder. I'm not so sure, but I can say I was beginning to feel a little like Victor Frankenstein as I watched my friend fall into that black hole named Tony Clifton.

Tony represented Andy's need to reinvent himself. And like a child who had just drawn a cool car or a giraffe he was proud of, Andy wanted to show off his new creation to everyone he could think of. One of those groups of people was his *Taxi* family. I use the word "family" only in the loosest sense, as Andy never truly felt at ease with the cast. Most of them socialized in one way or another, but Andy rarely made an appearance at any *Taxi* function unless it was directly related to performing his character. One of the few times Andy did attend a function, disaster occurred. Andy reluctantly went to a cast party at a restaurant, and soon a very drunken Jeff Conaway jumped on Andy's case about his infrequent attendance on the set.

"You think you're better than the rest of us, Kaufman?" said the toasted Conaway.

"No, Jeff," said Andy softly, trying to extricate himself. "I don't."

"Yeah? Well, I think you do," said Jeff, whereupon he punched Andy, knocking him into the chopped-liver canapés. From then on Andy had a practical excuse for not showing at cast functions. To his credit, a contrite and sober Conaway phoned

Andy the next day and apologized profusely. Andy forgave him but from then on was understandably wary.

But now Andy wanted to bring his new, improved toy out of the closet, and where better to do that than at the place which, at least to Andy, needed the most fun: his workplace, the set of *Taxi*. The show's producers, Jim Brooks and Ed Weinberger, had been good sports and gone along with the separate contract for Tony Clifton, but now the time came for them to make good on the deal.

The plan was for Clifton to star in an episode scheduled for production in October '78 called "A Full House for Christmas." Tony Clifton was slated to play Nicky DePalma, brother of Danny DeVito's Louie and a degenerate Vegas gambler, who was to take the employees of the Sunshine Cab Company for a ride at the poker table before getting his comeuppance at the hands of Judd Hirsch's Alex Reiger. The unwitting producers felt they would play along with Andy and get a credible performance from his alter ego, Tony Clifton.

Andy's plan turned out to be more anarchist than artistic. He wanted to show all involved that what he did was far beyond the commercial trash he felt they were peddling as a sitcom. That the show was quickly developing a reputation as a terrific production mattered not a bit to Andy. Sitcoms by their nature were garbage to him and though he took their money he wanted to hammer home the point of the futility of their treasured belief that what they were creating was great art. He planned to accomplish that by raining confusion and mayhem upon the set of *Taxi*. Andy was no less an ardent hard-liner than a crazed Palestinian with Semtex taped to his chest and a detonator and the Koran clutched in his sweaty hands. He prepared to attack the infidels of *Taxi* as the suicidal terrorist Tony Clifton.

The cast was told that Andy was to arrive as Tony Clifton and that they should all refer to him as Tony, not Andy. That irritated Judd Hirsch and Jeff Conaway from the get-go as self-indulgent nonsense, but they finally agreed to play along with everyone else. The paradox was that Andy would wholeheartedly have agreed with Judd and Jeff: it was indeed absurd narcissism. But Andy — like the kid with the chemistry set — really just wanted to see what would happen. Usually Andy's lab rats were the audience, but in this case it was the cast and crew of *Taxi*.

For the Tuesday rehearsal I went to Andy's home to "Cliftonize" him. He had finally moved out of his apartment and now lived in Laurel Canyon in a modest, slightly secluded house with a swimming pool, steam room, and, adjacent to his bedroom, a wrestling room with mats completely covering the floor.

Once transformed into Clifton he single-handed the helm of his Caddy as we sped down Crescent Heights to the *Taxi* set at Paramount. As part of the plan, I too was disguised in a wig and sunglasses. Andy didn't want Clifton and his "handler" to have any association with himself. At the studio gate we were stopped by the guard, who refused to let us in.

"I'm Tony Clifton, the guest star on *Taxi*, you fucking idiot!" he railed.

The guard was shocked when he called the set and found Tony's claim to be true. As the poor man began to give us directions to the visitor parking lot, Tony exploded, "I'm no fucking visitor, asshole! I got my own parking spot."

And he did. A moment later we squealed into a slot, as ordered, with his name stenciled in right next to the parking place marked Andy Kaufman. Walking over to soundstage 25, with the large *Taxi* logo, we met Ed Weinberger, who escorted us to Tony's trailer, an expansive Winnebago. Andy had his own dressing room, as did the rest of the cast, but it was small, and in his infinite wisdom and humor Ed knew it would not be an acceptable facility for the likes of Mr. Clifton.

Inside, we found the Winnebago to be fit for a Clifton. An extensively stocked wet bar, plates and plates of deli food, and the most salient feature of all: two hookers. Supplied by "an entity associated with the production," they were delightful young ladies, both quite attractive despite their de rigueur hooker makeup and tawdry clothing. Tony's eyes lit up and he immediately began barking orders to them regarding how things were going to be, sexually, that is, and Ed took his cue and beat a hasty retreat.

The second Ed disappeared, Tony ushered his "new friends" into the back bedroom of the motor home. In no time the Winnebago began to rock back and forth. I went outside where a small crowd of P.A.'s and various crew members had assembled out of curiosity. Drawn by rumors, the assemblage was rewarded as the huge vehicle now bobbed up and down, and given the noises from within, the reasons why were obvious.

"Is that Andy in there?" a fresh-faced kid asked.

"No," I snapped, cloaked in my disguise, "that's Tony Clifton, ass-wipe, and don't you forget it!" As I walked away I thought, *Oh my god, it's catching . . . I'm getting Cliftonitis.* Andy had gotten both girls to strip to their panties, and the rocking was actually caused by their energetic wrestling. The winner of the contest would, of course, get to have sex with Tony and would also receive an extra C-note for her efforts.

After I returned to the motor home, I sat down in its main room with a bottle of juice and waited for something to happen . . . something, that is, other than the moans of pleasure coming from the bedroom. The knocks on the outside door were drowned out by the animal screams of sexual gratification, and when I finally heard them I leaped to answer the door. I was gazing down at a very different Ed Weinberger. He looked stricken.

"I need Andy, uh, Tony on the set right away."

"What's wrong?" I asked.

Ed stepped up into the unit. "Some of the cast are upset. A couple of them walked by and were appalled at what was going on in here."

I would have given a million bucks for a tape recorder at that moment, because that last sentence would have been a highlight of Andy's career, possibly his life. Ed, his sparkle gone, scurried away after reiterating his request that I rouse Tony ASAP. I tapped lightly on the door, but Tony, like a dog in the act, would have none of my interruptions, and I certainly understood his position (or positions). Here he was, at high noon on another perfect day in L.A., nailin' two gorgeous bimbos, all on the nickel of Paramount Pictures' television division, and there wasn't a goddamn thing anyone could do to stop him. Man, *this* was the golden age of Hollywood.

Meanwhile, everyone on the set cooled their heels as Tony Clifton finished his "staff meeting." When Tony finally walked onto the set, his flossy arm pieces caused nearly as much shock as did his total lack of resemblance to Andy. It turns out I was wrong about the girls, whom I thought were simply prostitutes. In reality, they were prostitutes but also aspiring actresses. Silly me. They were only hooking until they got their big breaks as actresses, so of course Tony had sweetened the deal with them by offering them speaking parts in the episode. So enthusiastic were they at the opportunity to be in such an important production, they momentarily lost their heads and reverted to their hooker roles, offering to service Tony Danza for free while they were at it. Tony Clifton never passed on that offer to Danza, saying, "You dames are all mine, and don't you forget it!"

Ed Weinberger, gentleman that he is, introduced Tony, as well as "Buffy" and "Candy," to the cast. Tony had the girls pass out little mechanical toys, windup dogs that went *woof, woof* when activated. The cast had been forced to wait an hour while Clifton got his rocks off, and you could feel the anger boiling up in Judd Hirsch and Jeff Conaway as the Clifton circus strengthened its hold over the set of *Taxi*.

Judd and Andy had a rivalry stemming from the initial contracts regarding the show, when each was told separately that he was to be the primary star of the show. Andy didn't give a rat's ass who got the billing, but it gnawed at Judd Hirsch. Danny De-Vito, on the other hand, was one of the coolest members of the cast and loved every minute of Kaufman's antics.

The script read-through didn't go well, with Tony either fumbling his lines or stopping to ad-lib dialogue. When he began inventing lines for his two protégées, who were by then seated on each of his knees, the situation came to a head. As the girls uttered such Clifton improvisations as "Tony, you're the greatest," and the equally trenchant "Tony puts other men to shame," the mood of the room cut to black. But Tony had not found his way to the powder keg with his lit match — that is, until he began to change Judd Hirsch's dialogue. It was just the button Tony had been looking for.

Judd Hirsch leaped up and yelled, "Okay, that's it, this is bull-shit!" Stepping away from the table, Judd leveled his considerable gaze at Ed and Jim Brooks. "Either he leaves or I do!" and with that he walked away. Tony Danza ran off to get his super-8 camera, convinced a melee was about to occur. Wisely, Ed suggested the rehearsal be canceled. The cast stood up, looking slightly shell-shocked. As Jeff Conaway stormed off in a rage, he hurled his woofing dog into the wall.

I accompanied Tony and the girls back to the Winnebago. Soon, Ed arrived at the door of the motor home and asked to speak with Tony alone.

"Girls," Tony motioned, "take a hike for a minute. But Zmuda stays."

The fact that he called me Zmuda indicated that Andy was back. Tony would have called me Bugsy. As the girls closed the door, Andy dropped the Clifton persona.

"Are they freaking out?" he asked Ed.

"Judd is calling his manager," he answered.

Andy guffawed. "Oh, this is great! I'm surprised they put up with Clifton as long as they did."

"Andy," said Ed gravely, "I gotta pull the plug on this. I've got to fire Tony."

Andy held up his hand in accord. "Don't worry, I agree, but just do me one last favor. Announce you've fired me, but I'll come back tomorrow, and I want you to have security throw me out, bodily."

Ed was confused, trying to follow his star's perverse request. "Why?"

"I want Tony Clifton to be bodily removed from every major motion-picture studio in Hollywood," was his proud answer.

Ed shrugged. "Okay, I'll have security throw you out."

Andy nodded. "Great!"

The next morning we arrived at the gate with our female escorts from the previous day. Tony bullied his way in, and we went over to the set. They already had a new actor to replace Tony. Within five minutes Tony was in a shouting match with Judd Hirsch. Security arrived just in the nick of time. A guard on either side of Tony Clifton grabbed him by the arms and, amid a stream of foul-mouthed invective, hauled him back to the gate and threw him off the lot.

Of course we had an *L.A. Times* writer named Bill Knoedelseder present and his story ended up in the paper the next day accompanied by a photo. Andy was outraged the *Times* had been naming him as the éminence grise behind Tony

Clifton. He fired off an indignant letter to set them straight, claiming he merely did an *impression* of Tony Clifton, who was a real person, just as he did an impression of another real person, Elvis, but he was, quite obviously, neither Tony nor Elvis. They published that letter as well as the one sent by Tony Clifton claiming that he was most definitely *not* Andy Kaufman and that in fact Kaufman was just riding his coattails by using his good name to try to get places. The circus continued.

Unfortunately for our hooker-actresses, they were not mentioned in the article. Norman Mailer once said, "If a hooker can't fall in love with her customer, what chance has she?" With Andy the reverse was true. Andy rarely met a woman he didn't fall for, and women generally loved Andy. But Andy began dating one of the two hookers from the *Taxi* stunt, which included dinners and various outings. But when they didn't have sex he didn't feel the need to pay her. After a while she tired of his unpaid attentions and changed her phone number.

Tony Clifton was Andy's new ticket out of town, his next major leap in reshuffling the showbiz deck. Andy was working to reinvent the rules of engagement for performers: the audience doesn't have to like you, and you don't have to be funny . . . just interesting. With Clifton, that conceit went even further: you could be downright *bad*.

Failure and perceived mediocrity were concepts Andy toyed with his entire career. Andy's anchor character, Foreign Man, was a lovable schlemiel, a failure. Now came Clifton like an evil superhero, energized with the red kryptonite of excess and ego and over-the-top bravado that Andy as Andy could never summon. Clifton's style was not to entertain but to provoke, and his goal was not to be applauded off the stage but physically removed. Andy was getting into deeper waters by pushing audiences to reject him, but in some ways it was almost a compulsion, sort of like the murderer who cries, *Stop me before I kill again!*

Foreign Man had become too familiar and too acceptable, so Tony was reborn to carry on the tradition of dereliction of talent. In Tony, Andy had contrived the foolproof act. He would no longer be constrained by the faint tugs of concern about success on stage. Now his act was that in failure he would achieve success. No audience or critic could second guess him; he had just figured out how to beat the house at their own game.

Though I'm sure my role in the Clifton fiasco on the set of *Taxi* had nothing to do with it, after a few months had passed, George Shapiro got a call. He called Andy.

"They don't want Bob on the set anymore," said George.

"Why not?" asked Andy. "He's my friend, he can come if I want."

"They seem to think he's a distraction," replied George. "It wasn't really a request."

My being 86ed from *Taxi* hit Andy a lot harder than it did me. I knew my presence had worn thin with the producers. It was actually a relief for me and gave me a lot more time to pursue other activities and jobs. For Andy it meant he had to face his job sans his playmate, and that wiped out most of what little joy he derived from doing the show. Andy was really an outsider on the set. On Fridays when the cast and crew wrapped the show, they would party until all hours. That occurred every week and Andy never joined in, preferring to drive the fifteen minutes home to meditate or entertain a female acquaintance. When the occasion once arose that one of those young ladies was my ex-wife, it afforded me the perfect opportunity to pull off a prank on Kaufman.

My ex-wife, Brenda, came out to L.A. in late 1978. Shelly and I were moving, so she took over our old place. During this time I noticed Andy had developed an eye for Brenda. I knew by his hints that he was attracted to her and wanted to ask her out but feared I might disapprove of the courtship. Nothing could have been further from the truth. Over the years as Brenda and I grew apart we occasionally set each other up with dates. But that was something Andy was never aware of, for he and I never discussed it.

One day he approached me and, after figuratively digging his toe in the dirt, finally asked, "Do you mind if I asked Brenda out?"

"No, of course not," I said, playing the courtly former spouse. "I think that's a good idea, Brenda's a great girl, you two would get along great."

I made it a point not to discuss any sort of sexual development that might occur nor did Andy intimate such a possibility. But I knew Andy. That night they went out and the next day I spoke with Brenda by phone. After the niceties I bottom-lined it. "So, did you sleep with him?"

There was a slight pause, as Brenda, a proper lady, mulled her answer. But there was just too much between us to be coy. "Yeah," she said slowly, "yeah we did. Why?"

"Uh, no reason, just thought I might mess with him. Don't let him know I know just yet."

I figured Andy's guilt would eventually get to him and I'd be able to read it all over his face or in his voice. It wasn't long before he called. I answered the phone in an *almost* overly chipper voice — all the better for contrast.

"Hello!" I said.

"Hey, Zmuda."

My cheery inflection crashed. "Oh . . . hi." I'd plummeted from top-of-the-mornin' to sullen and withdrawn in two words. I could hear his heart stop. "Listen," I said curtly, "I gotta go, I got something going here. I'll talk to you later."

I might as well have told him I hated him. His voice dropped to a frightened whisper. "Uh, okay, I'll talk to you later."

I hung up without saying good-bye. He was mortified as well as terrified our friendship was over because of a woman. I immediately called Brenda and told her to play along and that she could now tell Andy she "admitted" to me what had happened between them and that I hadn't taken it well. Andy called her not long after, and she did her part. Now I had him by the balls.

My phone began ringing every ten minutes, and to heighten Andy's distress, I carefully avoided answering it. He didn't want to come over and confront me for fear of what I might do. I loved that he was sweating bullets — the prince of jokers was now unknowingly the butt of one. Finally, when I guessed he was ready to crack I picked up the phone.

"You're there," he said, taken aback that I answered. "I, uh, wanted to talk to you about something."

"Yeah," I said darkly, "I'd like to talk to you, too, Kaufman."

"How 'bout Cantor's?" he said, suggesting one of our favorite late-night eateries.

"No," I said. "It'd be better outside, a place near you," I said mysteriously. "Let's go to that park on Franklin, just before Highland. Half an hour."

Though he agreed because he was the one sucking up, I knew his suspicions were rampant as to why I wanted to meet in a dark, deserted park around midnight. I made sure I arrived at the park before he did. Dressed forebodingly in a long trench coat, leather gloves, and a stocking cap pulled down around my ears, I found a big tree to hide behind. Then I waited.

Andy showed up. I kept out of sight as I watched him wander warily around, looking for me. As he glanced nervously at his watch I pulled back and bit my tongue to stifle a laugh. The moment was beautiful: here was Andy Kaufman in a very rare moment of total vulnerability. After I felt he'd sweated long enough, I stepped out from behind the tree.

He saw me and as he automatically started to move toward me he looked into my eyes and they were cold as ice, a stare one gives a soon-to-be-dead man. His eyes bounced to the menacing bulge in the pocket of my coat where my hand was . . . a *gun barrel!*

"You filthy, wife-stealing son of a, bitch!" I screamed as I pulled the gun from my coat and his hands went up hopelessly to shield himself from the blast . . .

"*Bang!*" I said, as my "finger" gun pointed at him. "You're dead," I said with a smirk.

For a brief moment he honestly believed I was gunning him down. When he looked through his outstretched hands and saw my finger, I burst into hysterics and had to sit on the damp grass, I was laughing so heartily. It took him a few moments to comprehend he'd been had, having bought my story hook, line, and sinker. Once the shock washed away he joined me, and we laughed long and hard. It was a good reminder for both of us, as put-on artists, how guilt can leave you completely unguarded.

By now, the media were reporting on all Andy's antics. People had heard about the campus wrestling matches and Tony Clifton's bizarre appearances and the rumors that Clifton was really Andy Kaufman who was also that "cute little foreign guy" on *Taxi*. Suddenly the public was demanding Andy's presence, and we were eager to give it to them.

Because Andy was growing in fame and stature as a performer, we decided to mount a big show. Hollywood was our natural choice because it was home turf. Of course Andy played the Improv and the Comedy Store all the time but those venues limited the scope of what we wanted to do. The Park West had been a fun show, but we decided it was time to pull out all the stops and produce a *big* show, the show to end all shows, something that would have people talking for years. Like a couple of bargain-basement Selznicks, we sat down and started laying out our *Gone With the Wind.*

We booked the twenty-three-hundred-seat Huntington Hartford in Hollywood for two shows, December 15 and 16, 1978. No sooner had tickets gone on sale than they sold out. For some time, we had been flirting with the notion of a large show somewhere in New York, and we decided the Huntington Hartford shows would be the trial run. If they went well, then Hello, Big Apple.

On the night of our first show, Andy had done some extra meditation, and the only thing that kept me from worrying too much was the pressure of five thousand details before we opened. Then the time came, and we brought down the house lights.

After a moment of anticipation, Tony Clifton took the stage. I had set up a 35-millimeter projector, and as he began the first strains of "The Star-Spangled Banner," I played images of the Blue Angels precision aerial stunt team executing intricate maneuvers as their aircraft spewed great plumes of red, white, and blue smoke. The audience stood, hands over their hearts, and sang along with Tony as I unfurled Old Glory. It was the largest flag I could find and had to be trucked in from Texas. It was stirring, and the crowd suddenly felt more as if they were at an event, like the Olympics or World Cup, than at a comedy show. Then Tony went to work.

Drinking in the standing ovation, Tony took a number of bows before the crowd settled. This was a hip, showbiz crowd, and most everyone knew that eight weeks earlier Tony Clifton had been unceremoniously tossed off the Paramount lot. Now he had returned in triumph, and the who's who of Tinsel Town applauded the sheer courage of this legend, this god even (albeit tin-plated), for he had done something almost all in attendance had wanted to do but lacked the courage: tell Hollywood to go fuck itself.

Tony sang for a while (backed up by his band, the Cliftones) and, in between verses, berated various proximate audience members, but he was not as vicious as usual, and the crowd was still with him. After a while, Tony signaled his band and the music stopped. He then took the microphone and strolled somberly across the stage as he related a very personal story of profound pain and unbounded joy.

"My wife, Ruth, was the best thing in my life, and when we had our baby, Susie, I was overjoyed. They were the two most precious pearls of my life," said Tony in a rare moment of vulnerability. "And a few years back, when Ruth passed on after an untimely illness, I didn't know what I was going to do, I didn't know if I could go on, but every time I looked into that little girl's big brown eyes and she'd say, 'Daddy, it's going to be all right,' well, I knew she was right," he related, his voice nearly breaking. "Folks, I wanna bring out the light of my life, my twelve-year-old angel, Susie. Honey, come on out and meet these nice people!"

As the little girl parted the curtains and shyly shuffled over to Tony, most were on the edges of their seats, some even wiping their eyes, as Tony stood to embrace his beloved child and then sat her on his knee to sing a sentimental duet.

Certainly this guy wasn't as awful as they had heard; in fact, the big lug apparently had a heart of gold. And even if this blustering lounge denizen wasn't really Andy Kaufman, he had them in the palm of his hand. The band struck up a soft old show tune, and father and daughter began to sing. It was a wonderful, heart-touching moment, at least until the kid made a mistake by singing over Tony's part.

Suddenly his hand shot up, and the loud smack it made against her cheek couldn't have stunned the audience more had it been a gunshot.

"What are you, a fucking idiot?" screeched Tony. The stunned child began to cry.

"Shut the fuck up or I'll give you another one." Some of the horrified onlookers stood and booed.

"Hey," cautioned Tony, "don't boo. She's only a child and doesn't know any better. She'll think you don't like her."

He continued to sing as the little girl whimpered and tried to sing along. She fumbled her next verse and burst into full-blown tears.

"I said shut up, kid!" yelled Tony. "I'm tryin' to entertain da folks!"

With that, the pitiful, browbeaten youngster jumped down and ran from the stage, bawling her head off. Two security guards swiftly emerged from the wings and removed Tony, to the cheers of the crowd. I announced a short intermission as Andy got out of his Tony getup. And Tony's little girl? She was back-stage having a soda, laughing with the crew. Nowhere near twelve (she just looked it from a distance), she was one helluva good actress. A few minutes later Andy took the stage to wild ap-plause and began his act, which encompassed everything from lip-synching to his sing-along gibberish harvest song from Caspiar, to his Yiddish "MacArthur Park," and finally to his killer Elvis. It was two spectacular hours.

Just as the crowd gave Andy his standing O and was preparing to exit after a wonderful show, Andy threw a surprise at them: the Radio City Music Hall Rockettes suddenly took the stage, all 34 of them, high-kicking over their heads. Next, the back door opened and 350 robed members of the Mormon Tabernacle Choir marched up the aisle singing "Hallelujah" from Handel's *Messiah*.

Then, just when they thought nothing could top that, Andy introduced Santa Claus, who flew (on a special rigging I found) down to the stage, where he was greeted by Andy. It began to *snow*. Now the audience was delirious with joy, buzzing in de-light. Andy took the microphone and stepped to the lip of the stage.

"Everyone, I have a very special treat for you. If you will all proceed outside in a very orderly manner, there are twenty-five buses waiting to take you to milk and cookies."

Of course everyone thought it was another Kaufman smoke job until they went outside and saw he wasn't kidding. There *were* twenty-five school buses, doors open, waiting to take the twenty-three hundred guests to their treats. Andy came out and routed people into the buses, then they all caravanned twelve blocks down Sunset to the Olde Spaghetti Factory where, inside, the audience was welcomed by fifty volunteers wearing Uncle Andy T-shirts.

Each audience member was handed a milk carton and a package of Famous Amos cookies. Wally "Famous" Amos wasn't that famous back then, but he was on his way. Wally generously gave me twenty-five hundred bags of cookies to hand out to our guests. A little more than two years later, in February 1981, Andy would return the favor, and "Famous Amos" would star in a dream sequence on *Taxi* wherein he gives cookie-making Latka the comically cynical advice that family and friends are great, but success and cash are better.

The cookie-munching group was so thrilled it was as if they'd died and gone to Andy's version of heaven. We'd turned the tough, jaded Hollywood "insiders" into kids again. People came up to me to shake my hand, and men and women mobbed Andy so they could hug him and tell him it was one of the most magical experiences of their lives.

Every time Andy looked at me that night, it was with total admiration, for only he and I knew the truth, that his success that night was the direct result of my writing and producing the show. The Rockettes, the Mormon Tabernacle Choir, Santa Claus, the snow, and the buses were my ideas. Andy truly appreciated that I kept my mouth shut about it and let him take the credit. It was not just a matter of who was buttering my bread; after all, I owed everything to Andy and was content giving him back whatever I could.

I secretly enjoyed every time Andy did a talk show such as Tom Snyder's or Letterman's and the host would praise him for his brilliance in taking the audience out in buses for milk and cookies. It was almost as if the milk and cookies episode had become his new trademark. I was content to stay behind the scenes and pull the strings. In most print interviews, Andy readily admitted to having a writer. But talk shows were different. On those he had to maintain the mystique of being out there all alone and quite mad.

The day after the second show, Andy was admitted to Cedars-Sinai Hospital with debilitating hepatitis. Andy had performed his act while suffering from a 104-degree temperature. He took a few days to recuperate despite loathing downtime. Meanwhile, news of the amazing show spread. Soon we were in talks with the management at Carnegie Hall to stage our Huntington show there. We rolled up our sleeves and added a few surprises. This was a dream come true for Andy as he'd always visualized the apex of career success as playing Carnegie Hall.

In February 1979, a couple of months before the Carnegie show, we were in New York to wrap up some details regarding the show and for an appearance by Andy on *SNL*. After *SNL* wrapped we went out for some late dinner. We had just taken our table when an odd-looking young man with an improbably over-wrought haute couture look approached.

"Excuse me," he said, then focused on Kaufman, "but Andy Warhol is sitting over there and would just love to meet you."

We looked at each other, shrugged why not, then followed the artistic young fellow over to the table of the Pale One. Warhol stood, greeted us, and shook our hands. "Would you care to join me?" he offered.

What were we going to say? We sat down. The minion excused himself, so it was just the three amigos, Bob and Andy squared. I knew Kaufman had a deep appreciation for Warhol, for aside from seeing him as a very talented artist, he also respected Warhol as a fellow put-on master. Warhol's famous Campbell's Soup Can veritably screamed, *I'm art because he says I am!* Kaufman loved that brand of artiste's bravado. His own forays into such onstage put-ons for art's sake included doing his laundry — with a real washer and dryer — or leisurely eating while everyone just numbly watched.

The elevation of the ordinary to the level of art was something they shared. Despite their commonality as renegade creative intellects, they also shared another trait: excruciating shyness. Consequently, as soon as the hellos and idle chatter were memories, uncomfortable silence set in.

Eventually Warhol muttered a few compliments, then Kaufman muttered a few back, followed by more silence. After a moment, Kaufman perked up. "We did a special for ABC a year or so ago," he offered. "It hasn't aired yet, but I think you'd like it."

Kaufman was right, our special was pretty avant-garde, apparently a little too much so for that tight-ass Fred Silverman, I thought bitterly.

"What did you do in it?" asked the wan Andy.

"Oh, we did some funny bits and had some guests. Howdy Doody was my special guest."

"Howdy Doody? Really . . .," mused the producer of several Paul Morrissey movies.

Bingo. The dueling Andys suddenly bonded faster than you could say "pop phenomenons." Warhol was also quite taken by the little wooden man, and it turned out he had as much Howdy nomenclature tucked between his ears as Kaufman. Eventually the Howdy recitation wound down, but they were on to other subjects — once the ice was broken I couldn't get them to shut up.

Lorne Michaels years later saw a parallel between the Andys. "I call it the 'Warhol sensibility,'" he said. "In Warhol's *Sleep*, an eight-hour film of a man just sleeping, it's a nonclimax, he doesn't wake up. Like Andy's Gatsby, he doesn't read and fall into a hole. Nothing happens. It was conceptual and pure. I wish I could say it was popular. It was certainly popular in the small segment of society that I lived in. In the seventies, the kids called it Brechtian." When Lorne first spotted Kaufman, he had the insight and wisdom to see that in Andy he wasn't dealing with a simple comedian, but rather a bona fide conceptual artist.

On returning to New York a few months later we hit the ground running with the nearly overwhelming Carnegie show prep. A few days before the April 26, 1979, show date someone in management at Carnegie Hall mentioned that some crazy had been out front railing at potential ticket buyers not to patronize our show. They tried to underplay it but nevertheless thought we should know.

"No problem," I said dismissively, "it's New York."

Sure enough, a deranged man sporting long, scraggly, blond hair and swathed in street rags stood outside Carnegie Hall for a couple of days and screamed at anyone who passed by, let alone walked up to the ticket window. "Andy Kaufman is the Antichrist!" he wailed. "The *Antichrist*, I tell you!" To bolster his claim he wielded a cardboard sign: Andy Kaufman = Anti-Christ. The fervor didn't hurt ticket sales, as the show sold out during the lunatic's preachments to the deaf. We never told Carnegie Hall management that the insane man was Andy in disguise.

"When I was a young boy," Andy began, as he addressed the Carnegie audience that night after the boffo opening, "I'd tell my Grandma Pearl, who I love more than anything, that someday her little Andy would be famous and he'd be here, at Carnegie Hall. And I told her when I was, I'd give her the best seat in the house. Well, here I am . . . ," and with that a little old lady walked out onstage, "and this is my Grandma Pearl."

She and Andy had a heartwarming hug, and the audience went wild. "I said I'd make good on my promise, so I had her flown in from Florida. But you need a place to sit, don't you, Grandma?"

The frail oldster nodded, whereupon Andy gestured and two Mayflower moving men leaped from the wings bearing a frilly couch. They set it at the edge of the stage. "I also had your sofa flown in and it is now the best seat in the house."

It was a warm fuzzy moment and everyone in the place could see the pride on that little lady's face as she gazed adoringly at her Andy. Grandma watched the entire show from her sofa, and in the end, as at the Huntington, we brought out the Rockettes and the Mormon Tabernacle Choir. As the snow once again began falling, and just before he invited the audience out for milk and cookies, Andy coaxed Grandma Pearl to take a bow.

Her ancient, tortured joints forced her to rise ever so slowly, and then she ambled over to the footlights. Gingerly bending her sore old back she took a long bow, and as the audience's warm applause encouraged her, suddenly, in one incredible, lightning gesture, she pulled off her wig and sent it flying into the front row. Then, peeling back her face, she revealed to all that she was really Robin Williams! This was Robin's first rough sketch of what would eventually become his brilliant character in *Mrs. Doubtfire*.

Once again, we did the milk-and-cookies run, only this time it required 35 buses and four months of clearing red tape with the city of New York to get a permit to do so. For this incarnation of "Milk & Cookies" we hired magicians, sword swallowers, midgets, and fire eaters. We tried to find Turko the Half Man from our childhoods, but to our great disappointment, he had apparently passed on to that great sideshow in the sky. I guess as a half man you only got a half life in the bargain.

During the cookie-and-milk festivities, Andy made an offer to wrestle any woman in the house. Women began lining up, and the party continued unabated until I finally looked at my watch and was alarmed to see we were just passing 1 A.M. Fearing the awaiting bus drivers would soon be into some healthy overtime that could put the hurt on Andy's checkbook, I plowed my way through the partyers and whispered my concerns to him.

"What should we do?" he asked, surrounded as we were by a revelry with no apparent end in sight.

"Tell them to go home and get some sleep because the show will continue tomorrow morning at eight-thirty on the Staten Island ferry."

"Really?" said Andy innocently.

"Christ, Kaufman, I don't know, just say something, we need to get out of here!"

Andy repeated exactly what I'd said, and in no time the obedient crowd dispersed. When I got back to the hotel and hit the sack after a week of day and night preparations for the show, the last thing I wanted to do was get up at 8 A.M. Besides, I'd gotten lucky, and one of the Rockettes was slumbering next to me, having demonstrated into the wee hours how limber dancers really are.

At precisely eight o'clock my phone began ringing. I ignored three or four rings, and whoever it was gave up. I went back to sleep, and five minutes later there was a hard knocking at my door. I staggered out of bed and found Andy all bundled up and ready to go.

"Oh God, now what is it?" I said impatiently.

"Do you think anybody took us seriously?"

"About . . . ?" It was early and the notion anyone took us seriously about anything tasked my brain too much.

"About the ferry. Do you think anyone really went down to the Staten Island ferry?"

"No way," I said, but doubt instantly began forming. "They all knew it was a joke. Sure. Go back to sleep."

"You think so?"

"Yeah, absolutely, no one believed us."

"I was just worried," he said, then turned to leave. "Okay, you're right."

As he moved off down the hall I pictured the dock and that one lone, trusting fan standing there. I shook my head. "Shit . . ."

Andy turned. "What?"

"All right, let's go."

I left a note for the Rockette to stay put, and then Andy and I jumped in a cab.

"Staten Island ferry," I ordered the driver.

As we arrived at the ferry dock on the south tip of Manhattan we were stunned to see a crowd of about three hundred milling around — all familiar faces from the night before. In an instant, Andy and I were close to tears because our audience had thought enough of Andy to pull one over on him. A cheer went up as we alighted from the hack. Andy waded to the front of the group and bought tickets for all, then once aboard, treated everyone to ice cream. On the trip to Staten Island, Andy again made his offer to wrestle any of the ladies, so right there on the deck he took on five going and four more coming back.

And the Rockette was still there when I returned.

For the next few days we hung out in the city, basking in the glow of having just blown the lid off the place. Overnight, Andy became the talk of the town after our Carnegie Hall show rippled out as the cause célèbre of Gotham's trendy entertainment scene. People of all walks of life suddenly wanted to meet Andy.

One afternoon we were crossing Fifth Avenue, and a guy approached us and asked for Andy's autograph. Andy was always obliging, almost too much so. Then the man made an odd request. "Listen, Mr. Kaufman, Andy, my wife is your biggest fan, she loves you, and, uh, well, we only live a few blocks away and I was wondering if you'd wait a minute until I went and got her? She'd kill me if I didn't."

I couldn't believe my ears and looked to Kaufman to blow this clown off. I was even more stupefied when he said, "Sure, go get her. We'll wait."

As the guy ran off, I said, "What are you thinking? We're just gonna stand here?"

"Zmuda, c'mon, this guy's a fan," he said instructively. "It's my fans who've made me what I am. That's the difference between me and other celebrities. See, I remember that."

Okay, I thought, *that Kaufman head is swelling again and I need to lower the air pressure inside*. I decided to bide my time. After forty interminable minutes the guy returned, this time with his starstruck wife in tow. Now, more than ever, I wanted to get even with Andy for making me wait. I saw my opportunity to pounce and very loudly announced, "You see, that's the difference between Andy Kaufman and other celebrities. He knows it's the fans who made him what he is today."

Andy immediately realized where I was going and shot me a look, but the fuse was lit and there wasn't a damn thing he could do. As a crowd gathered I continued, laying it on with a trowel. "That's right. Kaufman knows it's fans like yourselves that have made him a star!"

After a few moments doing my best sideshow barker, enough people had assembled that I felt it was time to sink the knife. "As a matter of fact," I roared, pointing at the original couple, "I think you, Andy, should take this lovely couple out to dinner!"

Our small curbside audience registered their approval with whistles and applause, but the husband was reluctant. "Oh, you don't have to do that, Andy."

"Nonsense!" I said. "He wants to, believe me, he does! Don't you, Andy?"

He was on the spot. I'd served him back his words as an hors d'oeuvre.

"Yeah, sure, I'd love to," he said, giving me the glance of death. After politely declining the trio's invitation to accompany them by saying it was best Andy commune with his public alone, I chuckled to myself as the big-shot celebrity and his new friends went off down the sidewalk in search of an eatery.

The next night we went out to dine in a fashionable restaurant and concluded it was time for a little bit of our patented mischief. When the waiter arrived at our table, he took one look at Andy and was instantly repulsed by the massive ball of snot hanging from his left nostril. Of course he was too embarrassed to say anything and averted his eyes as Andy ordered his salad.

When I lowered my menu, the young aspiring actor nearly dropped his order pad when he zeroed in on the king-size booger cantilevered from my own snot locker. He blanched, then reflexively looked back at Andy, who now had monumental green chunks of solidified mucus poised under *both* nose holes. Then the kid got it and started laughing, so we removed the bogus boogers and laughed with him. Andy never left home without fake snot in his pocket.

We returned to Hollywood, and Andy began working on his first feature film, *In God We Tru$t*. It was a small but flashy role, and best of all he was to act opposite Richard Pryor. British comedian Marty Feldman (another Shapiro/West client) had sent Andy a warm letter some months earlier asking him if he would do him the honor of appearing in a film he had written and was planning to direct. Andy was more than happy to oblige and was assigned the character of Armageddon T. Thunderbird, a bombastic tele-vangelist.

The film debuted in 1980 and bombed, and poor Marty Feldman's heart also failed, less than two years later. And though the lack of success of that film didn't hurt Andy's chances in Hollywood, his next picture would be critical. Hollywood has a frightening habit of branding one "not movie material" on a second strike that can kill or severely hinder a career. Despite his seemingly anti-Hollywood leanings, Andy did one day want to succeed in the movies. He would get another chance in two years.

8

Mustang Sally

I said, "This man is outta his mind." But I dug it because I said,
"This man shows there are no boundaries."

SINBAD

After Andy's ninety-minute special aired, on August 28, 1979, Andy was as hot as he'd ever been. As his writer, I was the beneficiary of his success. Outside the industry's tight inner circle my abilities were unknown, but in the minds of the right people I was developing a rep as a very savvy and creative writer, the man behind the maniac. Of course, we had to keep my role semi-classified; after all, how could such a fluid talent, such an iconoclast, have a writer? That illusion was our carefully guarded secret. To the public, we worked hard to promulgate the notion that Andy Kaufman would never use a writer. *Writers? Writers? He don't need no stinkin' writers.*

Sure, yeah, absolutely.

Offers began coming in for Andy left and right. One of the propositions was from Harrah's Casino in Las Vegas. Though casino shows had long been the domain of the blue-hair set, the management of the gambling facilities realized they'd better approach a fresh, younger demographic before their current clientele died of old age. Yuppies were now lined up as management's latest victims, a new crop of hedonists they hoped would arrive in droves and happily surrender their paychecks to the cashiers and dealers. But sheer gambling alone was too naked an inducement to come to Vegas, and as it was in the beginning and now and ever shall be, entertainment was the guilt-softening ele-

So far, he looks normal!
Comic Relief Archives,
Courtesy of the Kaufman estate

Andy at camp (fourth from left)
Comic Relief Archives, Courtesy of the Kaufman estate

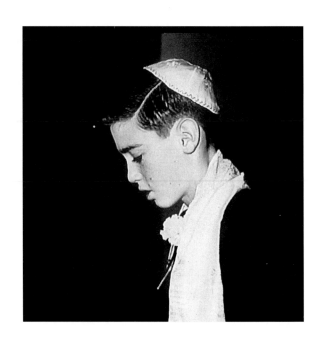

A good Jewish boy

Comic Relief Archives, Courtesy of the Kaufman estate

The Kaufman clan

Comic Relief Archives, Courtesy of the Kaufman estate

Following the beat of a different drummer
Comic Relief Archives, Courtesy of the Kaufman estate

The kid act that he would eventually do for adults
Comic Relief Archives, Courtesy of Grahm Junior College

His childhood idol

Comic Relief Archives, Elizabeth Wolynski

Following the beat of a different drummer

Comic Relief Archives, Courtesy of the Kaufman estate

The kid act that he would eventually do for adults

Comic Relief Archives, Courtesy of Grahm Junior College

Andy as the Hillbilly Cat
Comic Relief Archives

**Robin Williams—
a die-hard Kaufman
fan—backstage at
Carnegie Hall**
*Comic Relief Archives,
Elizabeth Wolynski*

<u>Saturday Night Live</u> sketch: Andy as Elvis, Zmuda as Red West
Comic Relief Archives

His childhood idol

Comic Relief Archives, Elizabeth Wolynski

I'm shocked Andy showed up for the the photo shoot.

Comic Relief Archives

Letterman and Merv fooled! They think it's Andy . . . it's really Zmuda.

Comic Relief Archives

Andy as the fakir, with the obedient Zmuda by his side

Comic Relief Archives

Tony Clifton makeup, designed for both Kaufman and Zmuda faces
Comic Relief Archives

International singing sensation Tony Clifton with the Cliftonettes— Harrah's Main Show Room
Comic Relief Archives

Two living legends, together at last!
Comic Relief Archives, Courtesy of Jim Henson Productions

Judd Hirsch yelling at Clifton while two prostitutes look on
Bill Knoedelseder

Tony Clifton getting thrown off the Paramount lot
Bill Knoedelseder

Over 300 wrestling matches. No woman ever won the money.

Comic Relief Archives, Elizabeth Wolynski

Andy stalking his prey, Zmuda as referee

Comic Relief Archives, Elizabeth Wolynski

Zmuda choreographing the Radio City Music Hall Rockettes for the Carnegie Hall Show
Comic Relief Archives, Elizabeth Wolynski

Zmuda and Kaufman triumphant as they receive a standing ovation from the Carnegie Hall Audience
Comic Relief Archives, Elizabeth Wolynski

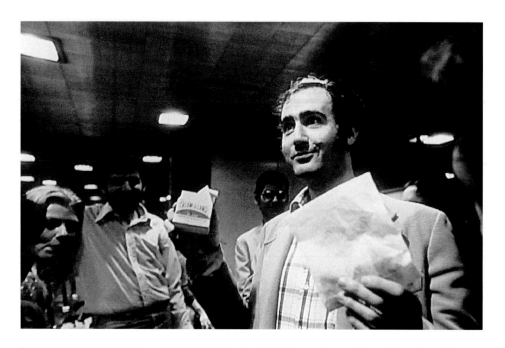

Andy takes the entire Carnegie Hall audience of 1,800 people out for milk and cookies.
Comic Relief Archives, Elizabeth Wolynski

**Bob Zmuda (above)
with Robin Williams,
Whoopi Goldberg, and
Billy Crystal**
Comic Relief Archives

Zmuda teaching Jim Carrey how to do Clifton

The legendary Milos Foreman, directing Bob Zmuda and Jim Carrey in Man on the Moon

ment necessary to bring in the largest contingent: *I paid for my trip and saw a couple of good shows.* Uh-huh, if you say so.

The only adjustment for casino management was shifting some of their entertainment resources from the traditional to the fashionable. They looked to the *Saturday Night Live* group as their yardstick of cool, and perceived Andy as the seminal artist among them. Because he was also on a hit sitcom, they thought he must be a big draw for young professionals. Thus strategized, Harrah's called and said, "Andy Kaufman? Come on down!"

Andy wasn't so sure about playing Vegas, despite its rich history and, of course, the important role it had served in Elvis's career. The rub was that he would be constrained from experimentation and would instead be required to offer up his "killer set" night after night. I saw it as a good career move and wanted Andy to take it, but he needed some convincing.

My family had been vacationing in the Tahoe area since I was around twelve, so I knew one piece of information that might inspire Andy to take a gig with Harrah's in Reno, if not the one in Vegas.

"You know, Andy, Harrah's has a club in Reno. It's huge."

"So? Why would I go there? I don't particularly want to go to Vegas. What's with Reno?"

"Well, Reno's surrounded by legal brothels."

"Really? But doesn't Vegas have them too?"

"They're way outside Vegas, plus they aren't as good, mostly rip-offs," I offered knowingly. "There's more in Reno and they're a lot better."

"Oh yeah? Lots of them?" I could tell I had him.

"Yeah, there's a ton of whorehouses up there," I assured him, "good ones."

"They're close by?"

"Fifteen minutes, tops. Most of them."

"Okay, but what are the girls like?"

"They're pretty decent, in fact lots of 'em are drop-dead beautiful."

Magic words. Andy got on the phone to George Shapiro, who got on the phone to Harrah's and made them a counteroffer: Andy would perform, but it would be at their club in Reno.

On September 13, 1979, we held a lavish press conference in

the major city nearest Reno: San Francisco. Harrah's flew reporters in from all over the country, and once the room filled I counted upwards of seventy representatives of the national media. It was all quite civil . . . then disaster struck. A youthful, longhaired reporter claiming to be from the powerful *Detroit Free Press* stuck up his hand. When Andy made the mistake of calling on him, the man's attitude spilled out like so much bile.

Apparently incensed by Kaufman's attempts to "buy" the press with such transparent incentives as free tickets, hotels, and piles of food, the subversive fledgling newshound, who was obviously trying to make a name by assassinating a celebrity, began a rapid-fire series of embarrassing questions that left Andy fumbling for answers.

"Mr. Kaufman, at Carnegie Hall, on December sixteenth and seventeenth of 1978, is it true the Radio City Music Hall Rockettes and the Mormon Tabernacle Choir appeared as part of your show?"

Andy nodded proudly. "Yes, that's true."

"And is it not a fact, Mr. Kaufman," continued the ardent scribe, "that members of the Olga Fricker School of Dance appeared in place of the real Rockettes, and that the Manhattan City Choir performed in lieu of the actual Mormon Tabernacle Choir?"

Andy looked stunned and hemmed and hawed, but the reporter continued.

"Is it true, Mr. Kaufman, that the wrestling match at this same concert was fixed?"

"No." Andy tried protesting despite his shock. "I, uh, we, the matches are all . . ."

"Mr. Kaufman," continued the Doberman with the note pad, "would you agree that the wrestling segments of your concerts have no redeeming entertainment value whatsoever, and are in fact a carefully contrived opportunity for you to fulfill your insanely perverse sexual fantasies?"

This stuff was below the belt, and Andy was reeling. The rest of the reporters stood by, struck mute by their vicious colleague as his mouth continued to consume Kaufman's ass. "Mr. Kaufman, isn't it true there is a petition now circulating in New York

City, containing more than five thousand signatures, demanding you be put under immediate and intensive psychiatric care?"

Andy's mouth was moving but nothing was coming out. He was all alone up there at the podium and there wasn't a damn thing I could do to help him. He swallowed hard, desperately seeking the answer that would end this attack, but it didn't come.

"Jaws" continued his merciless assault. "Isn't it a fact, Mr. Kaufman, that you are in the process of opening Andy Kaufman Wrestling Palace franchises in every major city? Are they not just thinly veiled arenas of sick pleasure where sexual deviants like yourself are provided an opportunity to grope young women under the guise of wrestling?"

"No, that's not true . . ."

"What exactly is your reasoning behind this wrestling routine? We'd like to know how you justify it." Before Andy could answer, the man moved on. "Mr. Kaufman, you are aware, aren't you, of the widely reported resentment growing among the cast of *Taxi* and in the Hollywood community in general regarding the fact you are uncommitted to your job, working on the *Taxi* set only two days a week while the rest of the actors are forced to work five? Don't you think you're trying to get away with a little too much? Don't you feel the least bit guilty?"

Andy was ready to flee, cornered as he was, but the next words were the gunshot through the head that bounced fifteen ways and hit Connolly too. "Mr. Kaufman, one last question. Are you in fact Tony Clifton?"

Andy stood to run away, when a Harrah's publicist descended upon this impossibly rude reporter and had him ejected from the proceedings. "Get your hands off me, you goons!" he screamed as he was carted off. Just as he got to the door, he grabbed the frame long enough to fire his last shot. "Isn't it true you've been under psychiatric care by Dr. Joseph Troiani for the past eleven years for acute multiple personality disorder? *Why are you hiding this from the American public?!*"

Then he was gone. But the damage had been done. The questions had hit him alarmingly close to home. Though he tried to put on a happy face, the rest of the reporters scribbled down every damning word, and a very chastened Andy thanked them and retreated out the side door. Devastated, he jumped into a waiting limo and headed for the airport. A half block away from the hotel, he glanced out the window and spied the reporter who'd just ruined his career. He rolled down the window.

"Hey! *You!*"

The reporter walked over. "What?"

"Thanks a lot. I'm dead. You happy?"

The door opened and I climbed in. "Completely. You?"

"Perfect," said Andy, and we laughed our asses off all the way to SFO. My accusations of the Rockettes and the Mormon Tabernacle Choir were accurate. Andy would have gone broke had I hired the real ones.

Embracing P. T. Barnum's conviction that "it doesn't matter what they say about you as long as they spell the name correctly," our barometer of success soon became the degree to which we could hoodwink the press. Andy's regular publicist, a lovely woman named Estelle Endler, was completely baffled as to what to make of our antics. Our brand of lunacy was something she had never witnessed, and she was constantly astonished by the amount of ink we were getting, not only in entertainment columns and the trades, but also in the sports pages and the hard news sections of various papers. We even developed an approach to con the "rags": the tabloids such as the *National Enquirer.*

I learned about a reporter for the *National Enquirer* who would hang out in the bar at a particular West Hollywood nightspot and keep her ears open for industry-oriented dirt. I knew who she was and she knew who I was, but she didn't know I knew who she was. Many a time when Andy and I wanted to plant disinformation I would go into that bar, feign intoxication, then spill my guts to some unsuspecting stranger as our "ear" eavesdropped. A week later the "bullshit scoop" would appear in black and white and Andy and I would die laughing and slap each other on the back for having pulled off a fruitful commando raid on yet another unsuspecting journalist.

We had to choose an opening act for the Reno gig. Tony Clifton was out of the question. He required far too much effort, given his two and a half hours of makeup and the draining commitment the character demanded of Andy. Andy settled on a pretty and ambitious young actress-singer named Lisa Hartman. During the '77–'78 season, Lisa had starred in an ABC sitcom called *Tabitha*, a spin-off of *Bewitched*. (Years later, Lisa married country crooner Clint Black.)

Momentarily forgetting the allure of the local brothels, Andy seized on Lisa as his opener not because he thought she was overwhelmingly talented, but simply because she was a babe and he wanted to have her. Andy's scheme was to get to Reno, settle in for a few minutes, then put the moves on Lisa. Unfortunately for the randy Mr. Kaufman, the best-laid plans didn't account for Lisa showing up with her mother (who was also her manager) or for the main deal-buster: her boyfriend. Andy felt screwed. He'd hired Lisa assuming she would be grateful and ball him all week, only to learn that their passionate love affair was over before it began. On top of that, Andy later discovered that he hated her singing, but he had to tolerate her warbling every night as it filtered down to him in his dressing room.

When one is the headliner for Harrah's in Reno you do not stay at the hotel, rather you are feted like a monarch in the sumptuous Harrah's House, a fabulous, exclusive resort just outside town featuring indoor tennis courts, pools, and kingly accommodations, with a limo and servants at your beck and call. Obviously frustrated by his undeveloped tryst with Lisa Hartman, Andy came into my suite as I was unpacking, ready to play.

"So, where are these brothels?" he asked.

Just outside Sparks, Nevada, which is directly adjacent to Reno's northeast side, lay the infamous Mustang Ranch, a collection of fenced buildings housing the most famous brothel on earth. We exited the limo and went to the first gate, and I buzzed, preparing to demonstrate to Kaufman my cathouse savvy.

We entered and the madam, a world-weary but cordial middle-aged woman, greeted us, "Good evening, gentlemen," and escorted us to the main room. There we were given a look at a lineup of young ladies and asked to choose. I politely refused.

"Hey Zmuda," whispered Andy, "what are we waiting for?"

I pointed to the bar. "Don't worry, Kaufman, I know what I'm doing."

We sat down in the bar, and in no time girls began hovering.

"This way," I said, after a few moments, "we can take our time and pick the ones we want. Have a drink, talk a little, you know, get to know them before deciding. Besides, if you choose one right away she'll hit you up for a fortune."

After fifteen or twenty minutes Andy had spoken with several girls but didn't seem able to decide. A couple minutes later he turned. "I want them all," he said emphatically.

"Don't we all."

"No, Zmuda, I'm serious, I want them all. Where's the head lady?"

"Andy, are you fuckin' nuts? There's gotta be dozens of girls. Don't play games here, they'll take you seriously."

"I am serious," he shot back. I suddenly realized he was.

Generally, Andy liked his women tall and pretty. But Andy liked women, period. To their credit, the cross section we'd seen so far ranged from decent to total knockouts.

"These girls are pretty good-looking," he said. "But the ones working, the ones we haven't seen, they have to be as good, if not better, right? That's why they're busy, wouldn't you think?"

"I suppose," I said, not disagreeing with his logic.

"So that's why I want them all."

"Be serious," I cautioned.

"I am. I've got a whole week. I can do it."

Andy caught the eye of the madam and waved her over. "How many girls do you have?"

The madam looked curiously at him, not knowing why he cared. "I think about forty-two this week. Why?"

"I want them all, all forty-two. I'll bet you I can sleep with all of them."

"Bet me?" repeated the madam rhetorically. "I don't take bets like that, honey."

"No, no," said Andy, "I'll pay. Just a gentlemen's bet. I'm here a week, over in Reno, so that's, what, six a day? I can do it."

Had he been anyone else, the woman would have had her burly security staff walk us to our waiting limo right then, but she knew who Andy was, and that sparkle in his eyes charmed the hell out of her. He negotiated a rate of around a hundred dollars per girl (*twice* the going rate at the time) and got started. Who but Andy Kaufman would walk into the Mustang Ranch and within twenty minutes make a package deal for the entire inventory? Mr. X came to mind.

That week became nuts. Get up in the morning, get Andy going, get him over to the Ranch to get started on his quota for the day, get him to Harrah's for his first show, then back to the Mustang to continue his other "work," back to Harrah's for the ten o'clock show, then back out to the Ranch to finish off his six-pack of women. Andy's act for Harrah's had been streamlined for commercial viability. He didn't push any of the audience's buttons. He simply came out, did "Mighty Mouse," played the congas, did Foreign Man, performed an old puppet routine, and closed with Elvis. Fifty minutes, no more, no less. His real performance was ongoing at the Ranch.

Andy's endurance quest became a joke at the Mustang and had the girls talking. As I've said before, Andy never met a girl he didn't love, and he made each one of them feel special. It got to be a contest for the girls as well, and as the week drew to a close, and time was running out, when our limo wasn't shuttling them back and forth, the working girls were carpooling over to Harrah's House to save Andy the commute time of the limo. Some were even throwing their bodies under him for free, so enthusiastic were they that he achieve his mark.

As our week came to an end, Andy not only was far too tired to remember he'd ever had a thing for Lisa Hartman, but also was actually in physical discomfort, his soldier rubbed raw by the friction of so many love canals. But if nothing else, Andy Kaufman was not a quitter. He was grimly determined to achieve his promised goal.

We were supposed to clear out of the Harrah's House guest artist's suite no later than two on the afternoon following our last night at Harrah's, because the next headliner, singer John Davidson, was scheduled to arrive at that time with his family. The servants waiting on us had been buzzing furiously about the scores of prostitutes coming in and out of our suites, and word had gotten back to management. With our limo sometimes ferrying six hookers at a time, our relationship with the innkeepers of Harrah's House had become strained, to put it mildly.

The woman managing the place had made a few "courtesy calls" to our door that morning to speed us on our way so her staff could come in and clear the carnage before the wholesome Davidson clan arrived. Unfortunately for her, Andy had just received his last order of a half dozen hookers and had his morning's work cut out for him.

Only moments before the Davidsons were to show, with the irate manager planted at our door and prepared to deal sternly with the "perverts," Andy still had a short stack of three hookers remaining on his plate.

"Mr. Kaufman?" she yelled through the closed portal. "We need the suite, now!"

I opened the door, and she began chewing me out because I was the show's producer and apparent ringmaster to my "problem child." "Mr. Zmuda, I must insist that you and Mr. Kaufman vacate immediately. We've been very patient . . ."

Suddenly some particularly heavy moaning penetrated Andy's closed bedroom door and wafted out over us like a foul stench. The manager's eyes widened in disgust, and I just shrugged. What was I to do? Andy was a goal-oriented man and was also just shy of a personal best. Who was I to spoil his hard-fought efforts? I winked and the manager slammed the door. A while later, the three remaining courtesans filed out of the bedroom, all short skirts and spandex, and just as Andy and I fled with them out the back door, the squeaky-clean Davidson family walked in the front.

Apparently Harrah's management was so happy with Andy's act they forgave our behavior, for they invited us back two years later. Only that time they would book not Andy but a friend of his, an entertainer by the name of Tony Clifton.

Leaving behind our experiences in Reno — Harrah's House, the casino shows, and, in particular, the beautiful ladies of the Mustang Ranch — was hard for us. We were already feeling nostalgic as we climbed aboard the plane back to L.A. It was as if we'd gone to summer camp, had fun far beyond anything we'd imagined, and now had to leave our new friends behind. We vowed to return.

Andy, always the childlike Don Juan who hated saying goodbye to any woman, kept in touch with many of the Mustangers and would, on occasion, fly one of them out to stay with him in

Laurel Canyon for a few days at a time. Andy appreciated the purity of prostitutes. Unlike the wannabes and starfuckers of Hollywood who would come on to you for who you were, looking for any edge to move up the ladder and deviously feigning regard for you to improve that position, the working girls exhibited no such pretenses. You paid them, and they were not required to like you or even pretend to, although it helped. That they always did like Andy was gravy to him, and he rewarded them with extended stays in town for which they were well compensated.

Some of the girls took no remuneration when they visited. To Andy that was the hallmark of sincerity in the world in which we lived, an often barren place where people, ideas, talent, and the ability to pose got you somewhere, and that somewhere was gauged only by power and money. That those young women made a living at having sex was of no consequence to Andy regarding his feelings for them — he was not judgmental and treated them like any other woman he knew, with courtesy and respect, and for that many of the girls became very fond of him. He developed some lasting friendships with the girls, and they kept in touch over the years. One of them even knitted him a sweater, and several made the trip to New York to attend his funeral. Andy once told me he admired their choice of occupation and added that if he had been born female he would likely have been a prostitute. It was the perfect occupation for someone who loved sex and wanted to operate outside of the system while making a comfortable living.

And a comfortable living was an understatement. Some of the more desirable prostitutes were making more money than Kaufman was. Do the math: Girls were on the floor for eighteen hours a day for twenty-one days straight, taking off the week of their periods. Some turned a trick every hour, so in three weeks they had serviced 378 customers at fifty bucks a pop. That added up to $18,900 a month. Multiplying that by twelve months equals almost $227,000. Even after paying the house its due, a young lady would walk away with $116,000 a year. That bought a lot of feminine hygiene deodorant. Some exquisite beauties could knock off *two* johns every hour.

What's even more shocking was that some of those women were happily married to men they had met at work. That may sound abhorrent by our Western standards of morality, but when asked how their husbands deal with their occupation, the response is matter-of-fact: "I only fuck the customer, I love my man." When one's bride is bringing home that kind of dough, it's easy to keep an open mind.

As soon as we returned from Reno, the next item on the calendar was a trip to Nashville, where Andy was to appear on the "Johnny Cash Christmas Show." As Santa Claus. Being a nice Jewish boy, Andy loved the irony, but the main draw of the gig was a chance to work with the legendary Man in Black himself.

We arrived in Nashville and were whisked over to the new Grand Ole Opry. Apparently that original hallowed hall of country music, the *old* Grand Ole Opry, was a firetrap, and the fire marshal prevailed in closing it. The new edifice to country western was constructed in the suburbs, along with an adjoining hotel, restaurants, a mini-mall, a television broadcast facility, and last but not least, a theme park dubbed Opryland.

Andy and I were somewhat disappointed that we were to work in a facility with hardly more history than a shopping mall, but our guide assured us the new GOO was the spiritual successor of the old GOO and took us center stage to prove it. There, embedded in the polished wood, was a one-foot-square piece from the stage of the old GOO. We stared at it for a moment, and I couldn't help but think of that scene in the movie *The Magic Christian* where zillionaire Peter Sellers buys the Mona Lisa and cuts out the smile because that's the best part.

That minor disappointment faded at the thought of meeting the mythic Johnny Cash, but he was nowhere in sight. We decided to arrange the sizable load of props we carried while we kept an eye out for Johnny. As we organized our things, everyone cleared the stage except for an old guy hunched over a desk in the corner, scribbling some paperwork. Assuming he was a stage manager or something similar, I glanced over and thought a few times of asking where Johnny Cash might be, but he looked so intent, staring through glasses as thick as Coke bottles, that I held off.

After a few moments the backstage intercom blared. "Johnny Cash, we're ready for you on stage." Looking around for the big man to finally appear, Andy and I were stopped in our tracks when the old paperwork guy suddenly stood to full, impressive height, shed his bifocals, shook his long hair back, and sauntered toward us in that trademark, manly gait. "Hi," he said, smiling as he passed us, "I'm Johnny Cash."

That the man was capable of flipping a switch and making the transformation from anonymous, seemingly old man to a virile superstar who strutted by like a panther was not lost on either of us. Like a couple of school kids, we said hello, and Andy's eyes locked onto and followed Cash, mesmerized by that star quality, that aura the man emanated. And as a student of character metamorphosis, Andy was particularly struck by that exotic transitional quality Johnny Cash had just demonstrated.

There is nothing that approaches southern hospitality, and fellow guest Tom T. Hall decided to introduce us to a large helping of it. After the taping, Tom T. invited us to his ranch for dinner. The consummate host, Tom T. laid on quite a spread, personally barbecuing our entrees, Tony Clifton–size steaks. Tom T. boasted that he had butchered the ruminant we were about to consume, and to my surprise, Andy the vegetarian wolfed down the immense filet without exhibiting a single Tony Clifton mannerism.

The height of the evening came after dinner when we retired to Tom T.'s back room and the artist took out his guitar. As he strummed away and began singing an obscure country ballad, Andy, to my and Tom T.'s surprise, joined in. Into the night Tom T. played and sang, and Andy accompanied him, knowing most of the songs Tom T. dished up. It was yet another discovery about my complex friend. As they sang, I reflected on one other benefit of hanging with Andy: not only meeting famous people but also relaxing with them in their natural settings, away from the artifice of that celebrity demeanor.

From Nashville we shot up to New York for Andy's October 10, 1979, appearance on *Saturday Night Live*. The guest host was *Monty Python* alum Eric Idle, and it was to be Andy's first wrestling match with a woman on national television. And as the ref, it was to be my first appearance *live* in front of that same national audience. I was scared shitless.

I had done the routine countless times on the college circuit, but this took my role to a new, frighteningly visible level. Suddenly all those ring moves I'd done dozens of times in the past, and taken for granted, were now rolling over and over in my mind. When I realized the surest way to fuck up was to overthink it all, I put it out of my mind and focused on making our first television wrestling gig work like clockwork. We decided, in honor of moving up to the big time, that we'd raise our standard five-hundred-dollar prize for defeating Andy to an even grand. Of course he wasn't supposed to lose, and he never had.

As the ref I was not only to officiate the match but also to lead the opponent-selection process by holding my hand above the head of each of our volunteers as the audience voted for their favorite with applause. The chosen lady was then cast in the role of challenger and candidate to win the dough. As the show went on the air, we prepared in our dressing room backstage. As usual, Andy annoyed some of the more zealous cast members when he changed the channel of the television in our dressing room from the live show feed to an old movie. They were all riveted to the myriad monitors backstage and they chose to acknowledge Andy's indifference as a slap in their faces.

We closed the door, and as Andy stripped down to his skivvies and prepared to don his tights, I held out a roll of fiber-backed gaffer's tape.

"What's that for?" he asked.

"You."

"Me? Whaddya mean, me?"

"You. We gotta tape you down. We can't have you on national TV with a major flagpole. I'm taping you down."

He considered the implications for a moment, then said, "You're right. Let's do it."

After laying on another pair of underwear I started strapping him, crisscrossing the sturdy tape around his waist and across his groin. When I was done he looked quite silly, as if he were sporting a metallic codpiece. "I'm going out like this," he said spontaneously.

"No, you're not," I snapped.

"Okay."

After his long johns Andy put on an additional covering, a pair of swim trunks, so eager was I to conceal his secret. Being wacky was one thing, but I understood how people could twist anything sexual, and I didn't want it to come back and bite us. Over the whole outfit I draped his dad's old bathrobe. Then we were ready for combat.

I was called to the stage first to choose the opponent. In a last minute twinge of either vanity or fear of seeing the camera and studio audience, I removed my glasses. They were hardly cosmetic props, and without them I couldn't see shit. I held the selection process, and as Andy was introduced, he entered the ring and lambasted me in front of the crowd.

"Zmuda, are you nuts? This woman's pregnant. You want me to wrestle a pregnant woman?"

As blind as a bat, I hadn't noticed when the audience offered up the pregnant would-be wrestler. I quickly put my glasses on, dismissed the future mother, and went to the alternate, a striking young woman named Mimi. Of course, everyone thought the pregnant bit was part of the act.

Mimi was attired in a skintight, sheer leotard that revealed every inch of her exceptional physique, including the fact she wore no panties, evidenced by the fabric coyly adhering to the cleft below her mound of Venus. That she also possessed a spectacular ass didn't help matters. Not only was Kaufman becoming aroused, but so was I, along with every other red-blooded male watching Mimi circle the ring. Mimi lunged for Andy and the thousand bucks, but they both evaded her. When she and Andy finally hit the mat and began to roll about he started in with the love talk.

"Can you believe it?" he whispered. "There are millions of people watching us right now. Come back to my dressing room . . . I've got to see you again."

Realizing Andy wasn't the enemy, Mimi was eventually pinned under Andy on the mat on stage and, later, in his dressing room. As Mimi emerged from Kaufman's room I couldn't help but marvel at how he'd taken public wrestling with a stranger and turned it into a sexual prelude.

Feminists everywhere decried Andy's Neanderthal attitude and were infuriated when he would utter such phrases as "Stay in the kitchen where you belong," or "God, man, woman, dog," indicating the hierarchy with a descending hand gesture. On the other side of the coin, cavemen in all walks of life loved Andy and mindlessly applauded his efforts to "keep women in their places." Both groups couldn't have been further from the reality of the situation or the nature of the man they were cheering or jeering.

That was part of Andy the Chameleon: make them believe something reversed from the truth. In fact, Andy was more of a feminist than many feminists. He respected women and harbored none of the prejudices that many other men did regarding equality of the sexes. Andy never felt women were incapable or had any less a role in the world than men, but he certainly knew that it was a societal hot button and delighted in standing at the control panel and punching it over and over to get a reaction.

As I've said, Andy revered women, and his sincerity and innocence caused many of those he came in contact with to fall for him. And he for them. He was a very sensitive man, in touch with, as they say, his "feminine side." Dates were often surprised to accompany him to a touching movie, watch him cry his eyes out, and note that afterward he exhibited none of the guilt many men would show.

I think he was surprised at the lack of sophistication our audiences showed regarding the put-on nature of our matches. He assumed they would know, as in mainstream pro wrestling, that it was all for show and that the insults, violence, and animosity were merely theater. That seemingly hip crowds sometimes became so incensed over his ring antics was a shock to him. But rather than wilting under the scorn, he used that knowledge to increase his effects on future wrestling audiences.

As for Mimi, that match was the start of a beautiful friendship, one that would last the rest of Andy's life. Many men can love 'em and leave 'em, and Andy could wrestle 'em and love 'em, but he was a failure at leaving them.

On returning to L.A., Andy went back to toiling on *Taxi*, and I found myself in a crisis with Shelly, my live-in girlfriend of three years. Shelly had had all she could take of L.A. and yearned for the good old almost-bucolic days of Ocean Beach, when schedules were simple and life was like an oil painting. She wanted to return to San Diego, and I, of course, was where I belonged and stubbornly held my ground. I sought Andy's advice, assuming he'd take my side.

"She says she has nothing here," I said.

"She's right," he said bluntly, to my hurt and amazement, "she doesn't."

The hopeless romantic, I threw up my best defense. "But how about me? *I'm* here. I'm certainly not nothing!"

Andy looked me square in the eye and said, "You're here for your career."

I was shocked by the cold, simple truth of it. He was dead right. It was moments like that in which that rare but strong Andy surfaced, as if a dispassionate and levelheaded business executive had subsumed the man-child for a moment. Shelly and I broke up and life went on.

Despite Tony Clifton's attempt at its destruction, *Taxi* was into its second season and going strong, a solid hit for ABC and a growing millstone around the neck of Andy Kaufman. As Andy's strength to endure the tedium of his television production schedule began to ebb he knew he'd better summon his superhero to deliver him from the bathos of sitcomedy — faster than a speeding insult, able to change the course of mighty stage shows. He needed an emotional rescue, like a life-giving IV, and that rescue could be found only in the chaos of Tony Clifton.

After he instructed George Shapiro to quit booking Andy Kaufman and begin booking Tony Clifton, Andy and I sat back and waited for some unsuspecting victim to fall into our web. It wasn't long before George called with news that the afternoon variety show *Dinah!*, hosted by its namesake, singer and actress Dinah Shore, happily wanted Tony. Used to has-beens and B-grade performers on their way down and out, the producers of *Dinah!* were giddy that someone as hot as Andy Kaufman would deign to do their show in any guise.

Andy had little respect for sitcoms and even less for poor Dinah's show, which was solidly in his "contempt" category, the ass end of television. Andy had done *Dinah!* before, as Andy, and had loathed everything about it. To Andy, it was worse than pornography, a homogenized effluent of mindless patter and less-than-trivial guests and features, all contrived to give its target — stultified, midlife housewives — an effect strikingly similar to fifty milligrams of Thorazine. If Andy had wanted to blow

Taxi out of the water, *Dinah!* was in the path of a strategic nuclear strike. The thought of his having to chatter away with Dinah, as the simpering Charles Nelson Reilly demonstrated how to concoct Cherries Jubilee, caused a seldom-seen hostility to well within Andy. Tony Clifton was called up for active duty and given his marching orders.

As I Cliftonized Andy at his home that morning, the rest of our entourage began to assemble: a new employee of George Shapiro's, a young agent named Jim Cancholla, whom we renamed "Jimmy the C" after presenting him with his Clifton-approved Ray-Bans, and three women, Andy's secretary Linda Mitchell and two other girlfriends of ours. The ladies did themselves up as tarts, and as soon as Tony Clifton emerged from makeup, we jumped into Tony's signature pink Caddie convertible with me at the wheel and sailed down Laurel Canyon to our two o'clock taping in Hollywood.

Tony spotted a liquor store and ordered us to stop for cigarettes and booze, a pint bottle of Jack Daniel's. Then we continued on to our destiny with *Dinah!* Noting it was spot on two as we approached the studio, Tony started in on the bourbon and told me to drive around for a while to make sure we were late. Half an hour later at the studio gate, juggling a cigarette and the three girls, who were in back with him, Tony barked a nasal command to the gatekeeper. "I'm Tony Clifton. I'm doin' *Dinah!* Lemme in." The guy looked over his drive-on sheet and made a mistake: he disagreed with Mr. Clifton.

"Clifton? Sorry, but your name's not here."

"You idiot, don't you recognize me? I'm the International Singing Sensation, Tony Clifton. I'm deeply insulted. Lemme in."

"I'm sorry, sir, your name's not on my list."

"I don't have to put up with this shit! Listen, asshole, I'll sue you and your two-bit studio for everything it's worth! You understand me?"

Recognizing what might have happened, I said to the rattled sentry, "Check the list, maybe you got the wrong name, maybe you got Andy Kaufman instead."

"What did you say? *What did you say?*" blasted the enraged Singing Sensation. "I told you never to use that untalented jerk's name around me . . . *ever!*"

Then he focused his rage on the poor guard. "How old are you?" demanded Tony.

The guard looked quizzical. "Forty-five."

"*Forty-five? Forty-five?*" mocked Tony. "You're forty-five, and this is all you've made of your life?"

The man's eyes narrowed angrily, so I quickly leaped out, apologized, and tried to communicate with him while Tony screamed for the man's full name, yelling at the girls to take it down and "spell it the hell right!"

I confirmed that sure enough, the talent coordinator hadn't heard the rules and had given Kaufman's name to the gate. After calling the set, we cleared that up and the guy let us through, but not before jotting down our license number. Having already gotten off on the wrong foot, I knew Clifton was somehow going to exact revenge for the slight. As we pulled into our parking place I glanced into my wallet and inventoried our potential bail money.

As Clifton and his retinue swept onto the set of *Dinah!* the producers and talent coordinator took one look and began getting nervous. With about twenty minutes to tape time, the plan was for Tony to go out, sing "On the Street Where You Live," then do a duet with Dinah, the cheery song "Anything You Can Do." After that, time permitting, they would do a cooking segment. One of Dinah's hooks was to get her celeb guests to cook something in the on-set kitchen, a little feature that "humanized" the stars for the folks in Iowa. Tony offered to whip up his favorite breakfast, bacon and eggs à la Clifton. His secret that made it so special? A dozen eggs, including some shells, whipped, tossed with raw bacon, then pan fried. Mmmmm, gooood.

When we'd settled into our suite, a shiny-faced assistant producer knocked on the door.

"Dinah has a cold today," she said, "and though she'd love to sing that duet with Tony, she's going to have to beg off. She says she hopes Tony understands."

He didn't.

"What in the fuck is this?" he screamed when I told him. "This is *outrageous!* Whaddya mean she ain't singin' the song? She can't do that and call herself a professional!"

As he ranted, the thin walls of the dressing room couldn't

contain him and soon we had another knock at the door, this time a senior producer.

"Is everything all right?" she asked, more to quiet us down than to solve a problem.

Tony strode out to confront her. "You bet, sweetheart! There's plenty wrong! Dinah's got a cold? Dinah's sick? As far as Tony's concerned . . . as far as Tony's concerned, the show must go on!!! It does not care if you are sick!! You must put on the show!!! I used to play the Steel Pier, fifteen times a day!! You tell her to get her ass out there and sing that song with me if she knows what's good for her!!"

The producer left, white as a sheet.

A moment later there was yet another knock at the door. "Five minutes, Mr. Kaufman."

"What did you call me? What did you call me?" yelled Tony.

After an appropriate pause came a sheepish little voice. "Sorry, Mr. Clifton."

We then sent Jimmy the C as an emissary to convince Dinah's people that Tony wasn't going to take no for an answer on the duet issue. Shuttling back and forth between peace talks, a minute before show time Jimmy the C delivered the death blow. "They won't budge. Dinah is really sick and is afraid her voice will crack." In retaliation, Tony upended the Black Jack, draining the bottle. "Well, we'll see about that," he said ominously, and headed for the set.

I whispered in Jimmy the C's ear, "Kaufman couldn't hold down a beer if his life depended on it."

We followed the now-weaving Tony out to the set. The studio audience was typical for *Dinah!* Lots of women, mostly overweight, heartland-fresh tourists locked into their style the day they left high school. They were well meaning, but not terribly sophisticated, and when Tony blew in with three floozies on his arms, they thought he was for real and applauded. I got close to Tony and saw that he was drunk, no, make that smashed. He smelled like a crashed Jack Daniel's truck.

As the floor director gave him the countdown, he seemed to sober up for a second. I held out hope he'd just do the act and we'd leave. Meanwhile, a nervous Jean Stapleton (Archie Bunker's wife, Edith, from *All in the Family*) was in her dressing room, preparing to go on next and quizzing the assistants about the commotion she'd heard.

As the show came out of the spot break, Tony was in the back, microphone in hand. On cue he waltzed down the center aisle of the audience singing "On the Street Where You Live," and, again, the ladies were all very impressed. At the end of his number, which was worse than usual because he was completely blitzed, Tony was welcomed by Dinah, a lovely, genteel southern belle. They shook hands and Dinah started in with the small talk that was sure to ignite Tony's powder keg.

"So, Tony, I understand you . . ."

"Woah, woah, woah . . . lemme stop you right there," he said. "I wanna introduce the three chickees, my 'assistants.'"

Our three female companions stood one at a time from their seats at the edge of the stage and were warmly encouraged by the audience. Dinah looked confused and I could see the crew scurrying to figure out what to do. Tony made them all wait as he introed the girls. That done, Dinah tried to continue, under the mistaken impression that it was still *Dinah!* she was hosting — she didn't know it had become the *Tony Clifton Show* the moment they'd let him on the lot. "So," she continued gamely, "I understand you have many albums out."

"What did you say?" he said challengingly.

"I understand you have many albums out."

"I don't have any albums."

"Oh, I'm sorry, I thought you did."

"Why are you bullshitting these nice people?" he asked, and with that the honeymoon was over. The audience tittered as Dinah reeled herself back and noted, "Well, we're going to have to bleep that out."

"I don't have any friggin' albums."

Dinah knew she was in a train wreck and tried to save herself. Realizing she'd just come out of a commercial and couldn't seek the refuge of another, she thought fast. "Well, Tony, why don't you sing another song?"

"Why don't we sing that duet?"

"Oh, Tony, I'd love to but, as I said before the show, I have a terrible sore throat and couldn't do it justice."

"A professional would sing," countered Clifton.

She smiled daggers. "Oh, some other time, Tony, I'd love to." Like when they were ice skating on the River Styx.

"I'll help you out," he said, looking to the audience, who, thinking Dinah was just being coy, began applauding. Screwed, Dinah smiled through the pain and agreed to sing with him, but with one caveat.

"I don't know the words."

Tony produced a lyrics sheet from his breast pocket and they commenced.

"I can do anything you can do better . . ."

"No you can't!"

"Yes I can . . ."

"No you can't!!!"

"Oh yes I cannnnn!!!"

At that point, it was evident that the poor, gentle Dinah would have gutted Clifton with a deer knife had she been wielding one. They finished their strained twosome and Dinah breathed a sigh of relief. Dinah wanted to get rid of him, but the floor director signaled she had several more minutes to kill.

"I understand you're quite a cook," she lied.

"Oh, yeah," said Tony, "I learned in France."

"Well, let's go over and watch you make your specialty."

They reset the cameras on the fly and walked over to the cooking area. Obsequious guest cohost Charles Nelson Reilly, usually zapping out numbing one-liners like a shtick-dispenser, was oddly quiet, apparently intimidated by the looming Clifton. Andy was over six feet tall and, with all his Clifton armor, looked formidable, less a lounge lizard than a lounge Komodo dragon.

"What are you making, Tony?" Dinah asked, watching the clock.

"Bacon and eggs, my favorite breakfast."

Tony proceeded to crack a full carton of eggs into a mixing bowl, making sure quite a few shells fell into the mix. As he stirred and dropped in the uncooked bacon, Dinah and Charles stood back, their postures oddly tensed, as if cringing in anticipation. Tony blithered on about his cooking skills, and finally, for Dinah, they'd run down the game clock. She smiled sweetly. "Well, Tony, we're out of time, but I want to thank you for coming."

Tony Clifton's next words rang like thunder. "I ain't goin' anywhere."

"What do you mean?"

"I'm not leavin'."

For a split second Dinah was speechless. "Well, Tony, I'm sure I'd like to have you stay, but I can't. You have to leave."

"No, I ain't leaving."

"Tony, you have to go, I'm sorry."

Again, Tony took his case to the people. "Everyone who wants to see me stay, applaud." There were some isolated claps. "Okay, everybody who wants me to go, do the same." The crowd erupted. After the noise died down, he shrugged. "Okay, it's settled, I'll stay." That got a good laugh, but now Dinah was looking to her offstage muscle to toss Clifton. As the security guards moved toward Tony, he grabbed the egg whip. "Okay, I'll leave, but not before I leave *you* with something, Miss Shore," Tony said, whereupon he committed assault with a gooey weapon by pouring the eggs over Dinah's head.

The producers went to a spot break, and the shit hit the fan. Tony dropped the bowl and began running from the pursuing studio gendarmes. "Stay away from me! I'll call a cop!"

The men tried to corner him, and by then the audience was really wondering if this was real or not. Some people in the crowd understood and were screaming appropriately.

"Get your hands off me," screeched Clifton. "You can't treat me this way! Do you have any idea who you're fucking with? I'm gonna remember each and every one of your faces, and if you come to Vegas . . . *you're not gettin' in!*"

Now it was a full-blown circus: Dinah was egg-dipped and ready for the deep fryer; Clifton was fleeing the authorities like Buster Keaton; and a panicked Jean Stapleton had rushed back into her dressing room and locked the door, fearing that that madman, whoever he was, had killed Dinah and was now after her.

Finally, as Clifton was grabbed and physically ejected, and as the rest of our motley crew, Jimmy the C and the counterfeit bimbos, all raced to help Tony, I ran outside, jumped into the rented Cliftonmobile, and spun around the corner. I slammed to a stop by the door to the *Dinah!* set as the guards heaved Tony into the back seat. We exited the lot, rubber burning. As we made Sunset, the import of Tony Clifton's coup d'état hit us, and like six high school kids who'd just put a flaming sack of dogshit on the principal's porch and rung the doorbell, we burst into hysterical laughter. Yes, Tony's act was irresponsible, childish, and impossibly rude, but it established one very important parameter for future potential employers: Don't fuck with Tony Clifton.

9

Smoke and Mirrors

I used to find myself really guessing which of those characters was closest to the real Andy. And I guess that is a tribute in and of itself, because you never really knew, and he would constantly surprise and fool me.

GARRY SHANDLING

Ninety-eight percent of Andy Kaufman's performances were never recorded or, for that matter, even seen by formal audiences, for they took place on streets, in restaurants, and in myriad other public places. Most of the witnesses to those incidents didn't know they were experiencing a performance, let alone that they had become an audience. But just as classic as Andy's "Mighty Mouse" or "Caspian Sea," those particular aesthetic treats were often as carefully planned as our stage shows and employed as much art of design. Yet because of their nature, much of Andy's best work (and mine too) was cast to the winds like dandelions.

If you flew in an airline's first-class section during the fall of 1979, there is a chance you were Kaufmanized without knowing it. We always flew first class as a perk of working with OPM (Other People's Money). Do you recall a nervous man with glasses and long hair, a frightened first-time flyer, who had the misfortune of sitting across from a man wearing dark glasses, a know-it-all on the subject of airline safety and crash survivability?

"So," said Sunglasses, "you're scared? Lemme tell you, there's nothin' to be scared of."

"Well," said Scared Guy, "I'm just nervous 'cause I've never flown. I've always been afraid of flying."

"Oh, I understand," soothed Sunglasses. "That's why I want you to know, should we crash, the chances of you livin' through it are decent, better than even odds, probably."

Scared Guy's eyes widened. "Crash?"

"Sure, it happens, but listen, unless we slam into a mountain or something, maybe clip a flock of birds or maybe another plane, we'll live to tell about it. Chances are."

"You think that could happen?" said Scared Guy, now bordering on Terrified Guy.

"What? Which one? Birds? Another plane? Hey, happens all the time, but don't worry, the odds are good less than half the people will get killed. Your job is to be in the good half."

"My job?" said quiver-voiced Terrified Guy.

"Sure," assured the ever-confident Sunglasses. "See," he said, opening his briefcase to display some graphic crash photos to bolster his case. "This crash, this one in Paris? Thoroughly avoidable, in my humble opinion." He indicated some other photos. "But no chance of surviving that one. Door failed or something and *boom*, three hundred fifty people ground into fertilizer. And this one? Now, this was a biggy . . . two jumbo jets crashed into each other on the ground . . . now, of course that's not gonna happen here 'cause we're airborne, but *this* one?" he said, pointing to another shot of carnage. "Whew, nearly three hundred people, engine falls off . . . *boom!* Hamburger."

"Hamburger?" said Scared-Shitless Guy, his voice faltering.

The people in the neighboring seats were now sickened as Sunglasses tried to calm Scared-Shitless Guy with soothing talk of missing limbs and human shreds smaller than packs of matches.

"Did you know," asked Sunglasses, "*Life* magazine said sometimes they find people's fingers embedded in the undersides of armrests? You know why?"

His mouth moved, but Scared-Shitless Guy couldn't even form a word.

"I'll tell you why," said the expert. " 'Cause they got so scared tryin' to keep the plane in the air they tore off their own fingers! Pretty wild, huh?"

A flight attendant noticed the poor man's extreme distress and warned Sunglasses. "Please, sir, you're obviously upsetting him."

"Hey," blustered Sunglasses, "he's scared 'cause it's all in his mind. Once you face your fears, you're okay."

The stewardess seemed unconvinced. "Well, I'd appreciate it if you didn't bother him anymore. Thank you."

The moment she left, Sunglasses turned back to the shaking man. "And this one?" he said, indicating a particularly gruesome crash photo. "See the dead man hangin' from the tree? Ooboy, he musta fallen outta his seat from a good twenty thousand feet. Plane blew in midair."

"Blew?" said Shitting-His-Pants Guy as the tears began to flow. "In midair?"

"Sure. Happens all the time."

That was too much, and the man burst into wracking sobs of agonizing fear.

Sunglasses himself called the stewardess. "Listen to him! He's a sniveling crybaby." He turned to the crying man and slapped his arm. "What kind of man are you?"

The stewardess was appalled. "Sir, please leave him alone!"

"I will leave him alone when you get him to stop that bawling!"

The stewardess tried comforting the stricken man but after a few more seconds of loud sobbing, Sunglasses was so irritated that, to the horror of everyone watching, he jammed a handkerchief into the guy's mouth to shut him up. As the battle between the flight attendants and the cruel air-safety expert continued, my tears were real, caused by painfully stifled laughter. The ladies finally got Sunglasses to leave me alone, never knowing their nemesis was a guy who'd probably made them laugh at some point, either on *Taxi* or *Saturday Night Live*. But on that day, Andy was merely a reduced-strength version of Tony Clifton.

Were you on that plane?

Some other aerial hijinks occurred on a flight with our new friend Kris Kristofferson. At the time, airlines were experimenting with inducements to use their services, and some had installed small cocktail lounges in their 747s. American Airlines called theirs Lounge in the Sky, and to get there one climbed a circular staircase from first class into a cozy space complete with a bar and small piano. It had been only a few weeks since the new facilities had been introduced, and travelers were still unsure of their function.

A curtain that separated the lounge from the stairs was drawn during takeoffs and landings, but was generally open in flight. We waited until there were five people in the lounge, and then I approached the flight attendants for their cooperation in our little scheme. They drew the curtain, and after a moment I stepped out and addressed the unsuspecting quintet, all seated around the piano, drinks in hand.

"Good evening, ladies and gentlemen. American Airlines welcomes you to 'Stars in the Sky,' an evening of merriment and song. Tonight, we have three of the biggest names in show business."

Now I had their attention. Five heads swiveled as they were all thinking, *Three big stars? He's gotta be fooling*.

I continued. "Without further ado, allow me to introduce them to you. First, you know him as the composer of such legendary hits as 'Help Me Make It Through the Night' and 'Me and Bobby McGee,' and as costar with Barbra Streisand a few years back in *A Star Is Born*. Ladies and gentlemen, give a big 'Stars in the Sky' welcome to Mr. Kris Kristofferson."

Their jaws hit the floor when Kris stepped out from behind the curtain, waved, and took a few bows. Before they could recover, I continued. "Next, you know him from numerous television appearances, from *Saturday Night Live* to *The Tonight Show*, he is currently the star of the hit sitcom *Taxi*, please give a warm welcome to Mr. Andy Kaufman!" Andy parted the curtain and bowed, and the people were now wondering, *How the hell can American Airlines afford this?* They applauded furiously, disbelieving their eyes, trying to figure out how to tell the folks back in Kansas about this encounter. I figured we had them, so I took it over the top. "Finally, he has been called the Chairman of the Board and Old Blue Eyes, but I call him Mr. Sinatra, ladies and gentlemen, please bring out the living legend himself."

Now they went nuts, clapping madly, completely in awe of American Airlines for assembling such powerhouse talent for such a small venue. But when Frank didn't show, I broke character and explained the prank, and they all screamed at such a good joke. Then Kris and I and our five audience members accompanied Andy at the piano in a hearty rendition of "The Cow Goes Moo."

Andy was a good Jewish boy who loved and respected his parents and siblings. He looked forward to family get-togethers and shared many a holiday with them and their extended family of spouses, aunts, uncles, cousins, and whoever else would join in. So when George Shapiro called a few weeks before Thanksgiving and told Andy that a well-known resort in the Catskills, Kutscher's, had offered him a gig for that night, Andy balked.

"That's the last place I want to be on Thanksgiving, George. I'm spending it with my family."

"That's the beauty of it, Andy," said George. "Kutscher's will cover your whole family for the night, plus whoever else you want to bring along."

The idea that Kutscher's would spring for the whole Kaufman gang appealed to Andy, who saw it as a chance to have a family reunion *and* Thanksgiving dinner all on someone else's nickel. Andy wanted me along, as well as Greg Sutton, Andy's musical director and childhood buddy from Great Neck. It promised to be a Borscht Belt kinda Thanksgiving.

Telling George to make it clear to Kutscher's that he wasn't going to do his standard show because it was a holiday and he'd be with his family, Andy set the date. When we arrived, the place was hopping, a classic Catskills resort with innumerable activities, from classes to friendly card games to nonstop eating. The band members, all guys over seventy, suspiciously eyed long-haired Sutton as he rehearsed them, probably thinking he was some degenerate druggie.

When it was show time, six hundred paying customers sat back and watched Andy Kaufman introduce his family one by one, who then crossed to center stage and performed. It was exactly what the Kaufman tribe had been doing around the dinner table for twenty-five years, and, like all family entertainment, it seemed killer to the participants. But for paying strangers, it was worse than watching paint dry. After the first few "acts" the crowd started rustling around in their chairs and within a few minutes quietly chatting among themselves. Their buzzing drowned out the real Grandma Pearl as she carefully related the tale of the rabbi and his dog.

At any second, Andy could have come to the rescue with Elvis or any of ten other bits, but he chose not to, rather he let his family quietly die one at a time. Since Andy was mesmerized by failure, he wanted his loved ones to experience it, to flop in front of a big crowd — a big crowd of *strangers*. As much as they loved and admired Andy, his family really didn't understand what he did or had gone through to get where he was, so by sacrificing them on stage he could give them all the gift of understanding of that initial elation of stepping out in front of an audience, followed by the agony of bombing. It was his little lesson for them, a small toll he exacted for their having enjoyed the fruits of his success for so long.

Foreign Man and Tony Clifton were magnificent failures, and now so too was the Kaufman Family, the unwitting stars of Andy Kaufman's gripping production of "My Family Dies On Stage." Andy even protracted the death scenes by gently prompting the singer or storyteller to warble another verse or chronicle another shaggy dog story, all to the audience's extreme discomfort. He was using his family as if they were a version of his Great Gatsby routine from the Improv.

At some point one of the older musicians took Greg aside. "If he doesn't stop this, we're walking off the stage." Civility prevented the crowd from throwing their dinners, but when it was finally over we felt the hostility and sought shelter in our rooms. In all my years in show business I have never seen such a mass bombing as I saw on the stage at Kutscher's that night. It was so catastrophic that when we got back to the rooms Andy's door displayed a note from the management demanding we vacate the premises *at once*. The failure was complete — another triumph for Andy.

As we exited like Russian refugees, clutching our bags and fleeing the onrushing Cossacks, some of the guests took the opportunity to cast some figurative stones. "That was awful!" yelled one man to Stanley Kaufman. "Your son should get out of show business!"

Stanley stopped and stared down the assailant. "You people are idiots! He's a genius. Someday you'll be telling your kids you saw him 'live.'"

We crowded into the limo, and as an assembled crowd readied to boo us off, Andy made sure he got the last word as he stepped to the waiting door and looked them over with mock contempt. "It's people like you who give Jews a bad name!" And with that he jumped in and we sped away.

Why would anyone want to self-destruct on stage, let alone allow their own *family* to do so? Perhaps it was his pure rebellion against the ethos that informs the lives of most, that conformity and acceptance are immutable foundations of our daily society. Iconoclasm and revolution, on the other hand, though noble behavior for historical figures, are merely disruptive and antisocial when exhibited by contemporaries.

On Saturday, December 22, 1979, Andy and I walked into Thirty Rock late in the afternoon to begin preparations for our segment on that evening's *SNL*. The powers at *SNL* had gotten behind Andy's wrestling matches, and a few weeks earlier, announcer Don Pardo had asked female viewers to send photos with a letter explaining why they thought they could beat Andy in the ring. Unlike our other matches, *SNL* was to pick the challenger. And therein lay the rub.

Their winner was a pro. After laying eyes on this sinewy Greek goddess as she warmed up, then discovering that her cornerman was not only her father, but also an ex-Olympic coach, I knew Kaufman was in trouble. To make matters worse, to sweeten the pot we'd brashly announced that Andy would allow his head to be shaved if he lost. The barber was setting up at ringside, and I cringed at the thought that the man was going to get to use those clippers and at the implications of it. Andy was the star of a national sitcom and his hair was of *mild* importance. If a cue-ball bald Kaufman arrived for work the next week, the resulting shitstorm would make the Tony Clifton appearance seem like a high tea. I sized up his statuesque opponent, and my stomach churned with the certainty that she was the real McCoy and was simply going to kill him.

As I took care of various details, Andy holed up in his dressing room consorting with his own cornerman, the redoubtable "Nature Boy" Buddy Rogers, a platinum-locked grappler from the Golden Age of wrestling. Andy had grown up watching Rogers defeat the forces of evil during numerous televised matches in the '50s and absolutely revered him. Lorne Michaels, on the other hand, was not as enamored of Mr. Rogers and in fact had decided, based on Buddy's lackluster run-throughs, that his appearance was merely "dead air" and needed to be cut to the absolute basics.

Lorne's motivation to chop Buddy resulted from a scheduling problem with another performer, Mr. Bill, the hapless, rudimentary clay puppet who often met a violent end at the hands of his nemesis, Mr. Sluggo. Mr. Bill was scheduled to appear in his pre-produced "Mr. Bill's Christmas Special," and, because some other sketches were already going long, Lorne was nervous that the time slotted for Mr. Bill was diminishing. Since the Mr. Bill sketch was date-specific, and since considerable effort had been expended on its production, Lorne viewed Buddy Rogers's questionable contribution as wholly expendable.

As we drew close to air, and Andy conveniently sequestered himself in his meditation mode with the standard "Don't bother me" warning, Lorne called me into his office to lay down the law.

"I'm cutting Rogers," he said. "My back's against the wall for time and I feel his contribution is not that strong. Please coordinate this with Andy."

"I'll tell Andy, but I won't make any guarantees. The man is Andy's idol," I countered.

"Bob, believe me when I tell you this is not negotiable. Cut Rogers."

I left his office with the sound of a ticking bomb in my head. Lorne Michaels had not yet learned that no one tells Andy Kaufman what to do. I also knew that Andy had worked closely with Buddy on the lines we'd written him and would not take kindly to last minute meddling — even from the executive producer. Andy had a deep desire to provide Buddy a few moments of nationally televised glory as partial payback for all the years of pleasure and instruction Buddy had given Andy as a kid. And Buddy not only had been Andy's spiritual advisor for years before they met, but also had coached another athlete, by the name of Muhammad Ali. Both Andy and Ali had borrowed the famous gesture — when they would point at their heads and say, "I got the brains" — from Mr. Rogers.

Moments before our sketch, I relayed Lorne's demand to Andy, who heard my words but proceeded to stare right through me. Whether he was still in a transcendent state or was going into a stubborn mode I'm not sure, but he said nothing to Buddy. Andy's friend and now coach was a VIP and was going to get the respect he deserved whether Lorne liked it or not.

When the prelim for the match began, with Andy and Buddy speaking on camera, I watched Lorne in the wings, arms folded, eyes narrowed. As Buddy droned on and on, I could as much as see the steam venting from Lorne's ears. As soon as the Mr. Bill window slammed shut from Buddy's inexhaustible verbiage, Lorne stormed out. Then the fun began.

As I helped Andy in his corner while his foe warmed up, he leaned close and whispered, indicating the barber, "Whatever happens, that man ain't shavin' me bald!" It may have been too late for that sentiment because, in the interest of further showmanship, I had brazenly announced that two large security guards would be retained to prevent Kaufman from beating a hasty exit should he lose.

I eyed the burly men who eyed Andy. "Just don't lose," I said.

Then the match commenced. As the ref, I circled the ring with the two and could see Andy was in no mood to try to pick this girl up, as she had a good chance of winning. With his hair at stake, Andy locked horns with the young woman with a vengeance and they fell to the mat, the crowd screaming for his blood. Andy had gone out of his way to get the studio audience against him and had been very successful in that.

After a few flips that didn't look good for Andy, suddenly he reversed on her, got her on her back, and *boom, boom, boom*, I slapped the mat. Andy leaped to his feet, the winner. The looks of astonishment on the girl and her Olympic-coach father were priceless. Buddy was grinning like the cat who ate the canary, for his pupil had listened well. It was then that I realized the match had been not between Andy and the girl, but between Buddy and the dad: real wrestling versus fake wrestling. The girl's dad held people like Buddy Rogers in contempt, but the truth was, Buddy, despite the theatrics, was actually an amazing athlete, just as Andy was a credible wrestler who always beat his opponents fair and square.

But the fireworks were just beginning. As I walked down the hall, Lorne descended on me like a hawk on a field mouse. "What did I tell you?" he screamed. "You fucked up Mr. Bill! I had to eat that, thanks to you and Kaufman!"

I was in no mood to hear Lorne's rants. After all, I was paid by Andy, not him. I had also made the effort to warn Andy, but it had fallen on deaf ears. As Lorne raged on and on, pursuing me as I walked, I finally turned and faced him down. "Hey, fuck off!"

"What?" he screamed, incredulous anyone would speak to him that way. "Nobody tells me to fuck off! I'm going to have you thrown out of here!"

"Yeah? You and what army?" With that, I spun on my heels and strode to the dressing room, where I related the ugly incident to Andy. He just laughed.

Many years later Lorne and I ran into each other while attending a barbecue at Danny DeVito's home, and I took the opportunity to remind him of that moment. He remembered and apologized profusely, saying he was wrong and shouldn't have acted with such anger. I copped to being wrong as well, and we finally buried the hatchet and had a very pleasant conversation.

I had heard many stories about Lorne over the years, and I think his sophistication is often misinterpreted as arrogance. His apology was unnecessary, yet very big of him and hardly in keeping with the rumors of a huge ego that have been circulated on his behalf. I've often thought it must be odd being Lorne Michaels, given the illustrious list of talents who owe their careers to him, including Chevy Chase, Bill Murray, Dan Aykroyd, Eddie Murphy, Mike Myers, Dana Carvey, Chris Rock, and Adam Sandler, as well as the late John Belushi, Phil Hartman, Chris Farley, and Gilda Radner, to name but a few.

On returning to L.A. as 1980 dawned, Andy and I kept audiences (and ourselves) entertained with occasional late-night experiments at the Improv. One night I had a refrigerator crate brought on stage and announced to the audience that for one dollar they could look into the box and view the star of *Taxi*, Andy Kaufman. They thought I must have been joking, for surely a big star wouldn't allow himself to be crated up like a pooch in an airline carrier.

To get things going I picked a young lady in the front row and told her she could look for free and tell the audience what she saw. I opened a small side panel and she peeked in. "My god! I can't believe it! It's really Andy Kaufman!" she shrieked.

I smiled confidently. "Tell 'em what he's doing."

She concentrated. "Uh, he's sitting on a chair in his underwear, and he's holding a flashlight . . . and he's balancing his checkbook."

I nodded. "Correct," I said, and the exhibit was officially open. We made eighty bucks that night. A few years later we did a variation where the audience was given an opportunity to touch a cyst on Andy's neck. Charging them each a dollar, we had a real nurse disinfect the person's fingers before they touched it. We called that "Celebrity Cyst."

Any chance to ridicule fame or stardom Andy seized with zeal. Though he used his celebrity as a career stepping stone, underneath he found the blind worship of fame silly at best and destructive at its worst. Over the years I've worked with countless so-called stars, and I have witnessed many who wallow in it. Andy didn't and would have dispensed with stardom had he been able to accomplish his career goals without it.

His loathing of the elevation by society of entertainers was often a subject of his routines. Tony Clifton, for instance, was an anticelebrity. On the theme of the abuse of celebrity power, Andy would sometimes go into a restaurant, spot an attractive young couple, and make sure he was seated next to them. Of course everyone in the place knew who he was. He'd chitchat with the thrilled couple and then focus on the girl, subtly coming on to her. When the boyfriend left for the men's room, he'd make his move.

"Would you go out with me?"

The stunned and flattered young lady would usually say, "What?"

"Go out with me," Andy persisted. "Your boyfriend . . ."

"Fiancé . . ."

"Fiancé. Okay, your fiancé, who is he? He's a nobody, I'm a star, I'm famous. I can do more for you than he ever could. Right?"

With stars in her eyes she saw the logic. "Well, yes, that's true."

"Of course it's true." Then came his only request in his inane bid for power over the girl's life, but it was a big one: "If you want to go out with me, you have to leave with me, right now. C'mon, let's go."

"What? I can't!"

"Sure you can, c'mon," he said holding out his hand, "we're leaving. Tell him you're leaving with me."

Dazzled by the brilliance of stardom, she'd stand hesitantly. By now the people at the surrounding tables were aghast at the cruelty demonstrated by the big celeb. Just then her swain would return, having drained the lizard. "What's going on?" he would ask innocently.

"I, uh, I'm leaving with Andy. I'm sorry, Tom."

"What?" he'd say, totally flabbergasted. "But you can't do that, I love you!"

"Love?" Andy would snort. "I can offer her something you can't. I'm a star, you're nothing!"

Then Andy and the girl would exit, hand in hand, leaving the poor shattered shlub to weep uncontrollably at the table just as their salads arrived. Andy, to his credit, would always pay their tab on the way out. The wounded man, blinded by his tears, would finally find the strength to shuffle to the door as the restaurant patrons buzzed about the power-mad TV star and how he'd destroyed the sweet young man's world. Outside, the "distraught" fellow would join Andy and our female accomplice, whereupon we'd often head to another bistro to perpetrate the fraud once more. I thank that Carnegie-Mellon training for my skill at being able to cry on cue.

Why did we do it? Simple: it was fun. But in retrospect, as I analyze our little psychodramas, they give great insights into Andy's own belief system. Did he feel celebrity was a necessary ingredient to meeting women? Absolutely. Was he suspect of such women? To some extent, yes. He understood that *everyone* would defer to him because of his status, so it was the divination of that shading, the motives behind the actions, that intrigued him, and often left him distant and wary.

Andy enjoyed a small circle of close friends, but they had generally signed on years before fame came to him and were therefore proven commodities. Our restaurant "presentations" not only were amusing diversions, but also served as outlets for Andy's welling disgust over the nature of fame and the nearly mindless permission people would heap on someone just because they had seen the person on television or in the movies. He hated such unqualified acceptance and sought to hammer the point home to unsuspecting diners during our histrionics. Would a girl shitcan her faithful lover just because some "star" wagged his finger? Sure, and we showed them how it would happen, in all its disturbing ceremony.

As a technical note, we took great care to keep the airlines and restaurants, as well as the other "stages" for our psychodramas, in the dark as to our purposes. We made separate reservations and always worked it so we sat either across the aisle or at adjoining tables, but always within earshot of others — as many others as we could reach. The "street pranks" were endless and we pulled them almost every time we ate or flew. Pulling pranks kept us sharp, and aside from being a lot of fun, it was our job.

10

On a Roll

It was now January 1980, Andy had just celebrated his thirty-first birthday, and we were on a roll. Suddenly, in a very short period, two amazing projects were offered to us, one in television and the other in film.

Happy with the results of our special that had finally aired in August, ABC called and asked us to come up with a concept for a weekly vehicle for Andy. That was music to our ears, especially given the fact we'd already fleshed out an idea that Andy had been waiting years to produce. We called it "Uncle Andy's Funhouse," a kids' show for adults. Picture *Howdy Doody*, but instead of Buffalo Bob, Uncle Andy would host. There would be cartoons and puppets and even a "peanut gallery" where the kids would be on camera too, only in this case the kids would be adults. Yet to maintain the illusion that it was a show for children, albeit adult children, Andy would speak to them as if they were kids. That was a way to embrace one's "inner child" long before the phrase was added to popular culture.

As we planned the pilot, I felt the action should be set in the place it all started, the basement of Andy's childhood home. I had been hearing stories for years about how Andy would eschew outdoor activities with the other kids to linger in the basement and stage his shows, playing to an imaginary camera in the wall.

According to Andy, that behavior constantly irritated Stanley Kaufman, who felt his son was solidly on track to becoming a misfit. Andy proudly acknowledged his dad had been right.

We decided, as an homage to the disdainful parents of that seemingly autistic oddball who secreted himself in their basement, that we'd cast Stanley and Janice Kaufman as themselves. Occasionally Stanley would open the basement door and yell down for Andy to quit farting around and come upstairs because his "lunch was getting cold." Of course Andy's parents never went downstairs to discover that his "imaginary" TV show was in fact real. Though Andy dearly loved and respected his folks, this was a gentle zinger for all those years they didn't "get" him.

We re-created the Kaufman household in the studio in painstaking detail. I even shot an exterior that looked like their home for the opening establishing shot, wherein the camera flew up to the house and made a trick dissolve through the basement window into our studio "basement." I was in my glory as the writer and producer — this was what I'd been dreaming of doing all my life. I gave Andy a dog to use on the show, my own dog Lazarus. We called him Laz, and Andy loved him as if he were his own.

As great a show as "Uncle Andy's Funhouse" was, we had a big problem: it couldn't be longer than ten minutes. ABC had commissioned the work to be part of a half-hour special called "Buckshot," which would consist of ours as well as two other ten-minute segments to be produced by other talent. As Roseanne Roseannadanna used to say, "It's always somethin'."

ABC's chopped-up format was ill-conceived, as ten minutes wasn't enough time to establish a feeling for the segment, particularly ours. In our pilot, Andy used up nearly two minutes with a film of his Grandma Pearl sleeping on her sofa. Thus, with such a slow pace set, the remaining six and one-half minutes (after leaving a minute-and-a-half hole for commercials) went by in a flash without giving us room to deliver a true taste of what our show could be. But, regardless of its length, we were happy that ABC had footed the bill to let us put the concept on tape, if only for ten minutes. "Buckshot" aired, and no one took notice.

*   *   *

The next foothold was offered us by Universal Studios. We were shocked yet deliriously happy when George called with the news that they wanted to do a biography . . . *The Tony Clifton Story*, with Andy starring as the title character. Even better for me, they wanted the two of us to write it. We thought we'd died and gone to heaven. Contracts were drawn and the money was going to be quite spectacular. We enjoyed some perks as well, including a fabulous babe secretary named Connie Bryant and individually assigned golf carts to be used to save our legs from the grueling walk between our beautifully appointed bungalow and the commissary. Actually, the Universal lot is pretty huge, so there was some practicality to that.

As we were settling in to our new office I noticed some workers out front, preparing to stencil our names into the parking places. I went out and watched with pride as David Steinberg's name was blotted out and mine filled in. I had seen Steinberg years before in Chicago's Second City troupe and he was a comedy god to me. But at that moment I felt like Caesar, rolling through the streets of Rome in triumph, my chariot's wheels crushing both foe and friend. It didn't matter: I had a deal with Universal!

Our benefactor, that is, the man responsible for our bounty, was director John Landis. At the time, Landis had replaced Steven Spielberg as Universal's resident enfant terrible, due largely to his extraordinary success with 1978's *Animal House*, a blockbuster hit. He was currently working on *The Blues Brothers*, and the scuttlebutt was it was going to be a hit. Landis was apparently a fan of Kaufman and me and had suggested to studio cheeses Thom Mount and Sean Daniel that we were the hot kids in town and they should hire us.

I was very grateful to Landis, and since we'd never met, I requested a meeting be arranged so that I could properly thank him for his support. On the day of the meeting I arrived two hours early at our office, did some work, and then, dispensing with the cart, walked in the stunning midday sun over to the commissary for some lunch and a chance to hobnob with my Universal brethren. As I ate I subtly dropped hints to my tablemates that I was about to have an audience with the Boy Wonder himself.

They were duly impressed, and as I walked back to get ready for my meeting, this goofy kid with hair hanging down in his eyes and with thick black Poindexter glasses accosted me. I remembered him from the Huntington show because he had wanted to chatter away with me as I tried to get people on the buses. He annoyed me then, and he was annoying me again. As we walked and I tried to outpace him, I wondered how he got on the lot and why he was bothering me *now*, just as I was set for an extemely important audience with the great John Landis.

He persisted, so I sped up, saying, "Sorry, I can't talk now!"

But he wouldn't listen, so I finally turned and, as firmly and rudely as I could, said, "Stop! Not now!"

I resumed walking and was relieved I'd scraped the pest off my shoe. After all, I didn't want to be late for my audience with Mr. Landis. When I got to Landis's office, I was about ten minutes early, and though he wasn't back from lunch, his secretary led me into his office, where I waited. I spent the time admiring miscellaneous memorabilia he'd accumulated, mostly from the *Animal House* project. Just then I sensed someone watching me, and when I turned, to my irritation, I saw that goofy kid again, this time staring through the window, smiling and waving.

But it was when he came around the corner and had the audacity to actually enter the place that I finally snapped. Leaping to my feet I sprinted to the outer office to prevent this chowderhead from embarrassing me in my big moment. Just as the nerdy kid had the temerity to pick something off the secretary's desk, and as my mouth opened to chastise him, the secretary beat me to the punch. "John, here are your calls while you were out." For a split second I looked past this nut for a glimpse of Landis . . . and then I realized he *was* Landis!

Completely mortified, I wanted to crawl under the rug and die. Since that day, I have held that lesson closely: never dismiss anyone who comes up or phones, no matter who I *think* they are or aren't. It was arrogance on my part and an element of that "creeping co-option" that Andy battled so heroically.

Landis took it all in stride and laughed generously when I confessed my sins. John and I have maintained our friendship to this day. The director of such hits as *Trading Places*, *Coming to America*, and *Beverly Hills Cop III*, John is a genius when it comes to his ability to see through the eyes of an eighteen-year-old, more or less Hollywood's target age.

With the Universal deal came such a feeling of well-being that I temporarily lost my head one day and threw an idea at Andy. "We should call Mr. X."

"Call him? Why?" he asked.

"Well, we've got a big-time movie deal and it would be fun to brag a little."

Andy's eyes lit up at the notion of calling that legendary lunatic. "You still know his number?"

"I never had it, but we could call his agent."

"Think they'd give it to us?"

"Let's try," I said.

We placed a call to Mr. X's agent and a woman answered. The conversation was short and sweet: *Mr. X's privacy is very important and we do not give his number to anyone.* End of story. After waiting a few days for our request to be forgotten we called again, this time employing a few theatrics. By taking our bungalow's phone to the end of its extension cord, we made it just outside the door to obtain the perfect street ambience we needed. Andy dialed the number.

The agent answered and Andy went into his act. "Ma'am, this is Officer Walters with the NYPD and we have a man in custody who claims to know you. He says he's Mr. X, a famous writer."

I confess to doing a dead-on Mr. X impression, so I stood in the background blithering on with alternating pleas and insults, as Mr. X would do. Andy continued, "Lady, I'm tellin' you, this guy looks like a street person, not no big-shot writer. Could you describe him?"

She described X perfectly, from the matted hair to the tattered, soiled uniform. "Okay," said Andy. "What's his home address and phone, to confirm?" She quickly gave it to us as "Mr. X's" screams and threats welled in the background.

"Oh, yeah, that's him," she acknowledged matter-of-factly.

"Thank you, ma'am," said Andy as he hung up.

Then we dialed the number. I got on the line, the plan now having been changed from our bragging about a movie deal to something more surreal.

"Hello," answered Mr. X.

"Hello," I said, *as* Mr. X.

"Who's this?" he asked.

"You."

"Who?"

"It's you, asshole."

"Yeah, whatta you want?"

Yeah, whatta you want? You get a call from *yourself* and you want to know *what you want?* I could barely keep a straight face, and Andy, on the extension, was in tears.

"I wanted to say hi. So, hi, asshole, how you doin'?"

"I'm fine. How're you?"

This Kafkaesque exchange went on for a full five minutes — Mr. X talking to Mr. X. That's when we finally came to terms with the true depth of his insanity. We could tell he wasn't playing along, but actually seemed to believe he was speaking to himself. We were in awe. Finally the conversation came to a natural end — natural for Mr. X, that is.

"Well, asshole, good talkin' to ya," I said.

"Yeah, likewise." And we hung up. We couldn't work the rest of the day.

Life on the lot held some of the best experiences I had in Hollywood. I hammered away on our script, and Andy stopped in occasionally when he could pull away from *Taxi*. He loved the direction the script was taking, especially when I cast Andy Kaufman as the antagonist to Tony Clifton's hero. When he came by the office we'd act out various characters and scenes. We were pumped knowing Universal was probably going to make the movie — unlike the other ninety or ninety-five out of a hundred screenplays developed by the studios.

During this time, since Andy wasn't at Universal helping me write the Clifton script and had managed to keep his schedule at *Taxi* down to a mere two days a week, the question was: What was he doing? Andy woke up when he wanted to, watched a lot of TV, and read his fan mail. But mainly, since he had met so many women, he was constantly on the phone promoting dozens of relationships. His little black book merits a place in the Smithsonian.

Andy had willed himself to be famous, and he had succeeded. The teenage alcoholic with bad grades and a pregnant girlfriend had pulled it out of the crapper with amazing style. Was it Andy, LSD, or TM that was responsible for his spectacular career arc? Probably all three. Andy's childhood friends would tell you that he would have been voted least likely to succeed, and they were awed by his success (though none were jealous), surprised by what this very strange friend of theirs was able to achieve. What Andy did was different from any other performer, with no rules seeming to apply. Dangerous? Frequently. Exhilarating? Every day with him was an adventure, every moment lived in the now.

When we finally handed in the first draft of *The Tony Clifton Story*, the studio loved it. I was on top of the world! Then, like the iceberg to our *Titanic*, something crept out of the mist to loom in our path: it was a movie called *Heartbeeps*. Universal set up the picture to star Andy and voluptuous actress Bernadette Peters and to be directed by Allan Arkush, whose previous credits included *Death Sport* and *Rock 'n' Roll High School*. When Andy told me he and Peters were to play robots who fall in love in the wildly futuristic world of 1995, I dug up a copy of the script. After reading it, even though I was new to the screenwriting trade, I was savvy enough to realize that the manuscript had "turkey" written all over it.

I warned Andy not to do it, and I gave him two reasons why. One was that after poor Marty Feldman's dog, *In God We Tru$t*, Andy had stepped into the wait-and-see spotlight as far as the movie side of Hollywood was concerned. Another stinker and his film career would probably be over. The other reason was that we had what seemed a sure thing in Tony's movie. Andy knew the character, we had the jokes down, and the material was tried and true. I felt strongly that *Heartbeeps* was going to tank and begged Andy not to sign the contract. I told him Tony Clifton was what we should focus on and that I didn't understand Shapiro/West's logic in risking Andy's film future on a likely loser. I guess the bird-in-the-hand philosophy won out.

Andy signed to do *Heartbeeps*, and when the dust from the deal had settled I was asked *not* to visit the set because this was "Allan's first major film and he'd be nervous" with me around.

Insulted by the suggestion, I also knew that it was a load of shit and that he'd had plenty of experience making bad movies, but I stayed away as requested. In some ways I was relieved, because the script stunk, and to see such expensive and talented manpower going to waste would have depressed me. Besides, I wasn't getting paid to be there, so I was content to hole up in our lovely bungalow and polish our masterpiece, *The Tony Clifton Story*.

Occasionally Andy would stop by, more downcast than ever, given that his schedule on *Taxi* now blended uninterrupted into his time on the *Heartbeeps* set. At least *Taxi* was well received. Andy tried to put a good face on it, but a good performer knows if things are working or not. He knew he was shooting a bomb, and to make matters worse, he had to endure hours of elaborate makeup each day to become the metallic character he portrayed. It was hell for him.

Many people in this town have worked on films they thought would be hits that in fact were bombs, while others have labored on what they regarded as fait accompli disasters that turned into huge success stories, so who knows? On the set of *Ben-Hur*, Charlton Heston was on the phone every day to his agent complaining that he looked ridiculous in a Roman "dress" and wanted off the picture.

Despite my shots at *Heartbeeps*, I honestly wanted it to be a hit for two reasons: because of Andy, and because it would mean *Clifton* would be a slam dunk. I cringed at the thought of it failing, for I could visualize the next guy to occupy our bungalow watching the workers rub *my* name off the parking place. When *Heartbeeps'* principal photography ended, in July 1980, we sat back and waited for them to cut it and then set a release date, figuring that would be sometime in 1981.

Around this time a new performer entered the airwaves and quickly developed a reputation for a razor wit and acid sarcasm. His name was David Letterman. Letterman's first outing with NBC was in the mornings, and Andy made two appearances on that incarnation in 1980. Andy arrived for one of the shows disheveled and panhandling the audience, claiming wrestling had ruined his career and that he was now forced to sleep on the street. Dave loved Andy's antics, and they clicked from the start. Letterman, like Lorne Michaels, was sophisticated enough to grasp Andy's off-kilter sensibilities and that knife-edge he swung against convention.

When Dave moved to late night and *Late Night*, he took Andy along, giving him carte blanche, knowing he'd always deliver — which he did. To this day he calls Andy Kaufman the best guest he ever had. In a 1993 interview with *Rolling Stone*, Dave said: "You know what I really miss? There's a song on the new R.E.M. CD that I listened to like six times before I finally realized, 'Holy shit, this is about Andy Kaufman!' Andy would orchestrate and rehearse each of his appearances for maximum impact. And when the impact worked, good or bad, he would savor it. If we could have one guest like Andy — to me that's worth six months of new material. There's nobody like that now."

We understood that while waiting for *Heartbeeps* to sink or swim it was vital to get Clifton out and generating press. The only problem was, after the eggs à la Dinah incident, and despite being the talk of Tinsel Town, he was very difficult to get booked — people actually feared Clifton. That pleased us no end, but George really had to dig deep to find anyone ballsy enough to have Tony. The guy with the brass *cojones* turned out to be Rodney Dangerfield. George hit pay dirt when Rodney made an offer to Tony to open for him during his upcoming two-day show at San Francisco's Fillmore West.

Rodney was an old hipster who ran with Lenny Bruce and got what Andy was all about. Rodney's stage persona was not unlike Foreign Man's, in that neither got any respect. In real life, Rodney is the antithesis of his stage persona; he is extremely articulate and very, very cool. But Rodney had created a golden cage for himself over the years, and that tension between who he really was and who people thought he was tugged at him. Though Rodney often wanted to tell audiences to go fuck themselves, he couldn't because his character was, by design, powerless. So, like hiring a hit-man, he could live vicariously through Mr. Clifton, who was guaranteed to assault anyone who dared think he was there to please.

Dangerfield's stamp of approval on Clifton emboldened Andy's management team, who had begun to wonder whether Tony Clifton wasn't becoming a terrible mistake for Andy. Dangerfield's career was undergoing a sort of rebirth with his popularity from the Miller Lite commercials, and he was finding acceptance among a younger audience. With such an endorsement, suddenly Tony Clifton — at least among the industry insiders — was seen as not only dangerous but *bookable*.

Andy knew he was headed into the lions' den. The Fillmore is a very large venue and would be full of screaming kids who were there to see Rodney, not some hack lounge singer. They'd certainly be indifferent if not downright hostile. Andy couldn't wait. Over the years, I've worked with most of the top comedians, and none have exhibited the sheer confidence of Andy Kaufman. If he ever had self-doubts, they were never even remotely apparent. He always plunged ahead full steam with the unwavering conviction that he was right. It wasn't ego or bravado, but rather the confidence of genius.

As usual, Tony Clifton's billing made no mention of Andy. Before the show, as the place was filling, Bill Graham, impresario extraordinaire and owner of the Fillmore, stopped by to say hello. Though Graham had helped launch the careers of Janis Joplin, Jimi Hendrix, and the Grateful Dead, Andy as Tony couldn't have cared less, and when Graham approached Tony he was soundly rebuffed by the brazen lounge indigene. Later, a spiteful Bill Graham would proclaim Tony Clifton the worst act he ever saw, worse even than the Sex Pistols, who pissed on his stage. Bill Graham may have been viewing Tony through the filter of negative emotions, because I'm surprised a guy so apparently hip could miss the point of Tony Clifton.

Finally it was show time. As the house lights dimmed I picked up a microphone offstage and announced, "Good evening, ladies and gentlemen, the Fillmore is proud to present Rodney Dangerfield!" The place exploded in applause. "But first," I continued, "before we bring out Rodney, I want to bring out our opening act!"

Now boos replaced the clapping. This was great — Tony hadn't even stepped out on stage and they were ready to kill the opening act, *any* opening act. Tony usually had to do a lot of work to get a crowd this hostile, and here he was, *starting* with blind hatred. It was perfect.

As I stood in the wings next to Tony and George Shapiro and watched the seething mass, Rodney stepped up in his shirt and boxers (Rodney never puts on his pants until he goes onstage). He was beaming. "Go get 'em, Tone!" he yelled. Rodney's comment stemmed from feelings from all those years he himself wanted to squash the audience, tell them he was no loser but a real ladies' man, a suave, sophisticated man of the world. That night, Rodney thrilled to the possibility that Tony was there to even the score for both of them.

I held the microphone close to my mouth to overwhelm the noise. "Ladies and gentlemen, please, our opening act, Tony Clifton, will not come out until all of you are silent." The crowd answered with a chorus of boos and scattered "fuck yous" and began to chant, "Rodney! Rodney! Rodney!" Tony took the microphone from my hand and stepped out on the edge of the stage. "You may want Rodney," he rasped, "but you're gettin' Tony." The boos and hisses notched up a few levels. "Rodney's not coming out until I perform for you first." He waited a second, then assumed a relaxed stance. "Believe me, people, I got all night."

The audience went insane as fights broke out between people arguing with one another about keeping quiet so they could get rid of this opening act. Tony, Rodney, George, and I thought it was hilarious — if any crowd was a Clifton crowd, this was it. Tony decided the people were "warmed up" and ready, so he hit the stage singing "I Left My Heart in San Francisco." No other song could have riled them more, particularly the way he sang it.

Tony occasionally stopped singing long enough to scream "Shut up!" After each interruption he would go back to the beginning of the song. If the audience members had been insanely mad *before* Tony sang, they were now much worse. A hail of bottles — beer, liquor, and soda — poured down on the stage and Tony had to bob and weave to avoid a beaning. "I want RESPECT!" he screamed, in a tribute to his headliner. Rodney was next to me, doubled over with laughter.

Suddenly an old man climbed onto the stage and went after Tony with a pocket knife. Security hauled him away before he could puncture Clifton. George turned to me, smiling with glee. "Great idea. When did you hire that plant?"

I looked over at George. "Never seen him before. He was for real." George blanched. Though the knife-wielding assassin failed, the crowd still posed a threat to Tony's well-being with the continuous storm of glass containers. Bill Graham finally ordered the curtain down fearing a direct hit might kill Tony. He ran over to Tony and apologized profusely, offering to pay in full despite Tony's having done only three minutes of his act. George and I and Rodney laughed our heads off, and Graham walked over, completely perplexed.

"What's so funny?" he asked. "The guy could get hurt. They hate him."

"Bill," I said, "that's the point. They're supposed to hate him, that's his act!"

Graham looked at us like we were nuts and walked away.

The next day we heeded Graham's concerns and went down to Fisherman's Wharf and rented a fishing net large enough to cover the stage. It was a little insurance for Tony against the night's bottles. By then, radio stations had gotten into the act and spread the word, so on the way to the show, many people stopped off at fruit and vegetable stands and stocked up on ammo.

That night Tony Clifton took the stage, but to the surprise of many of his hecklers he was clad head to toe in full SFPD riot gear, with a helmet protecting his noggin and his microphone attached to the full face shield. As he began to sing, produce and bottles cascaded down, so we lowered the net. That kept most projectiles from reaching Tony, although a few got through, to the delight of the audience.

When it was all over, the stage was littered with broken glass and the muck of smashed fruit and vegetables. It was a triumph for Tony Clifton. The audience had been assigned an interactive role, and they'd accepted it with zeal. Tony had come away more hated and reviled than any act either of us had ever seen — it was a stunning success. Our out-of-town opening had worked, and now we went back to Hollywood to continue our campaign to make Tony a household word, albeit a four-letter one. *Rolling Stone* helped when they ran a photo of Clifton dressed in full SFPD riot gear, singing his heart out while being pelted with debris. Taking that as a cue, I worked the Fillmore show into the Tony Clifton script for Universal.

*   *   *

The question most asked of me regarding Andy has been, Was he really as weird as he seemed? It sounds odd, but my knee-jerk reaction is always, "No, he was a regular guy." At times when I'd be falling apart at the seams from one problem or another, Andy's sound and sage advice would instantly straighten me out. But every so often, after I had concluded he was crazy like a fox, he'd do something so bizarre I would temporarily drop the fox qualification. After I had worked hard in Hollywood for a few years, and had had some good breaks, I'd accumulated enough savings to consider an investment, something to fall back on in my old age. I approached Andy, my best buddy, to see if he wanted to go in on it with me.

"I've found a great piece of property up in Santa Barbara. I'm thinking it's perfect for a restaurant. I'm just thinking ahead, since I probably can't be in this business forever."

That statement hit Andy like a two-by-four across the face. "My god, Bob, I just realized I don't know anything about any other business than show business."

"Well, that's not true," I said, surprised at how stunned he seemed. "You're a very smart guy, you could do anything."

"Yeah, but I don't know anything but performing. I've got no other trade."

I felt this was a very odd thing to say, particularly for a man making a decent yearly salary *every week* in his current trade, but I humored him. "Okay, so be a restaurateur with me. We'll have fun."

"But I don't know anything about the restaurant business," he said.

"So start from the bottom up," I countered. Then I added jokingly, "Get a job somewhere as a busboy."

He looked at me, eyes wild and intense. "Hey, that's not a bad idea!"

The next morning I got an excited call from him, and in the background I heard the clinking of dishes and glasses and silverware. I figured he was at a restaurant drinking in the vibes, pondering our foray into the business.

"I'm at the Posh Bagel," he said. It was a place we frequented, and my girlfriend, Shelly (we got back together), worked there.

Okay, I thought, *it's not the type of place I had in mind for Santa Barbara, but at least he's thinking about the investment.* Wrong.

"I'm doing what you said. I started this morning. I'm a busboy."

I paused, then deadpanned, "Sure, Kaufman, that's great. Something to fall back on, right?"

"Exactly. Listen, I gotta go, it's my first day, and I want to make a good impression on my boss. Call you later."

The phone went dead. I shook my head and laughed — typical Kaufman put-on. A little later Shelly called from work. "Did you know Andy was working here?"

Disbelieving it, I jumped in the stalwart Rambler Rebel — I hadn't put a drop of oil in it in two years and it still ran like a Swiss watch — and showed up at the restaurant. Sure enough, there was Andy, cap pulled low, in glasses and an apron . . . busing tables. No one recognized him, and why would they? A major star cleaning up your slop? Unheard of. He spotted me and ran over, as excited as a little kid. "Thanks for the idea! I love this job!"

Though he couldn't work a full-time schedule because of his *Taxi* duties, he did work a regular schedule of six-hour shifts. And he loved it. After Andy became established, the owner told me not only was he one of the best busboys he'd ever had, but also the rest of the staff was so pumped by his incredible work ethic that their demeanor and productivity had risen noticeably.

What prompted Andy Kaufman, television star, to take a minimum-wage schlepp job? First, Andy wasn't joking when he told me he didn't know what he'd do if he wasn't in show business. And on learning there was something he could do, aside from entertain, he became almost giddy. Busing tables liberated him and yet at the same time secured his feet to the ground, for it was an experience completely antithetical to being a star. Here, on the lowest echelon of the Hollywood food chain, he could observe his world through the same eyes as when he had been delivering meat to Alan King and admiring his beer tap — yet now his view was tempered by considerable experience. By now, Andy didn't care about beer taps; he was far past that, spiritually and politically.

Which brings me to the next reason he liked working at the Posh Bagel: Andy was a socialist. A staunch supporter of a classless society, he never looked down his nose at anyone, be they fellow busboy, street vendor, or prostitute. If the state would have subsidized his "art," as they do in some socialist countries, he would have been completely happy. Though Andy was an exceptional intellect and no doubt had his contracts — and subsequently his earnings — explained by Shapiro/West, I really believe he didn't have any idea how much money he had. Stanley Kaufman handled his son's finances, essentially giving Andy an "allowance" and managing the rest. When Andy upgraded his life — a new place, a new car for Tony — Stanley released the dough to him.

Andy's spare lifestyle could have made Gandhi look like Aristotle Onassis. His home, which he rented, was a modest, furnished two-bedroom. The place was isolated in the hills, but nothing special to look at. There weren't many personal items in evidence, except for props from his stage show and numerous pictures of Guru Dev and the Maharishi, always with incense burning beneath them. One notable feature of his living quarters was the temperature. It was always freezing. He kept the temperature very cool, just like a TV studio . . . or maybe a meat locker.

Most of the times anyone visited Andy he'd be in his underwear. Of course, you always removed your shoes before entering Andy's humble domain. You got the feeling that it wasn't so much his home as a shrine to the Maharishi, almost as if he was trying to re-create the setting of one of his TM retreats. Occasionally, he would have a roommate, Kathy Uttman, living with him, a fellow TMer. Their relationship was nonsexual, and she contributed to the ambience of the place as a tribute to TM. Had you known nothing about Andy you might have surmised the place was the domicile of a monk, or an indoctrination center for some cosmic cult. And if you looked around you'd be further confused by the ever-present Kaufman paraphernalia: congas, wrestling mats, and, of course, Howdy Doody.

Andy owned only a few shirts, a couple pairs of pants, basic socks and underwear, a dress jacket, and a heavy coat for colder climes. Until he rented the house several years after "making it," he had no washer and dryer and slogged down to the local Laundromat to wash his meager wardrobe. We certainly enjoyed limos and first-class seats and accommodations, but there were no personal drivers or butlers or cooks or security personnel for Andy Kaufman.

In many ways, he was an ascetic, a man who had simplified his surroundings just as he had complicated his position in the world, as well as the perceptions of most who knew his name. He feared co-option by Hollywood and in many ways went out of his way to prove he wasn't part of it: he became a busboy, was ardently nonmaterialistic, and dated trailer trash — all designed to say, *I'm not part of Hollywood, I have not been sucked into that world!*

Though I loathed the ungenuineness that pervaded the West Coast entertainment industry, Andy was even less sanguine about it. New York by comparison seemed much more egalitarian, a great metropolis where people of all walks of life mingled on the sidewalks and your class distinction was "New Yorker," not "struggling actor," "hack writer," "superstar," or "über-agent." Hell, in L.A. nobody even walked, unless it was to nowhere on a treadmill, and people oozed stock little snippets of insincerity like "Let's do lunch," or "I didn't love it," or "My people will call your people, darling." Yes, sports fans, "showbiz" people really do say stuff like that in "Hell Lay," and Andy reacted by fleeing to the kitchen of the Posh Bagel. Sometimes I wondered whether Andy had dropped in from another world or perhaps another galaxy and erroneously been branded a comedian. Many say he was twenty years ahead of his time; I think he was *from* twenty light-years distant.

On April 11, 1980, ABC launched its answer to *Saturday Night Live*, calling it simply *Fridays*. Also an 11:30 P.M. "live sketch show" with a musical act and a guest host, *Fridays* came out of the blocks with considerably less momentum than *SNL*. It tried to survive that traditionally thin Friday-night spot, but saddled with scattered affiliate disaffections brought about by material deemed objectionable in more conservative markets, from the get-go *Fridays'* ratings were abysmal and cried out for medical attention. By early 1981, the doctor they called upon to get the patient on its feet was Andy Kaufman. The offer came in for Andy to do the show with no restrictions. The only edict given him: Kick start this dog and get it some attention. There was never a concern that Andy was burning his bridges at *SNL* by doing *Fridays*. *SNL* was so far ahead of the pack that Lorne Michaels's take on the new show was that since imitation is the sincerest form of flattery Andy could do what he wanted with *Fridays*. The executive producers, John Moffitt and Pat Tourk Lee, contracted Andy to first appear on February 20, 1981.

Andy was to act in a sketch centered around two couples who are enjoying dinner together. The other actors were Maryedith Burrell, Michael Richards (of *Seinfeld* fame), and Melanie Chartoff. Occasionally each person, one by one, would be excused, go to the restroom, and return to the table stoned out of his or her gourd. A few days before the show's airing, Andy vehemently registered his offense at the drug humor, as he had forsaken drugs some years prior and no longer supported anything related to the drug culture. If the producers wanted to send such a message to the youth of America, they could do it without him. Producer John Moffitt, one of the sweetest, most reasonable guys around, patiently explained to Andy that the drug humor was done only in fun, and though the kids watching the show laughed at it, they understood it was just that, fun.

During the live cast, moments after the red cue lights on the big cameras winked at the performers to begin, Andy, who was in the middle of the sketch sitting with the three other actors at the dining table, announced he could no longer continue. This was live, on national television. None of the other actors knew what to do. Seconds of dead air seemed like hours as all eyes fixed on Andy, waiting for him to respond. When he reiterated that he wouldn't continue, Michael Richards walked over, grabbed a stack of the sizable cue cards, and slammed them down in front of Andy, warning, "Read the lines."

"You don't have to do that," retorted Andy, now offended. To punctuate his feelings he picked up a glass of water and threw it in Richards's face. Melanie Chartoff then tried to come to Michael's aid by hurling a plate of butter pats at Andy. The butter stuck to his face and hair, and he leaped up, ready to fight. As Andy and Michael squared off, producer Jack Burns jumped in from off-camera to mediate the dispute, screaming to the control booth, "Go to commercial! *Now!*"

When Jack told Andy to get off the stage and he refused, Jack shoved Andy. Suddenly all hell broke loose. They collided in a rage, and the studio security, along with various cast members, descended to pull the mad dogs off each other. A furious Kaufman and Burns were restrained from killing each other. Cut to commercial.

Luckily, when the show came back from the spot break it was the end of the program. As the cast gathered to wave good-night, one look at their faces and you could tell they'd been traumatized — and Tony Clifton had been nowhere in sight. The next day news wires shouted the headline across the country — Andy Kaufman was at it again, this time disrupting a live national broadcast.

ABC was bombarded with letters from irate viewers (some who hadn't even seen the broadcast) demanding Kaufman be banned from television. One incensed writer claimed that Andy was a "danger to himself and others." *Fridays* received so much mail that the producers decided to bring Andy back the next week to "smooth things over." During that appearance, a chastened Andy sat next to John Moffitt and read a prepared statement that sought forgiveness for his behavior. He performed our classic Viet Cong Confession, eyes blank, voice monotone, and rattled off his "sincere apologies." The ratings soared and a re-invigorated ABC renewed the show for the next season.

Six months later, a humbled Andy, his bad-boy ways behind him, appeared again on *Fridays*. Now a changed man, he sported a Pat Boone haircut and a suit and tie. Filled with joy, Andy had returned to the scene of his embarrassment to announce his new life. On his arm was a lovely young lady, a gospel singer from *The Lawrence Welk Show*, Cathy Sullivan. Facing the studio assemblage, Andy nervously announced he'd been born again and that he'd found the Lord. Then he dropped the bombshell: he and Cathy had fallen in love and were engaged to be married. It was a poignant moment for Andy as he and Cathy sang a beautiful spiritual and gazed moon-eyed at each other, all to the complete dismay of the studio and national audience.

Now, here's what really happened.

First, you must understand one thing: no matter how insane you are, no one but no one *ever* freaks out on national television without prior network approval. The reason is simple: do it and you will be blacklisted from television forever, no matter what kind of "artist" you are. Remember the name of the actor who uttered the word "fuck" on *SNL*? Exactly my point.

But that does not mean everyone need know what you're doing. Andy believed very strongly that the actors and crew should not know because their genuine reactions were what would make his little psychodrama completely believable. John Moffitt, Pat Tourk Lee, and Jack Burns all did terrific jobs of carrying out Andy's wishes and selling their anger to the rest of the cast, the crew, and, ultimately, the audience. John later confided that he had told Maryedith Burrell because she likely would have lost her cool. He was also concerned that if she were not let in on the secret she would not trust any of them in the future. Only recently, my good friend Michael Richards let me in on a secret: he'd been told the day before the incident and kept it quiet all those years. He did so because there were still many people who believed it was a real conflict, although there were those who didn't, and Michael didn't want to prove the naysayers right. His realistic reaction (fooling me as well) is a testament to his exceptional acting skills and his devotion to the Kaufman mystique. As for Jack Burns, the producer who rushed in to break up the fight that he only succeeded in fueling, he too did a wonderful job of acting. In *Man on the Moon* you can relive this incident in all its glory, with yours truly playing Jack's role.

Was Andy really disapproving of drug humor? Absolutely not. But because his devotion to TM was well known, and given TMers' disdain for drugs and alcohol, it was a natural plot point to allow Kaufman to find fault.

After we sat back and surveyed the "damage" done by our staged brawl, we became concerned that the public might begin to think Andy was literally insane, so we drew the line. At the time, it seemed every politician or entertainer who got caught doing something bad would suddenly announce they were born again, and the nation would always accept a loose nut or bad apple who'd turned to Jesus. That Andy was a Jew was all the better.

Thus we continued with our overall game plan: Andy as the good guy, then the bad guy, then the good guy again. Just like pro wrestling. Cathy Sullivan was actually from *The Lawrence Welk Show* and was relatively innocent to all the scheming behind the scenes. We decided Andy would really marry her on the show —just like when Tiny Tim and Miss Vicky got hitched on Carson's show, the only difference being we would cast Cathy as Andy's bride-to-be. That Andy didn't really have a relationship with Cathy, and in fact hardly knew her, didn't matter, as he was prepared to have her sign a prenuptial agreement and then have the marriage annulled immediately after the ceremony.

At the last minute, Cathy either wised up or got cold feet and backed out — I heard some of her *Lawrence Welk* crew talked her out of it. Andy just shrugged it off because he'd accomplished his goal: satisfy his responsibility to save *Fridays* while maintaining his artistic integrity. It was the '80s and the new phrase "win-win" was in vogue.

Tony and Me

Andy was traveling at the speed of life. It's amazing stuff.
ROBIN WILLIAMS

We decided we needed to get Tony out in public and stir up some ink on him. The Improv seemed like the natural place to begin. One night Tony made an unexpected appearance, and though he was warmly received, halfway through his act the crowd began shouting "Andy! Andy!" Furious, he stormed off the stage, and we left. It was bad enough that Foreign Man had been "bought out" and repackaged as Latka, *and* that both were automatically related to Andy, but now Tony Clifton was suffering the same fate.

Andy was pissed because fame was beginning to get in the way of having fun. It was similar to what happened to Allen Funt, the creator of *Candid Camera*. Before his show became an institution, Funt would go out and participate in the stunts himself, but his massive exposure eventually ruined his anonymity. The same was happening with Andy.

As we drove home to Andy's we decided a new strategy was in order, one that would once again turn the tables on the audiences.

"What if Clifton and I appear simultaneously?" he offered.

"Get somebody to play Clifton?"

"Exactly. Wouldn't that be hilarious? Tony's on stage, they're thinking it's me, and I show up."

"Yeah, okay, I like it, but who?" I wondered.

Andy looked over at me. "Oh, no!" I protested. "Forget it! No way."

From the moment I saw Clifton, I'd been doing his accent and mannerisms, and as we developed material as well as a persona for him, I had worked on getting him down. It was the quickest way for me to write a character: just become that character. I admittedly did a damn good Clifton, and many of the lines Andy uttered as Tony were my invention. I knew he was right about who should be the other Clifton, but I was scared.

Andy's voice was calm but firm. "Why not? It makes complete sense. You've got Tony down perfectly, his voice, the mannerisms. You *are* Tony."

It was a huge compliment from the man who was very proprietary about his characters, but Andy had given me, as his writer and best friend, a membership in a club so exclusive it had but one member, me. He trusted me completely, but knew I had to overcome one problem, a problem that was so foreign to Andy I didn't think he could possibly understand.

"You're afraid," he said quietly. "That's natural. We can work on that."

As the other half of "Albrecht & Zmuda, Comedy from A to Z," when we sucked I could blame Albrecht, and vice versa. And appearing on the *SNL* wrestling sketches, or at colleges in a background role, or even onstage at the Park West *in a mask*, well, that was a whole lot different from taking the stage all alone, figuratively naked, with no one to play off of. And on top of that, this character was not only front and center, he was one of the most balls-to-the-walls entertainers to stalk a stage, a guy who seized an audience by the throat and made them scream uncle! Tony Clifton was no shrinking violet. I didn't know how I could walk on stage and do what Andy did.

"You don't have a fearful bone in your body," I said. "Doing Clifton is . . ."

"Doing Clifton is no different in front of me or onstage," he said firmly. "It's all in your head. You know the character, right?"

"Yeah . . ."

"Well, we just have to convince you there's nothing to be afraid of. Would Tony be afraid?"

I laughed at the thought of Tony Clifton being afraid of anything. "No."

"Okay, then you will become Tony. Just like I do."

I pictured Andy Kaufman, the nonsmoking vegetarian, consuming steaks and chain-smoking as the polar-reversed Tony Clifton and worried about my own commitment to the character. Could I go there?

"I told you," he said, "when I was a little kid doing those shows? I was really scared, terrified even. I practiced in my basement for years before I could go in front of anybody, and then when I did, it was the neighbor kids, always younger than me. I never let the adults in because I was afraid they'd judge me."

We pulled up to his house and went inside. He continued. "What I've never told you, or anyone else for that matter, is that I'm still afraid. But that's why I meditate. So I won't be scared."

He had a meditation clause in all his contracts, allowing him time to release his tensions before going onstage or onto a set — it was de rigueur if you wanted to hire Andy Kaufman. He never told me it was because he was afraid — I figured he might now be telling me that to make me feel better. "You? Afraid?" I laughed. "That'll be the day."

"No, it's true. When I discovered transcendental meditation I learned to make those fears go away, to see they were nothing. And once I let go of that, that fear of being judged? Then I was safe."

"I think you're just saying that."

"No," he insisted, "I get scared, too, I just don't let anyone know it, you included. And when I do get scared, the meditation takes it away. Once I focus, I can do anything. So can you."

Andy was persuasive not only in his words but also in his eyes and his body language, which told me to be calm, everything would be fine. I believed him because he was by nature a scrupulously honest man and I trusted he wasn't saying those things just to get me to play Tony Clifton. There was an unspoken agreement between us to push each other not only to improve creatively but also to grow personally. We needed someone in our lives to whom we looked for guidance at times, someone whose opinion or judgment we held above even our own — we played that role for each other.

After some hours of his quiet persistence and counseling I started warming up to the idea of becoming Clifton. With Andy's help I began to visualize myself on stage, singing, smoking, strutting, and, best of all, berating unsuspecting audience members. I came to see it as a wonderful opportunity, with the payoff being the looks on the faces of everyone in the house when they began screaming to Tony for Andy . . . and got him! I visualized the shock wave as Andy entered from the darkness at the edge of the stage and stood side by side with Tony, and that clinched it.

"Okay, let's do it. I'll be Clifton," I agreed, not sure what I was getting into but excited by the promise of the unknown.

Andy smiled slightly. "You'll be good."

As we sat up late and planned what we'd do with our new creation, I came to realize what Andy had just done. Though his motivation was certainly "the big put-on," he also exhibited extraordinary generosity by gifting one of his signature characters to me. Though he and I had worked to hone Tony, Tony was, until that moment, Andy's. Now we would share Tony. That would be no small thing for any entertainer, because brilliant creations such as Tony Clifton are almost always zealously guarded, like secrets of state or family recipes. But Andy made the bestowal of Tony Clifton seem less like a business decision than one friend handing down a treasured heirloom to another.

Like his contemporaries Robin Williams and Steve Martin, when away from the footlights Andy was quiet and reserved, almost shy. What were often interpreted as Andy's offstage antics were merely a continuation of his act. To be alone with Andy and to be a member of his "club" was to spend time with a man whom some would consider boring. Andy himself felt he was boring when the mask came off, but he needed time to be "off" as opposed to "on," which required a phenomenal output of energy. Andy saw what he did as a calling, and his life was devoted to his art. His sacrifice was that the time afforded him to be just Andy was limited.

To pull off the illusion of a consistent Tony Clifton being played by two people of different heights and body types, great preparations were taken. Though I had been modestly successful in creating Tony's face with my limited knowledge of makeup, for the latest incarnation of Mr. Clifton I turned to the pros. Among those I interviewed were visual effects giants such as Rick Baker (*King Kong*), Stan Winston (who would go on to do the special effects for *Aliens, The Terminator, Terminator 2*, and *Jurassic Park*), and Wally Westmore (*Vertigo*). After careful consideration, I chose Ken Chase. Not only was Ken a certified effects heavyweight, but also I felt he could keep the secret of both Andy and me being Tony (a favor he has done me for the past fifteen years).

Ken made molds of our faces, hands, even teeth. The finished product had to fit us both and be consistent with the version of Tony that had been out there and that people were familiar with — no mean feat. Essentially, Tony's exterior would be the same regardless of who wore it, but the inner fit would be adjusted for our physical peculiarities. For instance, the bridge of Andy's nose was wider than mine, so I was fitted with a prosthetic piece. On the other hand, I was not as tall as Andy, therefore special lifts were devised to give me the trademark "towering Clifton" effect.

That Tony was a big son of a bitch merely enhanced his menace, and for that reason we made him slightly more heavyset than he had been. For consistency, there also was only one Clifton costume — if a button fell off, we'd still match. Our concern about the congruity of Tony's likeness stemmed from the knowledge that a fair amount of video already existed, and with the advent of the first portable video cameras, more and more footage would be generated, thus giving skeptics more of Clifton to compare. We required that my Tony be indistinguishable from Andy's.

Which brings me to another point of departure for our respective Tonys — we had diametrically differing goals as performers. Andy as Tony was a kamikaze pilot ready to die for the cause, so antagonizing an audience that they couldn't help but hate and reject him. I was the pilot ready to fly the dangerous mission, but I sure as hell wanted to come home — I needed acceptance. I soon rationalized we could each play our Cliftons: on one night he'd get dragged off the stage, on another night he'd *almost* get dragged off.

You'd think we were testing a new spacesuit for NASA given the countless tests, run-throughs, and adjustments we made dialing in the new and improved Clifton. But finally we were done. And he was magnificent. I had been channeling Clifton in preparation for my first big moment in the spotlight, and when we tried him out on some people we knew, and they thought I was Andy, we knew we were ready. Now our goal was one of despicable subversion: not only fool the public, but perpetrate our sleight on the hand that fed us, the industry.

Much of the credit for what happened next must go to George Shapiro. Putting his reputation on the line, he had the guts to book Clifton as Clifton, *not* as a manifestation of Andy Kaufman. Seeming to pull off the impossible, George secured contracts that called for Tony Clifton as a separate entity — making no mention of Andy — therefore technically allowing me to appear as the raffish International Singing Sensation. The clubs thought they were getting Andy in disguise, but George covered himself legally by insisting it was Tony Clifton, not Andy Kaufman. Everyone signed the contract as they winked accordingly, believing they were all in on the joke. It was a joke all right, but they sure as hell weren't in on it.

George's first miracle was getting Tony booked into the main room at Harrah's Casino in Lake Tahoe. Though Harrah's was forbidden to use Andy's name relative to Clifton in the advertising, the press, under no such restrictions, seized on it and widely reported "Andy's" appearance, much to our delight. The gig was for two weeks, so I suddenly had to create a slick Vegas-style show, with the requisite orchestra, charts, patter, and massive logistics. It was a little weird (and frightening) to know that this time it was I, not Kaufman, walking into the fire.

Another consideration was Clifton's voice. Two weeks of two shows a night were going to play havoc on my throat, given the vocal gymnastics Clifton required of me. Also, Tahoe's six-thousand-foot elevation worried me, as it was daunting even for experienced singers — a few minutes into the act and they're panting from lack of air. That Andy's voice was pitched slightly higher, more tenor than mine, and Clifton's voice was nasal and somewhat pinched initially drained me even in short bursts. I hired a vocal coach and worked closely with him to be able to deliver Clifton over the long haul and at altitude without blowing out my throat.

My first trial run as Clifton came when Shapiro booked him on both *Letterman* and *Merv Griffin* to give Tony a push for his Tahoe show. Waiting in the wings of the *Letterman* show, I was nervous until I got the cue to go on and remembered Andy's question — Would Tony be scared? — and suddenly I was Clifton. I went out and wowed 'em. As we went to a commercial, Dave leaned over and whispered, "Andy, that makeup is so good, if I didn't know you I'd swear it was someone else." Years later, Dave's longtime producer, Robert Morton, cornered me and asked about my appearances as Tony Clifton. Acknowledging that Clifton had been on *Letterman* three times, Morty asked, "How many times did you do the *Letterman* show as Tony?"

"Every time," I replied.

"You mean you were doing the show and Andy was home sleeping?" he asked.

"Yup."

I had passed the *Letterman* test and was ready for Harrah's. As *Late Night* was beamed out to the West Coast, Andy sat in his living room watching Tony Clifton pull the wool over the eyes of Dave and the nation, and he laughed till he cried. With makeup whiz Ken Chase sworn to secrecy, no one else but Andy, Shapiro/West, and I knew the truth.

As I was settling in at Harrah's (after making excuses to management that Andy was on his way), a masquerading Andy flew in to Reno and got a room at a place nearby called the Hormsby House, in Carson City. I mean nearby to the whorehouses, not so much to Harrah's. He was ten minutes from the physical pleasures we'd found two years before and thirty minutes from Harrah's, and he would occasionally drive in — cloaked in heavy disguise — and enjoy the show. It was surreal, because probably everyone in the audience thought they were watching him, and he got a huge kick out of that fact. He also derived great pleasure from taunting me from time to time with shouts from the middle of the crowd, like, "We know you're really Andy Kaufman. What do you think, we're stupid?" At one point he heckled me so much that I had him removed by security. If he couldn't be thrown out as Clifton, he had still managed to find a way.

A few times during the two weeks, he drove over and, as Andy

Kaufman, did a walk-through of the Casino, glad-handing fans and saying hellos to various Harrah's staff, thus establishing his presence. Then, when no one was looking, he'd head out the back door and back to the Mustang Ranch or the Hormsby House to order in "dinner," usually three or four of his "professional" acquaintances. Once he realized I was going to be fine, he even flew back to L.A. a few times.

Meanwhile, I was wallowing in the excessive world of Tony Clifton. As the first week passed I was like a kid in a candy store. Now I was the star and not Andy's sideman Bugsy — and it was a life really easy to get used to. One night after I'd finished my second show I was puttering in my dressing room when a lovely young showgirl knocked on my door. She claimed she was a big fan of Andy's, so I decided to stay in character, and within a few minutes was suggesting we go out that evening. Not one to miss an opportunity, very soon we were having sex (picture me still fully dressed as Clifton), and at that point, despite my pleasure, I realized it was the height of absurdity: she was blowing *Andy*, not me. I was now Tony Clifton, comic incubus.

She became suspicious after a while when I wouldn't remove my facial pieces or drop out of character, but by then the fat was in the fire and I dared not. I gave her some lame excuse that I had only the single set of latex appliances because the rest had been lost, and once removed they were useless. To shore up my argument I also pointed out I was an artist, therefore staying in character was essential and she should always address me as Tony. She bought it hook, line, and sinker, and we had no further problems. Sure, she was a starfucker, but she was a very sweet starfucker. My mind reeled over what her reaction might be if she found out her "star" was the *other* Tony Clifton. We dated for the rest of the run, and it was exciting, if not dangerous as hell. Not once did I remove the disguise.

The night of the last show I drove up to the Hormsby House, where Andy and I had agreed we needed to unwind with a prank. Since I was still wearing Clifton's facial appliances (each set lasted only one wearing, and we had plenty more in L.A.), I slashed the latex and then covered myself in fake blood. Looking like Jason Voorhees had been working me over with his ax for a good ten minutes, I lay down in front of the elevator and Andy stood in his doorway a few yards away to watch what happened. It was very late and people were coming back from various shows in the area. We didn't wait long before the elevator opened and an older couple in splendid evening attire prepared to step out. What they saw was Tony Clifton on the carpet at their feet, lacerated and bleeding to death.

"Get outta here! They're killin' people up here! Run away! Save yourselves!" Tony screamed, a frothy pink foam rimming his mouth. "Get away! *Live!*"

The horrified looks on their faces was worth a fortune. As soon as the elevator closed we darted into Andy's room and waited for the fun. It didn't take long before the place was crawling with security guards and police. They knocked on the door and Andy innocently told them he hadn't heard a thing.

Back in L.A., a few months passed, and Andy got a phone call — from my Harrah's showgirl. I had forgotten I'd given her Andy's phone number. When she'd asked for it, what was I to do? We'd been having sex for ten days, so I felt I had to comply and give her Andy's actual number, but I didn't think she'd really use it. She did, and Andy called me in a panic.

"She's flying in tomorrow. What should I do?" he asked.

"Pick her up," I said, loving that my move had backfired on *Kaufman*.

"What? I don't even know her. How will I do that?"

I described her again and pointed out her best selling point. "She'll expect to have sex with you."

Andy mulled that over for about one second. "Okay," he said. "But I may have to call you for information. This might be tough to pull off."

"You can do it."

And he did. The next day he picked her up at the airport, and she stayed with him three days. Of course, he called me every hour or so to find out things I knew that he was supposed to know, but he managed to fake his way through it. What baffled both of us after she left was that she didn't seem to know the difference between us, which was particularly odd given Kaufman was Jewish, I was Catholic, and only one of us was circumcised. I guess it's true that love is blind.

*　　*　　*

Our scam at Harrah's worked on several levels. When George Shapiro booked Clifton there, he never expected Tony to last two nights, let alone two weeks. That bastard Kaufman told me afterward (in spite of his pep talk) that he had figured I would survive no longer than ten minutes. I surprised them all. Actually, Andy felt *Tony Clifton* couldn't last longer than ten minutes, given his propensity for crowd antagonism. I pointed out that although his Clifton begged rejection, mine gingerly courted acceptance. Whereas Andy's Tony was a form of vicious catharsis for him, my Tony was just an *act*. And as an act I instinctively worked to keep most of the audience in their seats. (I say "most" as I could never forget that I was, after all, Tony Clifton.)

Prior to my debut at Harrah's, Andy warned me, "Clifton can get to you. You have to fight with him sometimes, he's pretty intense, hard to shake." During the filming of *Man on the Moon* I passed that warning on to Jim Carrey. A consummate artist, Jim discovered the wisdom of my words: Tony, once you fell under his spell, was a very tough demon to exorcize. Jim also had a choice over how to play Clifton: my version or Andy's. He chose mine because it was a more "accessible" direction for the way he wanted to portray Tony.

Much has been written on the Andy-as-Tony phenomenon, and some have suggested that Andy exhibited classic multiple personality disorder, or MPD. One expert felt Andy might have been demonstrating a rare case of "controlled" MPD in that, unlike most other sufferers of MPD, Andy could actually regulate his disorder, calling it up almost like a channeler.

One fact that seems to support the notion of MPD concerns a particular sexual preference over which Andy and Tony differed utterly: oral sex. According to experts, one cannot change hard-and-fast sexual proclivities, and though Andy was absolutely repulsed by oral sex, Tony Clifton lived for it. My friend psychologist Joe Troiani says that one cannot change such an orientation unless multiple personalities are involved.

But whoever Tony Clifton or Andy Kaufman or Bob Zmuda *really* were at that moment wasn't as important as that we achieved our two goals, getting Tony more press and proving you could book him and he wouldn't necessarily self-destruct. Now we had *two* Cliftons in our arsenal, bad Tony and worse

Tony, so I went back to work on *The Tony Clifton Story* and Andy returned to *Taxi*, as we awaited the impending premier of *Heartbeeps*.

On the weekend that *Heartbeeps* debuted, we held our breath, knowing Tony's movie future probably hung in the balance. Cut down to seventy-nine minutes, it was one of the shortest films Universal ever released. I was told by an eyewitness that when studio head Ned Tanen saw it in an early screening, he went ballistic. The picture opened and the word "bomb" was tied to it before the first reel unwound.

On the Monday after it opened, Universal conveyed a brief message to us that contained two statements: one, no way in hell would they ever make *The Tony Clifton Story*; and two, leave immediately. By comparison, the people on the *Titanic* had all day. When I fled to my Rambler Rebel I was stunned to see they had *already* stenciled my name out. I wanted to call David Steinberg and tell him I now understood. Suddenly the existential nature of the lyric "When you're hot you're hot, when you're not you're not" made a lot of sense to me.

That train wreck called *Heartbeeps* rolled over Andy as fingers began pointing in all directions. "Well, he kept us waiting with all that meditation" was one reason some of the perpetrators of the film claimed it bombed. Andy's meditation had been contractually approved by the studio, but in the aftermath of a disaster people play fast and loose with the facts. The bottom line was Andy's film career was dead, and with it our chances of making *The Tony Clifton Story*.

Adding salt to the wound of our loss of Tony's cinematic chance was the fact that the writers of *Taxi* had become so enamored of Tony Clifton's brazen demeanor, not only on their set but also in the trades, that they created a paler, more acceptable imitation called Vic Ferrari. When I heard of the Ferrari character I thought, *Quit stealing our material — write your own. You might have bought Foreign Man's soul, but not Tony Clifton's*. They had Latka, who was feeling inadequate about meeting girls, devise his own Mr. Hyde, the supercool Vic Ferrari, not unlike Jerry Lewis's Buddy Love from *The Nutty Professor*. The swaggering Vic Ferrari was so popular the show ran with him for a number of episodes. Though Andy used none of the Clifton features or props, you could still see glimpses of Clifton — as a younger man — in Ferrari.

Then (probably because in Hollywood nothing fails like failure) ABC announced that they were passing on Andy's basement comedy "Uncle Andy's Funhouse." It was another stake through the heart. Not long after, a similar project got mounted. It was called *Pee-wee's Playhouse*, and instead of Uncle Andy hosting a kid's show for adults, the host was Pee-wee Herman (aka Paul Reubens).

Despite Reubens being a fan of Andy's he more or less commandeered Andy's idea. I know that because Andy told me Reubens paid him a visit to break the news and ask for his blessing. What else could Andy do but be magnanimous about it? Legally, Andy couldn't claim ownership to a Howdy Doody–type show, but it bothered him that someone else pulled off his dream project. Yet in a town like Hollywood, where ideas are openly stolen on a daily basis, it's to Paul Reubens's credit that he sought Andy's permission. Andy considered Reubens a fellow artist and did nothing to stand in his way. That *Pee-wee's Playhouse* went on to become a major success was in some small way a validation of Andy's original concept. Though Andy never told anyone else, he once confided to me that it deeply bothered him that Reubens got the shot and we didn't.

Two other instances where Andy felt his ideas had been commandeered by others both revolved around Tony Clifton. The first occurred when Andy befriended one of the *SNL* writers in hopes the writer could persuade Lorne Michaels to allow Tony Clifton on the show. One day the writer called and gave Andy good and bad news: Lorne liked the idea of a sleazy lounge-lizard character; unfortunately he didn't see Andy in the role. Consequently, the recurring part went to Bill Murray. Always magnanimous, Andy gave the writer his blessing as Murray's Nick, the lounge singer, went on to become a signature character for the actor.

Kaufman also felt that Dan Aykroyd and John Belushi's creations, Jake and Elwood, the Blues Brothers, were influenced by the Clifton persona. One of the most powerful elements of the Blues Brothers' mystique was that from the moment they entered a venue to the time they left, they never broke character.

At that time, no act other than Kaufman was doing anything even remotely similar.

Going back home to *SNL* took our minds off the debacles of late. It was fun being a fly on the wall of the set. One day, during a dress rehearsal, I noticed Eddie Murphy walking around in a preposterous Gumby outfit. Dick Ebersol, who had recently been brought back to run the show after Jean Doumanian's short reign, was telling Murphy he wanted to cut the piece.

"Nobody remembers Gumby," he insisted.

Andy and I were happening by and overheard. "Oh, no," countered Andy. "Gumby's great! You should leave him in." And we walked away.

Ebersol must have listened, because a cigar-chomping Murphy as Gumby, railing, "I'm Gumby, *damn it!*" turned out to be one of Murphy's (and the show's) most popular characters.

During his tenth appearance on *SNL*, on January 30, 1982, Andy was slated to play Elvis in a sketch. Albert Goldman's tell-all bio, *Elvis*, was just out and had stirred up great controversy in its depiction of the King, particularly the sexual peccadilloes he allegedly exhibited, such as his fondness for girls wrestling each other while clad only in white cotton panties. That revelation was a stunner for Andy, who burst with pride that he and his idol shared such a fetish (women wrestling, not the white cotton panties).

Using the Goldman book for inspiration, Andy and I concocted a scene that played on the wrestling allegation. After a concert, Elvis (Andy) repairs to his dressing room where his bodyguard Red West (me) brings in two young girls to meet Elvis. Elvis dismisses Red and then asks the two (clothed) girls to wrestle. Just as they take a wrestling stance, Elvis stops them and says, "Hold it! Take off your clothes first — but leave on them white cotton panties."

The moment he uttered that line, Andy suddenly broke character, removed the Elvis wig, and turned to the camera. "I do not agree with this scene," he said angrily, "and I do not agree with Albert Goldman's book." He then walked out.

A few weeks later, on February 17, 1982, Andy appeared on *Late Night*. Dave gave him a forum to challenge Albert Goldman to a wrestling match. If Goldman lost, as Andy swore he would, he would be required to take back all those terrible things he said about Elvis in his book.

Goldman never accepted the challenge. Did Andy mean what he said? Was he really offended by Goldman's claims? Not at all. Andy wasn't really the kind of person to be offended by much of anything and in fact secretly enjoyed the book.

By March of '82 we were back in sweet home Chicago, playing the Park West again. We scheduled a few extra days in town just to hang out. Andy wanted me to take him to the locations of two of my greatest pranks. Like a little kid, he wanted to go to the exact locale and hear the stories all over again. As we drove down North Avenue, the scene of my first "psychodrama," I thought about my days with the guerrilla theater company, forty budding actors committed to complete lunacy.

"One evening, all forty of us spread out to various bus stops along here, probably over a mile or so," I began. "As the bus came along and picked us up, pretty soon everybody was on the same bus, all of us. So then at the appointed time, a fellow who was more or less the director of our little group of merry pranksters starts coughing. Pretty quick we all join in, all forty of us, hacking away."

"Of course, there was nothing to cough about," noted Andy.

"Nothing," I concurred.

"And there were other people on the bus, right?" asked Andy.

"Oh yeah, yeah, the thing was packed. Us and probably fifteen, twenty other people. Anyway, one of us starts it with, 'Hey, do you smell those gas fumes?' and the rest of us jump in, 'Oh, yeah, there're gas fumes coming from somewhere,' and immediately the others — the unsuspecting passengers — they're coughing too."

Andy grinned. "The power of suggestion . . ."

"Big time. So they're all coughin', and pretty soon so's the driver, he's coughin' his head off. He pulls over, everybody's eyes are watering. The driver radios in, 'We need another bus, *and send medics!*' That night we made the local news and the whole troupe died of laughter."

While we drove around, I told him my famous Escaped Lions

incident. That time the troupe went to the zoo and took up positions at specific locations. Suddenly all of us began screaming that we'd seen the lions get loose and they were after everyone. In no time our forty became four hundred, as everyone, even the hot-dog vendors — fearing the big cats would be drawn by their steamed tube steaks — fled for their lives. I told Andy that even after all those years, not one of the forty conspirators had spilled the beans.

"That's amazing. That many people, for that long," he said.

"Yeah, but it's necessary to keep secrets. We've sure got a few we don't want anybody to know, don't we?" I offered.

He paused. "Yeah, we do." After a moment he spoke again. "I've got a secret, something only my family knows, maybe one or two other people."

"Yeah? What's that?" I asked, feeling a setup.

"I have a daughter."

"Oh, Kaufman, what total *bullshit!*" I roared.

He was quiet for a moment. "No, Bob, it's true. I do have a daughter."

At that point in time, I'd known him going on ten years, and I could recognize the truth in his eyes. When you're someone like Andy Kaufman, you need at least one person with whom you can once in a while drop all pretenses, all the masks, and just be yourself, be *vulnerable*. We had that sort of relationship, so I realized he was dead serious.

As I mentioned earlier, the young lady Andy impregnated while living in Great Neck decided to forgo an abortion and keep the child. Although Andy had offered to "do the right thing" and marry her, both her parents and Andy's thought it prudent he not do so. When the child was born she was put up for adoption. Now, years later, as we spoke of her, this daughter whom he'd never seen was probably just about to enter her teens. Andy seemed slightly wistful as he talked of her, but soon we moved on to another subject, and he never again spoke of her.

Andy demonstrated an uncanny ability to obliterate any uncomfortable thoughts at will due to his TM training. As he had demonstrated on that tiny, wind-whipped airplane in the skies over Illinois, his years of meditation had given him the tools necessary to control his mind. Feeling such benefits of mind control were valuable, Andy not only had me promise to take a meditation course but also inserted that requisite into my contract and specified that I train for a minimum of one year, paid for by him.

I followed the TM methodology, accepting my mantra, a secret word each disciple is given to be used for the rest of his or her life. The word is repeated over and over during meditation, creating a sort of resonance in one's psyche. It is somewhat like holding down one key on a computer so that the screen of the mind fills with that one letter or, in this case, word; ushering off all other thoughts and bringing harmony — because there isn't room for anything else, just pure nothingness. That's the gist of it.

I underwent the training, and one year to the day after I began, I quit. I felt the techniques were good and certainly valuable, and I occasionally use them to this day to still my thoughts and refocus, but I took issue with what I saw as the cultish aspects of that "movement." But I respected Andy's devotion to transcendental meditation and appreciated its role for him — it was truly his religion and a safe place to which he could retreat when the pressures of big-time showbiz, or life in general, tried to overwhelm him.

For me, the movement demanded a rigid observance that didn't fit my philosophy or lifestyle. But it did fit Andy's. Despite his antics and seemingly freewheeling ways, Andy was actually a nut for absolute structure. Andy dealt with (or suffered from, depending on how you look at it) obsessive compulsive disorder, or OCD. Like Jack Nicholson's character in Jim Brooks's *As Good As It Gets*, Andy manifested some fairly quirky behavior.

First, his classic acts rarely varied. Watch his Foreign-Man-Becomes-Elvis routine and it is just that, a beat-for-beat pattern, every utterance and gesture duplicated time and again with unerring precision. Notwithstanding the myriad performances while pushing the creative envelope, left to his own choices Andy was comfortable with an almost assembly-line regularity. One of my primary functions was to shove him out of that creative rut he would slip comfortably into. Tony Clifton also gave him license to leave his self-imposed discipline and run rampant, but in general Andy's life consisted of evenness and special procedures that bordered on the bizarre.

He compulsively washed his hands, often dozens of times a

day, and frequently inconvenienced many others as they waited for him. Many of his girlfriends complained to me about how much time he spent in the bathroom. He had a different toothbrush for every day of the week, except Sunday when he carefully skipped brushing. Andy was always compelled to say good-bye to a room as he left it. After exiting his car and locking it, he walked around it exactly three times to make sure the doors were in fact locked. On visiting his home you were required to remove your shoes before entering. A creature of restrictive habits, when Andy dined out it was usually at one of a few known places — he didn't like taking chances on new eateries.

Though Andy's obsession with germs might not have been as dramatic as Michael Jackson's or Howard Hughes's famed phobias, there certainly were comparisons. Andy carefully washed his silverware at restaurants before using it. Into his drinking water he dunked each implement one at a time, then took it out and dried it with his napkin. He also had a fear of sleeping with germs picked up in daily life. He made sure that no clothing, with the exception of night clothes, ever came in contact with his bedding.

Since Andy was so compulsive when it came to his personal sanitation, he went to extreme lengths to purge his body after wallowing in that cesspool of excess called Tony Clifton. After all, Tony drank, smoked, ate meat, and picked up hookers right off the street corner — things Andy would never do. After a few days as Clifton, Andy's system demanded a total hygienic delousing. For this cleansing, Kaufman would call upon his hatha yoga skills, in particular, an extreme method employed by Swami Satchidananda.

The technique is not for the squeamish. After soaking fifteen feet of cheesecloth in warm water, the practitioner swallows it slowly and, through controlled peristalsis, threads the cloth through the alimentary canal. A more delicate way to describe it would be internal flossing.

That Andy had performed this bizarre ritual many times was not lost on the cast and crew of *Man on the Moon*. Director Milos Forman regarded the practice as so depraved that he quickly nixed the idea of portraying it in its technicolor glory. Nevertheless, this didn't prevent jokester Elton John from dropping by the set and presenting Jim Carrey (who plays Andy in the film) with sixty yards of cheesecloth. Lynne Margulies still has the canister containing Andy's original cheesecloth. Has that cheesecloth been used, or not? Don't even ask.

One of his oddest eccentricities related to air travel. Whenever Andy boarded a plane, he did so with his right foot first — and as his traveling companion you were required to follow suit.

Just going somewhere on foot with Andy required vigilance. If you were walking down the street and passed a light pole or some other hazard, it was mandatory you both did so on the same side. If you split up and walked on either side, Andy made you return so you could both run through it again and get it right.

Andy was aware of his peculiarities and would make light of them with others as if pulling a prank, but I knew they were rituals he could not let go of. Often, the most mundane tasks took far more time than for anyone else because of his eccentric observances. If you didn't really know Andy, as most didn't, his behavior could be construed as manipulative. Many saw his strict customs as just the controlling behavior of a big star. The truth was, he had no control over it.

It was not uncommon for us to change hotels two or three times if the establishment did not lend itself to Andy's very particular requirements. One of those was privacy. Despite my warnings to innkeepers, invariably a mistimed phone call from the operator or a knocking maid who had ignored the Do Not Disturb sign would drive him bonkers and usually send us fleeing to another hotel. I took to carrying a screwdriver so that I could disconnect the phone in his room (this was before clip-in phone jacks).

One of my strangest functions was to patrol the hall outside Andy's room, just after checking in, while striking a small saucepan with a mallet, like the medieval undertaker during the plague yelling, "Bring out yer dead." My task was to check sound levels. If Andy could hear the pan resonating at a certain range we'd immediately change rooms or hotels. More than once I was spotted late at night in my bathrobe, wandering the halls of a hotel banging my pan, hoping we wouldn't have to repack and run.

Andy's other aberrations would surface in his dressing room before he went onstage. He'd check his props over and over, ad nauseam, often keeping the audience waiting forty or fifty minutes beyond his scheduled show time. That practice made me extremely anxious until I realized it was part of the act. I finally understood that Act One began in the dressing room, before the audience ever saw him, and consisted of him pissing them off. It was pure Kaufman brinkmanship: work them up, get them angry, stomping their feet — almost like foreplay — then *boom*, make his entrance and reel it back from the edge. It was the kid with the chemistry set again and again, taking the crowd to its limit — *How far can I push until you hate me?* — then saving it at the last second, a comedic Michael Jordan, shooting the game winner at the buzzer.

Over the years I've searched my memories for some key that would unlock this enigma named Andy Kaufman. I might be straying too far afield into some Freudian morass from which I might not be able to extricate myself, but I keep coming back to one incident in his life.

The closest relationship Andy had as a very small child was with one of his grandfathers, the one he lovingly called Papu. Andy and his granddad played games and sang songs together and were the best of pals. Andy so idolized the old man that on the day his parents, Janice and Stanley, told their son his grandfather had "taken a trip and gone very far away," the puzzled little boy began sitting in the window for hours on end, patiently awaiting the return of his best friend.

When the weeks became years and no postcard or letter ever came detailing how or where Papu was, Andy's folks realized the error they'd made in not coming clean and telling Andy his grandfather had died. By then, a melancholy had come over the boy and in many ways stayed with him his entire life. Because of that incident, I believe the die was cast for Andy to assume the philosophy "Never give yourself over totally to anyone else, you'll only be hurt." I also submit that, aside from the trauma directly related to his loss, the incident also taught Andy that reality could be altered, adjusted to deceive the beholder. That the element of reality that had been faked on his behalf was no less than death was not lost on him.

During April and May of 1982, a drama was playing out between the producers of *Taxi*, Paramount, and ABC. Though the ratings had faltered somewhat, the show still had a loyal following, and the producers felt their baby was a very viable program. ABC felt differently and on May 4, 1982, canceled *Taxi*. After a hue and cry in the media orchestrated by the producers and picked up by television critic Tom Shales, HBO made some overtures to acquire the property, but on May 21 *Taxi* went to NBC. Andy had a love/hate relationship with the show. He loathed the daily grind but was accustomed to the sizable paycheck that subsidized his TM classes and his love of prostitutes.

Despite his complaints, there were a few times he had fun on *Taxi*, with Latka and Vic Ferrari and even the occasional dead-on mimicry of fellow actor Judd Hirsch. Andy showed his gift for impressions in an episode a few weeks into the fourth season. Called "Mr. Personalities," it had first aired on October 22, 1981, and featured Latka assuming Alex's traits in a manifestation of the multiple personality disorder that had overcome him. Latka's Alex seemed to improve on the already generous, warmhearted Alex Reiger. In the final scene, set in a psychiatrist's office with Alex, Latka, and the doctor, just as the extemely insightful Latka-as-Alex is about to figure out the secret of Alex's life, he's cured, reverts back to Latka, and leaves contented — while the real Alex is left hanging over the all-important answer that never comes. There was no love lost between Andy and Hirsch, and the episode gave Andy an officially sanctioned chance to take shots at Hirsch. When the show got picked up by NBC, Andy secretly breathed a slight sigh of relief.

12

Is This for Real?

I would scream at my television sometimes, "Is that a joke or not?"

JAKE JOHANNSEN

On April Fools' Day, 1982, Andy went on David Letterman's show and told viewers he had decided to wrestle a man. He wasn't joking. Also, it was not just any man Andy was planning to take on, but a formidable opponent, a real wrestler, pro champion Jerry "The King" Lawler. No weak suck, Lawler was a burly man, probably around our age, sporting a goatee, a sort of modified Caesar haircut, and arms damn near as big as Andy's legs. Andy announced the match would be held in Lawler's home turf, the Mid-South Coliseum in Memphis. Dave patiently let Andy rattle on about the match, probably believing the veracity of Andy's statements no more than any of his viewers did.

Though I made a pact with Andy never to reveal the truth behind that ill-fated evening and the events leading to it, I have decided to break that vow and come clean. The reason I am doing it only now is that Universal Studios, the entity behind the film *Man on the Moon*, has chosen to be truthful about Kaufman's antics and disclose in the movie what really happened. I feel it is my duty to take their lead and expand on their revelations accurately and in detail.

Andy's childhood dream had been to be a professional wrestler. Had he had the chance to walk into a room featuring Marlon Brando and "Nature Boy" Buddy Rogers and be required to choose a conversation partner, he would have made a beeline to Buddy. We knew from the first day Andy began wrestling women that he would one day have to face a man in the ring. We always tried to take our lead, our direction, from the audiences, and every time Andy took to the mat with a female we heard catcalls like "Why don't you wrestle a man, Kaufman?"

In fact, during the Carnegie and Huntington shows Andy did just that. During both shows, a man came out of the audience to wrestle Kaufman and subsequently beat the shit out of him. As the ref, I was also maimed by the brute, and in retaliation I managed to crawl back into the ring and, to the prerecorded strains of "Popeye the Sailor Man," pass a can brimming with spinach to my friend Andy. Quickly consuming the strength-giving leaves, the now superhuman Andy rebounded to give the blackguard what for, all to the delight of the crowd. Of course, it was all done comedically and with a plant, but we knew the time would come when circumstances forced Andy to meet a man, and that man might not be in a joking mood.

That day came when Andy got a call from a local Memphis promoter offering Andy a chance to wrestle a real sportsman, Jerry "The King" Lawler. A few days earlier, Andy had wrestled some women in Memphis. Right after the match, Jerry Lawler, standing just outside the ring, shoved Andy onto his ass. Andy was furious. When Andy went back to L.A., he began talking about his feud with Jerry Lawler. As I've explained, Andy understood that the basis of pro wrestling was theater, so when he calmed down he felt that if he accepted the offer to wrestle Jerry Lawler, the match would be all in jest, and he and Lawler would have a chance to vamp. He decided to allow Jerry Lawler a membership into Uncle Andy's Funhouse.

Several weeks before the match, the promoter got in touch with Andy and gave him the bad news: ticket sales were dismal. "We need to create some heat here," he said. "You got any ideas?" Well, being idea guys, Andy and I sat down and came up with a series of videos designed to exploit the strongest aspect of pro wrestling: the good guy versus the bad guy. Lawler was the hometown favorite, so we cast Andy as the malefactor. Required to be the sweet, adorable Latka every week, Andy was dying to play a heavy.

Using the backdrop of a palatial (but rented) home in Beverly Hills, Andy approached the camera, clutching a piña colada adorned with a tiny umbrella, and started in. "I'm from Hollywood, I'm smart, I make movies and television shows . . . I'm not a hick like you people from Myemm-phisss Tenn-uh-seeee . . ." He really hammed up the enunciation when he named their city and state, hoping to inflame people just by mocking their speech patterns. Then he introduced his lawyer, a guy with slicked-back hair and dark glasses, wearing a brown suit any ambulance chaser would be proud of: "This is my lawyer, Bob Zmuda, and he'll tell you, Mr. Lawler, what kind of trouble you're in."

I proceeded to go on and on in some fake legalese about how much trouble Lawler would be in and how we were filing a huge lawsuit for his unexpected shove. After my speech Andy repeated, "Mr. Lawler, I have the brains, I'm from Hollywood and you're just a hick. If you want to wrestle, fine. I'll mop the floor with you."

The reaction was exactly what we wanted. The people of Memphis were driven insane by the cocky television star, and suddenly tickets were vacuumed out of the drawers of ticket agents and into scalpers' pockets. Almost overnight it became the hottest event in years. Enjoying the hype, the promoter encouraged us to send more tapes. Since it was so much fun we complied.

We hired a very sizable young woman, and she and Andy stood on a small wrestling mat poolside at the rented house. "Okay, Mr. Lawler, you think you're so tough?" taunted Andy. "I've wrestled women tougher than you . . . and bigger! Like her." He turned to the hefty girl. "How tall are you?"

"Six feet," she said.

"And what do you weigh?"

"I weigh three twenty-seven."

"Three twenty-seven? You see, Mr. Lawler," he said, addressing the camera, "that's a lot bigger than you. And I can beat her."

They then proceeded to grapple, and Andy quickly slammed her to the mat and then got her on her stomach and began "bashing" her head into the ground. I, as the lawyer, raced out and stopped him, but it was too late — the poor, endomorphic young lady was "unconscious." I leaped up and, before I could stop the camera, yelled, "Andy, I think you've really hurt her!"

To which the callous Kaufman snapped off, "So what? She's poor, she doesn't have any money, she can't sue me."

And with that, the image of the prostrate whalelike victim and the strutting "bad guy," the camera went to black. That video was a big hit.

One of our favorite taunt tapes had Andy holding up a roll of toilet paper and instructing the poor benighted "bumpkins" of Memphis on its use. In others he showed them how to use soap and informed Memphis women on their personal grooming habits and the use of the safety razor. The reality was, he actually loved Memphis and found most of the citizens as sophisticated and charming as those in any other place he'd been. But Andy's performances were so convincing that soon the promoter informed us there were numerous death threats circulating. Thinking it was a big joke, we couldn't wait to get to Memphis.

When Andy and I and George Shapiro and Andy's latest squeeze arrived in Memphis, we realized how seriously the residents of that fair city had taken Andy's taunts. At the hotel we were turned away, the reason being that management claimed more than half a dozen bomb threats. I checked Andy into another place just outside town, disguised and under an alias, and the rest of us found a place nearby.

Twenty-four hours before the match Andy complained to the promoter that he was getting anxious to speak with Lawler regarding their plans but that Lawler wasn't returning his calls. The promoter smoothed things over, saying, "Jerry's just no good 'bout gettin' back to people," and said he would try and intercede. The promoter reminded Andy that he and Jerry were set to appear the next day on a local morning show to pitch that evening's match. Andy got off the phone, looking slightly irritated.

"What's wrong?" I asked.

"Oh, the promoter wants me on some show with Lawler at eight in the morning. I have to be there early. I wanted to sleep in, get my energy up for the match."

Despite the intrusion on his sleep time, we were up early and got to the TV station a few minutes before eight. We were escorted to the green room, where Jerry Lawler sat with a few local media types. We walked over to Lawler and Andy extended his hand. "Hi, Jerry, I'm Andy, and this is Bob Zmuda."

Lawler stood slowly, sized us up, then hocked up a luger and spat a significant, juicy green oyster at our feet. "Share that among ya, you Yankee assholes." As Lawler turned and strode from the room, Andy's hand was still outstretched, his face a mask of complete surprise. The wags with Lawler smirked and retreated with him. A few minutes later, on the air, Jerry "The King" Lawler was just as rude and obnoxious. After the show Lawler quickly exited.

As Kaufman and I prepared to leave, Andy began voicing his doubts, now unconcerned that the station personnel could overhear.

"Do you think I've been set up?" he asked.

"I don't know. It doesn't look good," I said. "Lawler doesn't seem to understand this is a joke."

"I think the promoter's in on it. He's gotta be," said a worried Andy.

"Probably is. You've made a lot of enemies here," I said, bringing a snicker from one of the set assistants, now embarrassed she'd been caught eavesdropping.

"I think Jerry Lawler is going to use me as an example to prove pro wrestling is real. He's gonna kill me."

"I think you're right, Kaufman."

"That's it, I've gotta cancel this thing. It's my only choice."

Andy went back to the hotel, where he and George got the promoter on the phone. "I want out," said Andy.

"Well, if that's the case," said the promoter, "then you'll owe me thirty grand. Just send over a check before you leave town."

"What are you talking about?" asked Andy. "What thirty grand?"

"Actually," interjected George, "he's right, Andy. It's in the contract you signed. Thirty grand if you're a no-show."

Andy's eyes were circles. "We'll get back to you," he said to the promoter and hung up. "I gotta pay them that much if I walk?"

"Yeah," sighed George, "it's in the deal. Sorry."

"What am I contracted to do? I mean, if he beats me in the first round I'm okay, right?"

I said, "I don't think you want to risk that."

"No, you're right," said Andy, "but isn't there some time limit or something?"

George nodded. "Yeah, two minutes. I believe that's what the contract called for. To make the match legal."

"Okay, okay, I can do that . . . I can stay in the ring two minutes."

"Be careful," I added, knowing Andy was scared of Lawler.

"I think that goes without saying," said George.

"He won't lay a hand on me," decided Andy. "I'll just keep running away from him until two minutes are up."

That night we arrived at the Mid-South Coliseum completely unprepared for what awaited us. A thick, angry mob pressed against a police barricade as we climbed warily from the limo. Fifteen Memphis cops in full riot gear formed a phalanx around us and pressed through the spitting, hissing crowd. A few of the more vicious taunted, "Kill the Jew!" Suddenly it wasn't just Andy in danger, it was me, George, and Andy's girlfriend, all vested partners in some impending mayhem. Despite the anti-Semitic cries, I couldn't help but feel like the early Christians as they proceeded into the Coliseum to face the lions.

We entered the arena and marched to the ring, the atmosphere within even more hostile than outside. Andy turned to me and said aloud, not caring if anyone heard, "I'm not doing it. I'll give them the thirty grand."

I added, "You're right, let's get the fuck outta here."

But it was too late. As the announcer took to center ring and began the rundown, Andy warmed up and looked across at Mr. Lawler. The pro wrestler returned one of the most menacing blood-into-ice-water stares I've ever seen. Once introductions were done (delayed slightly because of the intense booing), Andy Kaufman, the smart guy from Hollywood, stepped toe-to-toe with Jerry "The King" Lawler, the angry "hillbilly" from Memphis. The entire assemblage could see the fear in Kaufman's eyes, and they reveled in it.

The referee (a real one this time, not yours truly) laid out the rules, and the grapplers went back to their corners. Then the bell rang and the match was on. Lawler came out of his corner, and Andy did so briefly but then began running away every time

Lawler came near. All Andy had to do was last two minutes and he'd be home free. Every time Lawler zigged, Andy zagged, sometimes even leaping outside the ropes when his stalker came near. He carefully avoided destruction although the crowd's angry boos and yells escalated in fervor. But Andy didn't care because he was going to live.

As Andy got closer to his two-minute safe zone, managing to thwart the grasp of Jerry Lawler time and again, he seemed to relax slightly, as if the worst was over. That's when Lawler did a peculiar thing. Stopping in the center of the ring, Lawler just bent over and clasped his hands behind his back. "Go ahead, Kaufman, put me in a headlock," he offered. "Go ahead, I won't stop you."

Andy had always prided himself on his headlock, and therein lay his downfall. The crowd screamed its approval as Andy gingerly approached the bowed Lawler. It seemed Lawler had forgotten his revenge and sought to engage in theatrics. Taken in by Lawler's apparent supplication and lulled into a sense of security that perhaps Lawler didn't really mean him harm, Andy positioned his arms around Lawler's thick neck. I screamed from the side of the ring for him not to go near the beast.

What happened next occurred with dizzying speed, but it was the moment the crowd was hoping for. Lawler quickly unlocked his hands, reversed on Andy, lifted him high, and, in what wrestlers call a suplex, slammed him hard onto the mat. A stunned Andy, the wind knocked out of him, writhed slowly on the canvas, trying to regain his bearings. The crowd screamed in glee as the invading Hebrew from Hollywood got his comeuppance.

George and I were in shock and moved to stop the match, but we weren't fast enough. Before we could do anything, Lawler gathered up a dazed Andy and, in an impressive grasp, lifted him straight up, with Andy's toes reaching for the ceiling. For a split second everyone in the house held their breath, and then, like the final plunge of a doomed airplane, Andy's head, now nestled between Lawler's meaty thighs, was driven into the mat with the force of a jackhammer. Game, set, and match. Lawler's application of wrestling's most dangerous move, the infamous "pile driver," resulted in Andy being knocked completely unconscious.

Lawler was immediately disqualified for that illegality but pressed on.

Despite the ref's attempt to stop the fight, bad turned to worse as Lawler repeated the death blow, hefting the limp Andy once again and crushing his head in yet another pile driver. The bloodthirsty townsfolk cheered madly over their joy that if the arrogant Kaufman next addressed them, contritely admitting he had been wrong, it would be from the confines of a wheelchair. Or maybe they'd been really lucky and Jerry had done what they'd asked of him and actually killed the Jew.

Andy's body was lifeless as Lawler stormed over him, bringing other wrestlers from outside the ropes into the ring to prevent further crimes against the fractured Kaufman. About ten minutes later, an ambulance backed up to the ring, and two paramedics assembled a two-piece gurney (a special device used in transporting critical back injuries) and spirited Andy to the vehicle. As he was settled in, George and I and Andy's girlfriend huddled at the door to the ambulance, half concerned over Andy, half seeking refuge from the rabid crowd. George and the girlfriend were waved in, but the paramedic held up a hand to me. "Sorry, only enough room for two family members. You'll have to get another ride to the hospital." *Another ride to the hospital?* As I sized up the mass of hateful Memphisites, I thought, *Yeah, probably the ambulance that takes* me *to the hospital.*

Staring at the exit thirty yards away and the ten thousand maniacs in my path, and with nary a cop in sight, I pushed off on what would be the hardest, loneliest walk of my life. People were pushing and jostling me, and debris pelted me. It was only a matter of time before someone just hauled off and knocked me out or the crowd closed in and ate me like wild dogs. "He's Kaufman's friend!" someone screamed. "Get him!"

What I did next was completely instinctual. Using every ounce of my acting training, I put on the toughest fuck-you scowl I could muster and notched up my gait to John Wayne proportions. A few yards later, I found the biggest, meanest looking guy I could and slapped him hard as I passed. My gesture worked, and like Moses with his staff, I parted the Red Sea of inflamed trailer residents, and the toughest motherfucker they'd ever seen, including Jerry "The King" Lawler, passed through their sullen ranks without further incident. Of course, once that metal outside door fell shut with that reassuring *thwump*, I dropped all of my puffer-fish pretense and ran like hell, quaking with blinding fear.

At the hospital, Andy was being ministered to in a private room, and we released to the waiting press all we knew: he was drifting in and out of consciousness, and though he had received a CAT scan indicating three of his vertebrae in the lumbar region had been badly compressed, his doctors were almost completely certain he would be able to walk again. As some news outlets were reporting that Andy would be paralyzed for life, George decided to phone the Kaufman family with the doctor's more hopeful prognosis. Though the doctors gave Andy a week of recuperation before he could be released, the media reported Andy left one day short of that week, clad in a bulky neck brace.

About a month after the match, on May 15, 1982, Andy appeared on *Saturday Night Live*, humbled, his damaged neck buttressed by a sizable brace, to thank those who had sent cards wishing him well. Chastened by his near-death experience, Andy promised he had seen the light and was through with wrestling. Meanwhile, an angry Stanley Kaufman was in the preliminary stages of filing a lawsuit against Lawler and the promoter. A few months later, on July 28, 1982, Andy, still in the neck support, gathered the courage to face his nemesis for the first time since his near-crippling injury. Jerry "The King" Lawler and Andy were scheduled to "bury the hatchet" as Dave Letterman refereed from behind his desk.

Using the *Late Night* forum to extract an apology from Lawler for traumatizing him, Andy became heated immediately, still angry that Lawler had betrayed him and then seriously hurt him and had completely discarded the code of ethics among wrestling pros that you never intentionally do harm to your opponent. As Andy and Lawler traded remarks, Dave sat helplessly by, unable to calm Andy and fearing Lawler might get mad. Just as they were to go to a spot break, Andy said something, and the muscular Lawler snapped. Standing up, Lawler towered over the taunting Kaufman and suddenly, like a striking cobra, slapped Andy hard across the left cheek, knocking him completely out of his chair. As chaos erupted they cut to a spot. Andy picked himself up and fled the set.

Coming back from the commercial, Jerry and Dave continued their interview. Suddenly a mad-as-a-wet-hen Kaufman flew out from the wings, slamming Dave's desk and screaming bleeped-out obscenities at Jerry Lawler. Andy *never* swore (as *Andy*, not Tony Clifton). His eyes bugged with rage. Andy, standing to Dave's left, seeing his furious words elicit little reaction from Lawler, grabbed a cup of hot coffee and flung it on Lawler. That did it, and Lawler leaped up as Andy raced backstage and out the back door.

Letterman, who had given up control of his show to the two combatants, made one of his trademark mocking observations: "You can say some of those words on TV, but what you *can't* do is throw coffee!" The next day, Andy Kaufman's antics were the talk around every coffee urn and water cooler in America. Within a week, Andy's publicist had accumulated over eight hundred clippings from news sources coast to coast. It had nearly cost him his physical mobility, if not his very life, but once again Andy had people buzzing.

Now, for the first time anywhere, the *truth* . . .

The entire series of incidents was staged. It pains me to say so, but as the movie is going to let the cat out of the bag I feel compelled to fess up. The depth of the conspiracy was what was most interesting: no one but Andy and I and Jerry Lawler really knew. And speaking of Mr. Lawler . . . is he the brute I've portrayed on the past few pages? Not in the least. Jerry is quite the gentleman and a helluva good sport. As a matter of fact, the night before the match in Memphis he secretly hosted me and Andy at his home as we planned our hijinks.

Jerry was very, very careful not to hurt Andy, and it was Andy who insisted Jerry take more chances to heighten the reality. Jerry's pile driver was perfectly executed both times, leaving Andy completely unharmed. That night I was actually the only one in danger, as I made my escape from the Mid-South Coliseum. At the hospital, Andy was taken into a private room where the examining doctor pronounced him unscathed.

"Do I need a neck brace?" asked Andy.

"No. You're perfectly fine," replied the doctor.

"Can I wear one anyway?"

The doctor was puzzled. "It would serve you no purpose."

"That's okay. Give me the biggest one you've got."

Andy quietly slipped out of the hospital, and we released the information that he was laid up for nearly a week. On the *Letterman* show, Andy instructed Jerry beforehand, "Go for it and slap me hard."

"I'm afraid I'll hurt you, Andy," said Jerry.

"No, it's okay. We gotta sell it. Go ahead and whack me good."

Jerry was concerned he might really knock Kaufman for a loop but played along brilliantly. Andy had told Jerry he had to strike him before the commercial break — that's why you see Jerry standing, anticipating having to slap Andy. When they came back from the spot, Andy was really swearing, the bleep-outs in the tape being authentic. I told him that to make it all believable, particularly to those who knew Andy, he had to swear for real, something he never, ever did unless, as I explained before, he was Clifton. Andy's barometer of reality was his family — if he could get them to buy something, he knew everyone else would fall into place. Andy eventually had to take Stanley aside and tell him the truth before Stanley's suit against our friend Jerry Lawler got out of hand.

Andy and Jerry continued for some time with their comedy in the ring, elevating their "feud" to Homeric proportions with various matches and rematches and tag-team combinations and even the red herring of a supposed "teaming" of Andy and Jerry. The beauty of it was that when Andy "betrayed" his new partner, Jerry, against another wrestler, Jimmy Hart, it was still part of their big deception. Oh, and did Dave know that that "scalding" coffee Andy hurled at Jerry was only lukewarm? You'll have to ask him.

Did Andy look at such stunts in terms of a career strategy, or did he work intuitively? And how did I feel, working outside the box on such "projects" that amounted to mass hoaxes? Were we worried that people would find out and that our credibility would be destroyed? No. First, what credibility? We were performance magicians, devising sleight-of-hand tricks that went on for weeks, even months. We were forced by circumstance to pull the wool over the eyes of everyone, including our friends, families, business associates, and colleagues.

Was it uncomfortable? Sure, especially those times we stared a close friend in the face and lied our heads off, but it was all done for the cause. For better or for worse, this was Andy Kaufman's career and, by association, mine too. As his best friend, writer, and producer I was as involved as he in pulling off the stunts. In fact, it was often I who had to prevaricate the most, since Andy could hide behind the facade of "stardom" or retreat to meditation while I carefully explained to others what was happening. Or seemed to be happening. As they say, it was a tough job, but somebody had to do it.

After the months of madness and energy expenditure involving the wrestling flimflam, things quieted down a bit. In August of '82 Andy called and explained he was doing a small project and needed some help. He asked me to meet him at Sambo's restaurant the next morning. When I arrived I found he was shooting a sort of impromptu student movie. While real patrons moved in the background, Andy and his costar, pro wrestler Freddie Blassie, sat across the table from each other and simply shot the shit. Designed to parody *My Dinner with André* starring André Gregory and Wallace Shawn, Andy's film dispensed with such pretense and offered a glimpse into the mind of the man who invented the caustic appellation "pencil-neck geek."

Though loosely directed by the notorious Johnny Legend, *My Breakfast with Blassie* was more of a cinema verité homage to wrasslin' and pigs in a blanket than it was a gripping drama. Made for about a buck ninety-eight, it's quite funny and a must-see for anyone interested in Kaufman trivia. I had the most demanding role of all: cast as a bystander, I happened by and vomited on cue. Of course, as did Marlon, I had Sacheen Littlefeather pick up my Oscar.

The most significant item about *My Breakfast with Blassie* comes in an unplanned moment when Andy meets a cute girl and tries to pick her up. That girl's name was Lynne Margulies, and she is Johnny Legend's sister. Portrayed in *Man on the Moon* by Academy Award–nominated actress Courtney Love, Lynne is a phenomenal Renaissance woman. Of all Andy's girlfriends, she is the only one who really ever knew how to handle him.

At first I didn't believe him when he called and told me he was moving in with Lynne. The great Casanova settling down? It didn't sound possible, but then Andy explained he'd devised a way to have his cake and eat it too. They would live together, enjoying mad, passionate love, but the rule would be they could both retain their freedom to have sex with others. Andy wasn't sexist and the woman he was with had to have the same rights he had. Lynne was as open-minded as Andy in that regard and readily agreed. It was not unusual for Andy to call Lynne from the telephone booth at the Mustang, and it didn't bother her in the least. Andy couldn't stand any control over him, culturally, creatively, or sexually. As Marilu Henner, his *Taxi* costar, put it in her autobiography, Andy was "an absolute original, a thoroughly fascinating, unfathomable, complex, uncompromised, tortured artist who marched through his short, strange life to a very different drummer."

Lynne was very feminine and also smart enough to know not to engage Andy in verbal confrontation. Her mature, open-minded demeanor set her apart from the scrambled-brain bimbos he'd been dicking for years. Though she had done a full nude layout and centerfold for *Gallery* magazine a few years before, that only bespoke her wild, rebellious side. She was a find, and even the great Andy Kaufman knew it. Andy would carry the magazine around with him and show it to all the guys. He'd finally found a woman who was a highly intelligent artist in her own right, and he knew he'd met his match. She was the love of his life, though his ego would never allow him to admit it. After all, he was Andy Kaufman, and that demanded he be the center of the universe.

Meanwhile, Tony Clifton got another job. Though Andy and George had lobbied to get Clifton on *SNL*, management of that show was only lukewarm to the idea. However, the producers of *The Fantastic Miss Piggy Show* welcomed Tony Clifton with open arms. On August 14, 1982, we flew to Toronto and met the legendary Jim Henson. He and Andy hit it off from the start. After all, they were both very much in tune with that child most refer to as "inner." In a way, Henson understood Tony almost better than we did. To him, Tony Clifton was just another big puppet, as grouchy and condescending as some of his own lovable inventions, such as Oscar the Grouch and the Cookie Monster. Though Henson had no problem with Tony's rep of obnoxiousness, the lounge singer was on surprisingly good behavior around all the Muppets and their handlers. It was probably either his absence from Hollywood or just being in the company of others who never completely grew up that caused Tony to be so friendly.

As I strolled around the set I saw that Henson had built a warm and friendly creative environment outside the hubbub of Hollywood, and I admired him for it. The set buzzed with busy teenagers, all assistants and interns in Henson's dream factory, building scenery and making molds for various Muppet characters. I had heard that Jim Henson's only formal agreement with his manager of twenty years, Bernie Brillstein, was a handshake. One afternoon while Andy meditated, Jim and I struck up a conversation.

"So I understand you worked with Howdy Doody," began Jim. "How was he?"

As I started in on the story of Howdy's visit to Hollywood and Jim asked questions, he referred to Howdy, as Andy would have, as if he were another actor, a real person. Jim's sense of open wonderment and lack of guile endeared him to me immediately, just as it had to another guy, named Kaufman. As I detailed Andy's encounter with Howdy — first Andy's sense of betrayal, then his unqualified acceptance — Jim's eyes misted a bit. "I know exactly how he felt," he said.

A few years ago I was saddened to hear of Jim's passing. Like Andy, that gentle man left us all too early. I couldn't help but wonder if men like them, children at heart, weren't destined to grow old.

If I had to pick a favorite Kaufman/Zmuda routine, at the top of my list would have to be our performance at Rick Newman's "Catch a Rising Star Tenth Anniversary HBO Special." Andy could be very cryptic about business matters, and one day as we prepared to board a plane (right foot first) after a college gig, I saw we were not going back to L.A. but on to New York.

"What gives, Kaufman?"

"We're going to New York. I have some HBO special or something like that."

Back then HBO didn't mean what it does today.

"What are you going to do?" I asked.

"I don't know," he admitted, "but I've gotta do something, I'm supposed to do a whole set."

"You haven't even planned it yet?"

"No. Maybe I'll do Elvis."

For Andy, pulling out Elvis was like most people putting on their socks. As we got on the plane and sat down, Andy turned to me. "Hey, what if we do something different? Something fun. I'll do my standard set, and you can be in the audience. You be a plant and we'll do something."

"How 'bout I heckle you?"

Andy's eyes lit up. "Oh, yeah, that's good! Really criticize me."

"I'll jump on you with all that bad shit the critics say."

Andy nodded gleefully. "Great! I love it!"

So as we winged our way to the Big Apple, we worked out the beats of our scam. As his attacker, I would be believed, because only insiders in the business knew who I really was. My assault would focus on the repetitiveness of Andy's routines, so he girded his loins for my onslaught. I decided to hold back a few items during our airliner conference — I figured it might be interesting to see him *really* sweat.

On the bill that night were Billy Crystal, our old buddy Robin Williams, Richard Belzer, who was also a friend, and rocker Pat Benatar. This was sort of a homecoming for Benatar, who had been discovered some years earlier by Rick Newman. Consequently, she invited her aunt and uncle to attend the show. Residents of nearby New Jersey, her aunt and uncle had never seen her perform live because they feared the dangers of the rock element drawn to such shows. Though somewhat provincial, Pat's relatives felt since the show was to be televised, what harm could come to them? Another inducement was that the uncle loved Billy Crystal, so once it was decided they'd saddle up and ride into the big city, Pat's uncle slipped a modest revolver into his boot for protection, and off they went. Rick Newman gave them a wonderful table in the center of the room and the show commenced.

Belzer introduced Andy, who came out and began his standard Foreign Man set. He wasn't a minute into it when I started walking on his jokes, repeating them about a half second after he said them. Then I started getting *ahead* of him, nailing his lines a second or two *before* he said them. This seemed to rattle him, and he paused several times as I coldly let each joke out of the bag before he could finish. Finally, when I wouldn't let him complete any of his Archie Bunker bit, he stopped and leaned past the microphone. "Sir, you got a problem?"

"The only problem is I'm doin' your act for you," I said from my table about six feet from the stage.

"Is there a problem?" he repeated, as rivulets of sweat started to streak down his temples.

"No," I said, "there's no problem. If you did some new material I wouldn't know what you were gonna do next."

"Look," he said defensively, "they asked me to do this."

He started explaining he had a lot of new material.

"Oh, yeah?" I said. "Well, I've followed your career for a long time, Kaufman, and I haven't seen anything new in years. Wrestling women? That's not entertaining."

A few in the crowd applauded at that, and Andy winced. "I was on *Fridays,*" insisted Andy, "and I did something that got a lot of people talking."

"What?" I asked. "You pushed some other actors around and call that real? That was a put-on, Kaufman, everybody knows that. It's not original, it's not comedy."

I was hitting nerves, and Andy's streams of sweat were not all products of the conscious effort of a trained yogi. I was really getting to him. We went back and forth for a while, then Benatar's aunt said something, and I turned around and said, "Fuck you." Well, that didn't sit well with her husband, and suddenly he was threatening to come over and straighten me out. Rick Newman, who knew nothing of the gun, was at that moment crawling on the floor toward the uncle — trying to stay off-camera — to inform him I was but a harmless plant.

243

As Rick was talking the uncle out of murder, I was pointing out to Andy that he was on his way down, indicated by the certain failure of his film career. *"Heartbeeps?"* I said. "What a piece of shit."

"That wasn't my fault, it was the writers, the director . . ."

"You got any other offers?"

Andy looked furtively about. "No . . ."

"You can't even do Elvis anymore," I said, and then looked around at the audience. "He's gotta wear a wig 'cause he's losin' his hair!" I declared.

Andy was very sensitive about his spreading hair loss. The look on his face when I proclaimed his secret to all was one of honest shock. In a world before Rogaine or Propecia, Andy had lathered all manner of creams and potions on his head in an effort to halt the recession of his hairline. That I had made his fear public staggered him slightly, mainly because there were several young ladies in the audience who had caught his eye. He took the gunshot and moved on but didn't talk to me for a while after the show. Finally I busted him on his withdrawal. "What's a matter, Kaufman? Sensitive about the hair? So you can dish it out but can't take it, huh? Is that how it works?"

Irritated with me at first, he finally caved in and we laughed about it, agreeing the below-the-belt shots at him helped create believability.

After the show Pat Benatar approached me. "You don't know how lucky you are."

"How's that?" I asked.

"Those people you were insulting? He's my uncle, and that was my aunt with him."

"Oh, sorry," I said.

"No, that's okay," she said, "it's just part of the act, I know that. But he didn't, and he always carries a gun in his boot when he has to come over to the city. He almost shot you."

I wilted. If you watch the tape closely you will clearly see him reaching for his boot just as Rick approached the gun-toting Jerseyite before he could wreak havoc. That was the chance I took with that type of act. Working without a net had its dangers but it was almost always wildly rewarding.

On Saturday, September 23, 1982, we were scheduled to board a bus for a nine-day trip with one of the oddest collections of people you'd ever hope to assemble. A political Magical Mystery Tour, the Jerry Brown tour was a mission of goodwill designed to stir up votes among a populace apparently more motivated by various celebrities than by exercising their rights as Americans. Jerry Brown wanted to be governor of California again, and it was time to hit the stump. Rather than assemble a group of tired politicos, Jerry sought to look hip.

Thus, the tour gathered an eclectic mix guaranteed to hit the spot with just about anyone's taste in artists. First, there was folk/rock icon Stephen Stills; our friend Kris Kristofferson; composer and Kris's guitar player, Billy Swan; actress Diane Ladd; the manly Nancy Culp (Miss Jane Hathaway) of *The Beverly Hillbillies;* and of course the urbane candidate along with his dad, former governor Edmund "Pat" Brown.

Aside from me and Andy, last but by no means least was little Patty McCormack. I say "little" because Patty's claim to fame was the 1956 film *The Bad Seed,* wherein she played an eight-year-old indeed gone bad, all while stealing the picture. Having received an Oscar nomination for her role, Patty never quite reached those heights again in her subsequent appearances in such epics as 1988's *Saturday the 14th Strikes Back* and 1995's *Mommy's Day.* But in 1982 she was hell on wheels, and with her rounding out our band of gypsies we took to the road.

The routine was pretty undemanding — tool up the California coast, stop in small towns, put on our brief dog-and-pony show for stalwart Jerry Brown campaign workers, then move on. Up the coast a ways we cut inland and headed for the likes of Oakland, Fresno, Redding, and Eureka. The schedule was a cakewalk, and being on the road was, as always, fun for us. I realized that that was precisely why we had come: the lure of the road. Andy never voted, we weren't getting paid, and with all due respect to Jerry, Andy didn't give a shit who was governor. But he did love the road.

Once we reached our final destination for the day, the bus would roll up to modest lodging, such as a Holiday Inn or sometimes a Hilton. While we were unloading I would notice some number of cars all populated with attractive women. This intrigued me, so I stopped Billy Swan and asked him, "What's the deal with the girls in the cars?"

Billy smiled. "They're waitin' for Kris. Happens every place we go."

And it did. Everywhere we went, women showed up on cue, motoring up to our places of rest as if summoned by that "da da da tuh daaa" tune from *Close Encounters*. Despite his appearance — the previous year — in what was considered the biggest box office bomb in history, *Heavens' Gate*, Kris's popularity didn't seem to have diminished. I wondered about that as we pulled into a town like Ventura at two in the A.M. and saw the hopefuls in their cars, faces pressed to the glass like puppies in the pet store. *Well, a girl can dream, can't she?*

One evening as we were about to board the bus and head for our base for the night, we did a head count. No Kaufman. We waited and waited, and finally it was decided the bus could go on, because Patty was driving her own car and offered to take us. Patty had planned on being with the tour only a few days, so she'd been following the bus in her fast little roadster. The hotel was about an hour away, so with our tourmates now gone, we sat down to wait for Andy, thinking he'd be but a few moments. He showed up forty-five minutes later. By that point Patty was fuming as she slid behind the wheel of her overpowered sports car.

"Where've you been?" I asked, since he didn't offer an explanation and I felt Patty was too infuriated to inquire. Given her demeanor and the fact she was about to spirit us into the night in her hot car I was hoping Andy's excuse would help calm her down.

"Oh, I don't know, I just sorta lost track of the time."

Patty's foot crushed the accelerator and our heads snapped as the ragtop fishtailed onto the freeway. As the speedometer climbed past ninety I looked over in the dim lights of the instruments and saw Patty's jaw clenched in anger. Suddenly I flashed on the parking lot with all the women, and a lightbulb winked on: Patty herself was intent on bedding down with Kris.

As we hurtled down that dark road at better than a hundred I looked back into the jump seat, and sure enough, Kaufman's face was plastered with that really annoying shit-eating grin. I flashed back to our nearly disastrous small-plane experience and had a sickening déjà vu, but this time I saw a slightly different headline: "*Taxi* Star, *Bad Seed* Actress, Other, Perish in Car Crash."

Miraculously, we arrived intact. Early the next morning Patty's car was gone, and I wondered if she'd been successful with Kris. By 8 A.M. as we shuffled out to board the bus, there were still several cars in the parking lot containing a handful of unrequited lovelies waiting for that chance with the unattainable Mr. Kristofferson. None of those women-in-waiting were the least bit interested in Andy, and it infuriated him. "Latka is such a dork," he grated. "If I keep doing him, I'll never get laid." An interesting statement from a man who, by any standards, was wildly successful with women. I guess it's true that you can never get enough.

The idea of voting for a candidate was of interest to Andy not from a political standpoint, but from one of onstage performance. Fresh from the Jerry Brown tour, and inspired by an event that would occur on *SNL*, Andy decided it was time to pull off his greatest feat of audience participation yet. Andy's plan was to give the national audience of *SNL* a chance to decide his fate: should he live . . . or die? Figuratively, of course.

Around that time, during a broadcast of *Saturday Night Live*, Eddie Murphy grasped a live lobster from the hands of a chef during a cooking sketch (seconds from the lobster's demise in a pot of boiling water) and warned that the fate of the crustacean was now in the hands of the audience. Murphy then invited viewers to phone in to one of the two 900 numbers on the screen, depending on whether you wanted Larry to survive or become dinner.

During the broadcast, updates were given on the voting, and seventeen minutes before the polls closed, Brian Doyle-Murray announced the tally: 116,207 "he crawls away" versus 123,074 "start melting that butter." It didn't look good for Larry, but when the next commercial aired, the save-Larry contingent had pulled ahead, and things looked promising for the decapod. A short background on the highlights of Larry's life was aired, including his childhood on the floor of the Atlantic Ocean, that he'd been captain of the swimming team, devoted time to disadvantaged youngsters, and was a member of Crustaceans for Christ.

That did it, and in the end the kind-hearted demographic outweighed their cold counterparts 239,096 to 227,452. Larry lived, and the little drama dazzled Andy with its impact and potential. With an upcoming appearance on *SNL* scheduled, Andy fixed on the idea for a little conflict of his own.

On October 23, 1982, Andy arrived at Thirty Rock for *SNL*, and something went wrong. Andy and producer Dick Ebersol got into a screaming match that was heard by cast and crew alike. Ebersol assumed the role of Dr. Frankenstein and reminded his monster of the pecking order. Asked to leave the premises, Andy did so, never making his appearance that night. A few weeks passed, and on November 13, 1982, Ebersol read a statement on the show:

> *Hi. I'm Dick Ebersol, the executive producer of* Saturday Night Live. *In recent weeks we have received inquiries from many of you, including even the editors of* TV Guide, *as to why, prior to our last two telecasts, we heavily promoted Andy Kaufman and then failed to present him as advertised. So tonight, let me set the record straight by saying, in my opinion, that in both cases Andy misled us into thinking, right up until airtime, that his material would be up to the show's standards. It was not. It was not even funny, and in my opinion Andy Kaufman is not funny anymore. (audience applause) And I believe* you, *the audience here, agrees with me. (more applause) So thank you, and I hope this sets the record straight. Good night.*

After the Ebersol statement I phoned Andy in his hotel room and was alarmed at how distraught he sounded, so I went over. He met me at the door, obviously glad to see me, but there was also a fire in his eyes. "So, they think I'm washed up, huh? I'll show them!" Before I could console him he grabbed the phone and dialed Shapiro in L.A. "George? Andy. I want you to book me on *Letterman* — now!" George called back and had Andy set for November 17. Andy was on the comeback trail. Though failure intrigued him, he figured a fun, noncontroversial appearance

248

might help him with the vote. He may have been Andy Kaufman, Master Investigator of Failure, but he was also human.

We stayed up all night and wrote his *Letterman* piece. Needing something different, something he'd never done before, we decided Andy would come out dressed only in a large sort of diaper and a turban and emulate the abilities of a Hindu fakir. Dancing to some exotic music, Andy would stand on his head and then roll his belly muscles in a demonstration of body control. (Being an accomplished yogi came in handy.) Soon a butler (me) would come out and hand him a sword, which he would proceed to "swallow."

Andy and I went over to *Late Night* that Wednesday, November 17, and his set went exactly as we'd planned. At the end of the act he strapped on a guitar, slapped on a fake mustache, and did a wonderful impression of Slim Whitman singing "Rose Marie." The song was one of Andy's favorites and invariably moved him to tears every time he sang it.

On November 20, 1982, one week after Ebersol's stinging rebuke and three days after Andy's appearance on *Letterman*, it was announced on *SNL* that a vote would be taken that night to determine whether Andy Kaufman lived or died . . . at *SNL*. Andy was the new Larry the Lobster. The stakes were all future appearances on the show. If the vote went to him, he stayed; against him, he'd walk away and never come back. Given Andy's reputation for a pugnacious attitude (based in part upon Ebersol's statement as well as the *Fridays* incident) no one took the vote too seriously, and when the results came in 195,544 to 169,186, against Andy, it wasn't any big surprise. People knew Andy begged rejection and were all too eager to give it to him.

Meanwhile, I went back to L.A. to continue work on a picture with director Joel Schumacher. I had returned to Universal (they'd resprayed my name onto the parking place), and Joel and I and another writer had cowritten a film called *D.C. Cab*. The film had been green-lighted for production and we were busily in preproduction. I'd even been cast in a role. It was a dream come true.

Back in New York, Andy was going through a nightmare. He called me many times during that period to give me constant updates as well as to have a shoulder to cry on. For the first time,

I'll reveal the extent of our conversations. Andy and Dick Ebersol did in fact lock horns in a screamfest backstage on *SNL*, but it was wholly staged, designed to build momentum for the vote they planned soon after. Dick read the statement to build conflict, and so far, so good. Then came the vote.

"Well, didn't you know it was going to go against you?" I asked.

"Of course I did," said Andy. "I'm not an idiot."

"So why are you pissed? You got thrown off the show. That was the plan, right?"

"That was only half the plan. The only reason I went along with it was because Dick and I had a secret agreement."

"What kind of agreement?" I asked warily.

"Okay, it's true I would not be allowed back on the show, but guess who would?"

"Tony Clifton?" I wondered.

"Exactly."

"That's great! So what's the problem? Who's going to play him? Me or you?"

"Neither," he said with a sigh. "Ebersol screwed me. He won't return my calls."

The joke was on Andy, and he wasn't laughing. Ebersol had suckered him with the vote and then went back on their agreement. Both Andy's agent, Marty Klein, and his manager, George Shapiro, were appalled over Ebersol's treachery. A few years ago, George Shapiro ran into Ebersol at a party and confronted him, saying, "It was a shitty thing to do."

Andy had always courted rejection with audiences and then either pulled success out at the last minute — or fled the building. For the briefest moment I wondered if this was just another Kaufman stunt, but Andy was being completely sincere. He loved his appearances on *SNL*, not only for the freedom and exposure, but for the feeling of security — almost of *family* — they gave him. Though the cast had changed over the years, walking into that studio fit him like an old pair of slippers, and the loss of it hurt him profoundly.

After all of Andy's hard work to examine and exploit failure, with this very real expulsion from his beloved *Saturday Night Live*, his wishes had come horribly true. His desire to succeed at failure had come full circle. A good friend of mine, who is a psych professor at Northeastern University, speculated at the time that Andy had been flirting with the threat of being "shut down" for some time. He was constantly amazed at the antics Andy pulled on television and, because of the "sedative for the masses" nature of the medium, thought it inevitable that TV's gatekeepers would one day rebel against the rebel and switch him off. With Andy Kaufman on camera, their precious connection to the American consumer was in danger of being interfered with by that man, pushed to its (and the viewers') limits, thus diminishing its primary goal of selling, not entertaining. Kaufman jeopardized that relationship and had to go. Someone had to remove the madman from the controls. Andy underestimated his own impact, and when he was thrown off the stage of *Saturday Night Live* as Andy, not Tony, he was shocked.

But the shocks were just beginning.

13

Over the Cliff

*I knew an essentially shy kid who had gone from his parents' home
to a stage to national television.*
LORNE MICHAELS

One day as Andy and I sat around his place reading his reviews, he happened upon one particularly vicious article. "Hey," he said, with that boyish enthusiasm, "this one says I've gone as far as I can go, short of killing myself on stage. What do you think?"

I lowered the review I was reading and fixed him with my patented "get serious" look. "So, you're gonna kill yourself on stage?"

"What do you think?"

I smiled wryly. "Sure, why not. You've already died on stage. Remember Kutscher's?"

"No, not like that. What if I faked my own death?" he said, with a gleam in his eye.

"Count me out. That's too much."

"But why? It's perfect!" he said, suddenly thrilled at the notion.

"I'll tell you why, because faking your own death is illegal. I'd be an accomplice to a crime. I don't want to do that for a living, be a criminal. Besides, it's nothing new, that's why it's a crime . . . people fake their deaths every day."

"They do?" he asked. "Why?"

"Sure. Insurance fraud, child support, bankruptcy, maybe they pissed off the Mob, you know, lots of reasons."

Andy was intrigued by this, never having thought about such scenarios. I continued. "You know, some people just want to disappear and start again from scratch, a whole new life. No, Kaufman, if you really wanted to fake your death, you couldn't tell anybody, and I mean *anybody*."

"Why?"

"Well, because I don't think anyone would be able to stand up to questioning. Plus they have lie detectors and stuff."

He got it. "You couldn't tell a soul."

I went back to the article I was reading. "Not a soul."

That was the last time we discussed the subject — Andy never brought it up to me again, but he did to two others, Jack Burns and John Moffitt, producers of the television show *Fridays*. John recently related the following story to me: "I remember the conversation quite distinctly. It was after the telecast of one of our shows Andy was on. He joined myself and other cast members at Jack's house. Later in the evening, Andy asked to speak privately to both me and Jack. We moved into a quiet room away from the others, and Andy closed the door, making sure no one besides us could hear. He told us he was about to embark on the greatest prank of his career and made us swear we would never repeat it to a living soul. He then told us it would be the biggest thing in the history of show business, then he lowered his voice and said, 'I'm going to fake my death, go into hiding for ten years, and then reappear.'" John understands the explosive nature of this story but stands by it and is willing to take a polygraph test to prove it.

In addition to John Moffitt's startling revelation came another, from Mimi Lambert, the young lady Andy wrestled on *Saturday Night Live* and with whom he established a lifelong friendship. Mimi said that Andy once told her he was seriously considering faking his death. But the detail Andy disclosed to her that he held back from me and Burns and Moffitt was how he would "die." Andy told Mimi that if he did go ahead with his plan, he would do so by pretending to have cancer. Mimi said she was disgusted by the idea and told Andy it was anything but funny and to never speak of it again to her. He never did.

*   *   *

A few months after his confession to Moffitt and Burns, on January 6, 1983, Andy brought his parents, Stanley and Janice, on *Letterman* for one reason, to go before millions of viewers and tell them how much he loved them. He also hugged Dave, telling him how much he loved him too. In retrospect, it was almost as if he was saying his good-byes.

Following his dismissal from *SNL*, the next blow to him was *Taxi*. Though the show was picked up by NBC and seemingly revived, the reprieve was short-lived, and by February 1983 the last episode had been shot. *Taxi* was toast, and Andy no longer needed to fret about the tax it exacted from him.

From the start, *Taxi* had been hard for Andy to accept. It had provided excellent employment and made him a star, but it had short-circuited one of his romantic aspirations of being a highly regarded but esoteric artiste. Though he had dreamed of being famous since he was a child, when it finally happened it was not what he'd expected, like Alan King's beer tap he'd so coveted. Andy felt he had become just another highly successful schmuck and in some ways had missed out on the romance of the pain and the struggle.

A few months later, on May 26, 1983, an L.A. television interview show called *Tom Cottle: Up Close* featured a very unusual interview with Andy. It was the only time he appeared on television as himself, totally unaffected, totally Andy. Among many things, he spoke candidly about losing his beloved grandfather and how his folks kept that news from him. He even told Cottle how, on hearing the news that Elvis had died, he wondered if it was really true, how a guy that young and vital could die so young. Another thing you don't notice unless you look for it: throughout the interview Andy coughs occasionally.

During that time I was very busy with a career that had slowly separated from Andy's, and I remember watching that show and wondering out loud, "What is he up to? This is very un-Andy of him." Since the contact between us had dropped off to two or three phone calls a week, I suspected he was planning something, and this was the setup. Though I wanted to be in on it, the press of my own schedule prevented me from exploring it with him.

Fifteen years later, while working on the film *Man on the Moon*, I was having dinner with its director, Milos Forman (*One

Flew Over the Cuckoo's Nest, Amadeus, The People vs. Larry Flynt), and we were discussing Andy's psyche. Milos believed that people often instinctively know when their days are numbered, even when they haven't been "formally" informed, and unconsciously begin wrapping up their lives.

Paul Giamatti (*Private Parts, Saving Private Ryan*), the talented actor who played me in the movie, had his own contribution to that theory. Paul's father, the late great baseball commissioner and former president of Yale University, A. Bartlett Giamatti, despite having no inkling of trouble, began to put his life in order a few months before he died. No sooner had he made his last will and testament than he dropped dead of a massive coronary.

In September and November of 1983 Andy made appearances on *Letterman* and, during both visits, introduced a theme he'd never broached with anyone: his "own" children. Bringing out three young black men on one of the shows, Andy insisted they call him Dad. Also, that he was thirty-four and they looked to be in their early twenties was unimportant: Andy told Dave they were his kids and he was proud of them. As usual, Dave played along patiently.

Why did he introduce as his sons three men who obviously weren't his sons? On the lines of the above ruminations about impending death, some suggest Andy was playing out some sort of last-minute "family life" psychodrama because, at least on an unconscious level, he realized he wasn't long for the world. Probably Andy was merely extending his wrestling persona, first being the "bad guy," wrestling women and insulting the people of Memphis, then being the "good guy," showing he was all heart. And the fact that the three young men were very ethnic recalled the bit we did with the four tough-looking guys accompanying Andy on "It's a Small World." That a nice Jewish boy could father three inner-city youths is ludicrous, and therein lay the humor.

To Andy everything was theater, and this was just more role playing. If Andy needed a family, he already had one in his loving parents and brother, Michael, and sister, Carol; if he needed a child, he had that too, a daughter whom he'd never met nor ever made any attempt to contact.

*   *   *

So now here was the score: he'd been summarily kicked off *SNL*, *Taxi* was gone, and what motion picture career he'd hoped for was now beyond his reach. Andy and his managers saw no hope of landing anything in films. When George Shapiro and Howard West called him with a possible sitcom, his knee-jerk reaction was, *Oh, no, not again*, but, like it or not, he had gotten used to that fat weekly paycheck. He grudgingly agreed to consider it, but there was one catch: the producers of the sitcom wanted him to audition. Such a command could have been a slap in the face to a guy who'd just done five years on a very successful show, but Andy complied, assuming it would be a mere formality. He didn't get the part.

Deciding Broadway might hold a creative outlet and critical success, he signed on to a British import, a play called *Teaneck Tanzi: The Venus Flytrap*. What intrigued Andy was that its theme was wrestling and that he would be starring opposite songstress Debbie Harry of Blondie. They rehearsed in earnest for many weeks, but when the play opened on April 14, 1983, it did so to such scathing reviews that the first two performances were also the only two.

Demoralized by *Teaneck*'s head-spinning demise, Andy received another punch to the gut: his mother had a stroke. That all of those crises happened around the same time is almost unfathomable, but Andy hung in there, weathering one shot after the other, a series of setbacks that probably would have sent most others into a spiral of irretrievable depression. What kept him out of the abyss was his faith. Transcendental meditation was his religion, and now more than ever he needed the refuge its practices and teachings could offer him.

TM was Andy's safety net, and by making a pilgrimage to the meditation center in Switzerland he would be able to spend time among the other initiates and get his balance back. He was in a crisis and desperately needed that haven to retreat to and mentally sift through the wreckage that had become his life. Each one of the recent blows had knocked down his confidence and stripped away that facade of invulnerability he had been building since he entered the movement and found his inner peace. He made the call to the transcendental meditation center to make his reservation and received a heart-stopping reply: "We don't want you."

Finding his behavior unacceptable, that is, wrestling women, creating arguments on television, and so on, the leaders of the movement informed Andy (who had by then ascended to a very high ranking within) that he was no longer following their path and would not be allowed to take another course. If his ousting at *SNL* hurt him, this news was a knife through the heart. For Andy such rejection was tantamount to a Roman Catholic being excommunicated. Suddenly he was rudderless, cast adrift by his own religion at the lowest point in his life.

Then he received the coup de grâce.

A few months later, during his Thanksgiving visit with his family, everyone noticed Andy's small but persistent cough. He promised he'd see a doctor back in L.A. and did so in December of 1983. When he got the verdict the news was absolutely stunning: *cancer*. It was not something that could be easily fixed. This was deadly, a nearly hopeless type of carcinoma sometimes called large cell or undifferentiated cell carcinoma that had attacked his lungs with a vengeance. When he was told he had about three months to live, he couldn't believe it. This was the worst kind of smoker's cancer, a strain so malicious and advanced that doctors could do nothing but suggest counseling and a good hospice. Andy didn't believe it. After all, except for occasional forays into Tony's world, where cigarettes and booze abounded, Andy was by no means a smoker.

I really believe Andy never thought he was going to die. How could he? He had the supreme confidence a self-made man has. He was Andy Kaufman: *This just can't be*. As long as he meditated twice a day, every day, he was invincible. The cancer was a temporary inconvenience, a bad cold, nothing more. *Terminal*, the doctors said? *Ridiculous*, for TM had taught him any adversity could be overcome through meditation.

Because of the shock to me of such news I cannot recall who told me, Andy, George, or Lynne, but Lynne assures me it was Andy who called. Despite our having pulled a hundred hoaxes, whatever he told me did not hit me like a joke. I flashed on our discussion some months before of his faking his death, but it struck me as unrelated: Andy wouldn't do that to me, therefore, this was monstrously real.

As the days after the revelation unfolded, Andy calmed down and fell into a pattern of casual dismissal, as if the cancer were a minor inconvenience and would soon pass. I thought of my friend Stan Martindale and his tales as a U.S. Marine on Okinawa. As the sergeant, Stan would get the "stats" from HQ every night, telling him, based on various sources of intelligence, what his casualty rate would likely be during the next day's battle. Often the numbers were extraordinary and, according to him, usually accurate within 3 or 4 percent. Stan had the option of informing his men beforehand so they could pen letters to loved ones or mentally prepare for almost certain death. He chose to do so, and despite the predictions of a 30 percent or worse casualty rate, not one man thought he'd be in that category. Shot? Okay, sure. My arm blown off? I'll accept that. But killed? Never.

We live in an era where we are surrounded by vivid death, from the evening news to graphic movies. But we have an exceptionally difficult time accepting it, and when personally faced with death, we are always amazed it could happen to us or near us. It is the nature of death that we shrink from: the end of it all, depending, of course, on your spiritual beliefs. But death is certainly final for this existence, and it is that finality, that closing curtain on all that we know, that is so very, very hard to accept.

Like Andy, I chose not to believe, not to accept it, because it was not real. This couldn't happen to Andy Kaufman. His life force was so powerful he could ward off anything, particularly something like cancer that he had no business having in the first place! To this day, I beat myself up over that, my inability to take it seriously, at least at first. Lynne now comforts me by saying it was just my way of denying it and dealing with it. She also reminds me that we all took our cue from Andy, and since he wasn't taking it so seriously, how could we?

But it brings me little comfort that I scoffed at the needs of my friend out of disbelief. Yet to take the illness seriously would have meant the end of everything, of every dream we shared. There were TV shows and films and spectacular stage shows in our futures. There was the Ninety-Nine-Cent Tour I was working on, which would take milk and cookies to the next level. This time we would take an audience on buses to a port of call. Totally unsuspecting and with no notice, they would be taken aboard a vessel and sent on a six-day cruise. We not only would have had luggage packed for them but also would have notified their employers in advance and brought them in on the whole thing. I was already in negotiations with a major cruise line to pick up the entire cost in exchange for the promotional opportunities. If anything happened to Andy, it would be the end of that. No, I had to side with Kaufman — death was not an option.

Andy refused to own the disease for a long time and sought, along with a few confidantes, to keep it quiet. Andy's brother, Michael, was told with the caveat that he not tell anyone else, particularly their parents, at least for a while. George called and asked if I knew who else knew, because he feared the news could further damage Andy's already ailing career. Like those involved in the Manhattan Project, we were sworn to keep this dark secret to ourselves. George's motivation was not commercial in the sense of receiving personal gain; he just didn't want any more harm to come to Andy, whom he loved like a son. Letting such information out into the already skittish Hollywood community would draw sympathy, and with sympathy comes a price: everyone loves you, but no one will hire you. George knew Andy's first love was his work, and therefore, he needed to keep Andy working, keep him busy and feeling vital while he fought the battle of his life.

On January 26, 1984, Andy appeared on a television program called *The Top*, a showbiz euphemism for finally making it. It was fitting, for it was Andy's last appearance on the medium he loved so and had dreamed of conquering since that little kid played to the imaginary camera in the wall of his basement so many years before.

Typical of Andy, he dismissed the dire prognosis given him by the purveyors of Western medicine and looked to heal himself by his own methods. Practitioners of Eastern holistic philosophies, where symptoms are merely the body's signs that it is attempting to heal itself, use the judicious application of natural herbs and remedies, along with mental and physical harmonics, to rid the body of the invading disease. Though he knew something was wrong with him, Andy did not believe what the doctors said, choosing to follow his own path toward healing, at least for a while.

Always careful what he ate (again, when Tony Clifton wasn't around), Andy stepped up his regimen to a full-blown macrobiotic diet, a holistic approach that incorporates grains, beans, and vegetables, with moderate seafood and fruit, to create a harmony with nature — what the body *really* needs, not what we *like* to eat. Then he contacted a counselor, a man he'd met in the TM movement who, despite Andy's banishment, offered to help. His name was John Gray and he would go on to author the wildly successful series of books beginning with *Men Are from Mars, Women Are from Venus*.

Andy hoped to expose via John Gray's counseling sessions some deep-rooted, unresolved psychological malaise stemming from conflicts in the primary relationships of his life. His theory was that if he identified that problem or problems, and dealt with them, he might shut off the poison that was infiltrating his system.

When I heard that he'd called in his family and George, I was frightened I'd get the same summons. He had baggage with his family as well as with George, having fought with him for years over much of his "avant garde" work. I feared a confrontation with Andy over something I may have done to let him down. One day, after stewing over that scenario, I was with him and mustered the courage to ask about the counseling sessions and my possible role in them.

He smiled and shook his head. "You? I have no bones to pick with you at all. You're my best friend."

Despite his commitment to holistic healing, Andy covered his bet with a course of radiation and chemo. But as the months went by, it didn't seem to be working: not even holding his own, he seemed to be slowly slipping away. Finally, when his "Western" physicians solemnly told him, "There is no hope," he didn't accept it and turned to another means of salvation. Having recently seen a documentary about "psychic surgery" in the Philippines, narrated by Burt Lancaster, Andy made some inquiries and decided to go. He would leave the United States a sick man and come back whole and completely healed: it would be his greatest trick ever.

*   *   *

As I said before, I was in a state of shock or denial about all of this, and when I got the news, I blocked much of what happened from my mind. As I was preparing to write this book, Lynne and I agreed the trauma had erased much of those sad times from our memories, so it was with great excitement that I told her I had uncovered a series of diary entries I had made during that time.

Contained in three large boxes of Kaufman memorabilia I had collected over the years were papers, clippings, mementos, and, incredibly, those valuable pages chronicling my pain and observations during Andy's last months. Though I had been through the boxes in the past, I had forgotten about the diary until I discovered it just as I was about to begin this book. Providence? Maybe, but I prefer to think someone I know had a hand in my finding it.

I've decided to incorporate some of the passages into the next chapter. The excerpts are exactly what I wrote fifteen years ago and contain none of the cheery revisionism that writing can undergo when time has softened the pain, anger, and incredulity that one endures at difficult times. The diary entries helped rekindle my memories of the worst time of my life, and I hope they serve to honestly convey the profound hurt of losing your best friend.

14

Closing Act

He did these fringe reality things where you didn't
know where his reality was.
ROBERT KLEIN

It was a Thursday, March 15, 1984, and I was particularly worried about Andy because I hadn't spoken to him all day. I kept
calling well into the evening and getting the answering machine.
Finally, out of frustration and fear, I drove over to the house he
and Lynne had rented in Pacific Palisades. On the way I spun all
sorts of horrors in my mind — that I'd find him, dead. His treatments were not really helping, and for the past few weeks I could
see he was deteriorating quickly. Holed up in his house, he had
taken to screening all but a few of his calls. He always took mine,
and that's why I was worried.

I drove by the house and the lights were out. I drove around
the neighborhood for a while to kill time and gather my
thoughts. Later, around midnight, I passed the house and saw
him through the window. I was afraid to stop, maybe because this
man was changing and wasn't the old Andy — perhaps I was
afraid to see him that way. I reminded myself that he was my best
friend and needed me. I put aside my fears and parked the car.
He answered the door and was heartened to see me. The radiation treatments had taken their toll by stripping off a lot of
pounds he didn't have to spare. His hair had fallen out in large
clumps, so he'd fashioned it into a Mohawk. Andy and Lynne
and I sat around chatting for a bit, and when the mood lightened,
Lynne seemed to relax slightly and got up and went to bed.

"I look like that guy in *The Hills Have Eyes*," he joked, referring to a scary-looking bald character from a recent horror film. I laughed with him. Now that we were alone, I decided to hit him point blank. "So what do you think caused the cancer?"

"I talked to this girl I know about a year ago," he started out, seemingly in a non sequitur. "We talked about suicide. She said she'd toyed with the idea."

"You thinking about it now?" I asked, trying to keep my calm.

"No. Not really," he answered softly. "You know, I think I peaked with *Taxi*. That's what people will remember me for," he said with a touch of sadness. "All the stuff I did, and you and I did, all the important things, I don't think will be remembered. Maybe me dying will make people see they blew it with me. Maybe they'll realize what I really did." I sensed a slight bitterness coupled with resignation.

Then he started in on the potential reasons for his illness. He'd read a book called *Sugar Blues* five years ago and told me he should never have read it and strongly advised me never to do so. It planted the idea in his head that sugar was killing him. He felt there might be some mind-over-matter connection, that his belief in the book may have contributed to his getting sick. And since he was addicted to sugar and there was no stopping, the only cure would be for him to go on a strict macrobiotic diet. He said he felt for the last five years that every time he indulged in sugar he was poisoning himself. He said he was almost relieved when the doctor told him he had the cancer because now he could quit worrying when it would actually happen. Now he could finally go macrobiotic and save himself. I thought, *Just like the old bombing routine: bring it to the point of disaster and then turn it around.*

Then he launched into a dissection of the problems with his parents as well as his own strange childhood. "I never joined in with the other kids," he finally observed. "I stayed by myself all the time. I was aloof and got lost in my own world. I'm not so sure if that was such a good choice. Maybe it was unnatural."

"What would you have done different?" I asked.

He shrugged. "I don't know. I really don't know."

We sat for a moment, pondering. It seemed Andy's fate may have been set many years before. Andy joining in with the other kids? Organizing a kick-the-can game or hide-and-seek? Impossible.

"You know," he said, "I would have loved to re-create the *Howdy Doody* show. This time, no Peanut Gallery, just me and Howdy and the other puppets."

I felt like just letting him talk. He talked about the wrestling days and how much fun we'd had. He also admitted his last attempt to wrestle in the South the previous year had been met with "lack of interest at the gate," and the two weeks he'd scheduled had been canceled. That hurt him, though he never showed it until now.

"*Heartbeeps*," he said simply. "I really screwed up with that one. You warned me."

"It doesn't matter now," I said, fearing this might degenerate into a session where Andy might start to beat himself up — a quality very unlike him. He was self-critical but not self-loathing. Avoiding that trap, he brushed it off and laughed. "You know, I'd always dreamed of being in the movies."

"You were," I said, acknowledging he'd been in some films.

He smiled and shook his head. "No, not really." Then he changed direction. "The whole thing with Dick Ebersol was hard to take. I really wanted to stay on *Saturday Night*." He sighed, letting go of any hard feelings. "It doesn't do me any good to get into that. It's against my therapy to lay blame," he said. He paused. "But I can't help but think every dog will have its day."

"When do you go?" I asked, referring to his trip to the Philippines.

He brightened. "Less than a week."

"Have you got a guy picked out?" I asked, regarding his surgeon.

"Oh, yeah," he said. "His name is Jun Roxas, and he's supposed to be the best. I noticed in the documentary he carried a Bible. I wanted to fit in, so I got one, too." He reached to a table to show me his new Bible. I thought, *Andy Kaufman with a Bible, how weird is that?*

He thumbed through the book absentmindedly. "Nobody believes I'm sick."

He wasn't wrong about that. I even harbored some tiny

doubts, and there I was sitting five feet from him. "I know," I said. "Does that bother you?"

"Sometimes, I guess so," he said. "I just think it's funny that if I really do die no one will believe it."

"You won't die," I said, not so sure.

Andy came back, "If I did it might make me a legend."

I joked. "That's all you think about — career, career, career."

He laughed at this, then switched gears. "Hey, maybe you should write a book. If I die, then you've got to do it."

"Tell the stories," I said.

"Yes," he answered. "Tell it all. You know, it's too bad Universal never did *The Tony Clifton Story*. He was our best creation . . . brilliant. George and Howard never really got Tony, they weren't as supportive as they could have been. Well, maybe George was."

We talked for quite a while, then Andy paused and looked out the window, even though there was nothing but blackness. He truly believed his cure awaited him in the Philippines. I hoped with him. His energy was high and strong and I felt for the first time since accepting the news that he might be okay after all. When we parted and I walked out to my car, I had the reassuring feeling that he might pull it off. Andy had controlled most everything in his life to now, so why was this different? I laughed to myself that he was going to cheat me out of my book about him.

A little less than a week later, *My Breakfast with Blassie* was set to premier at the Nuart on Santa Monica Boulevard. I worried that the strain of it all would completely drain Andy, but the *Blassie* debut was something he wouldn't have missed. It was also a chance for him to hold his head up amid the Hollywood community and show he was a fighter, despite many still thinking he was putting it all on. In an attempt to keep our "secret" under wraps, we had not made any announcement, so few knew of the grave nature of his illness.

Tuesday — March 20, 1984

Premiere Night of My Breakfast with Blassie. Nuart Theater.

I almost missed it. Coping with my depression. I tried to oversleep, going to bed at 4:00 P.M. and waking up at 6:45. Usually waking up from a nap later in the day causes me to wake up "out of it." Almost on the brink of terror. Somehow going to sleep when it's light and waking up in the dark. Throws off an equilibrium, maybe because it's the opposite of the correct way to do it.

Anyway, I woke up in terror, more so knowing it will be the last time I see him . . . seeing he was planning [on] going to the Philippines in search of a psychic surgeon the next day. The dread of seeing him in such an environment — the premiere, the crowd, the cameras — I loathe the thought of going but I went.

When I passed the theater my worst suspicions had come true. The place was a zoo. A group of young wrestling fans had gathered in the vestibule, gulping down toasted waffles that were served before the screening. A truly obnoxious wrestler dressed in a loose-fitting gold outfit, wearing a wrestling mask that concealed his identity, was apparently hired for the event. Perhaps if I didn't know the horrible truth of the evening, I would have written it off as just harmless press or even fun. Tonight the juxtaposition was deadly, a party for a corpse with only a few of the inner circle knowing it.

I considered turning around and going back home and jumping back under the covers. Hoping that when I woke I would find that it had all been just a nightmare. I had already loathed myself for taking a nap and knew if I chickened out of this I wouldn't be able to look myself in the mirror.

So I pulled the car into a restaurant parking lot a few blocks away. I walked back to the theater slowly. Hoping I would enter just as the lights would go down and the film started. Was I wrong.

I was a half block from the theater when the limo pulled up. Andy got out. A couple photographers started shooting away. He stood there with his Mohawk and leather jacket. (The Mohawk was to disguise the loss of the hair from the radiation treatments.) He was a pathetic sight — frail, punked out, dying. To the crowd, though, he had it all — money, fame, notoriety. They had come to see him on film and had the bonus of now seeing him in person.

Lynne gently held his left arm, protecting it from the crowd. The cancer had eaten the bone away. It dangled lifelessly at his side. Forever useless. Her holding it would give the impression it worked. All I could think was that he'll never play the congas again —

no more ah-be-dah-bay-
ah-be-dah-bay-
dah-bay.

I found myself running up to him, like I had countless times in the past, perhaps out of habit. When I got near, I did my best impression of being normal. "Hey, Kaufman" — like I had done countless times in the past. He spotted me and said, "Hi," just as normally.

Then I saw Estelle [Endler]. It was the first time we had seen each other since "The Top" taping. Back then she didn't know about Andy; now she did. Our eyes studied each other for any telltale sign. Telltale of what, I'm not sure either one of us could ever explain. Neither of us spoke a word to the other. I doubt we ever would again.

We all entered the vestibule of the theater where the crowd, now seeing him, lit up their face and stood on their toes to get a better look.

By now, friends could be seen. George Shapiro and his secretary Diane, and Linda, Andy's secretary. Before it became more of a nightmare, the wrestler in the mask announced that the film would be starting shortly, so everyone should take a seat.

As everyone hustled into the theater, Kaufman was swept away in an unknown entourage. I planned on possibly standing in the back of the theater, just in case I couldn't take any more of this. Linda, Andy's secretary, comes up to me and asks me where I'm sitting. I tell her nowhere in particular. She said, "Great!" 'cause I've got to do her a favor. Would I sit between her and her boyfriend? At first, I couldn't understand for what reason. But she explained another boyfriend of hers would be sitting on her other side and could I be sort of a "buffer." I never did exactly figure it out, nor cared, for that matter. But the silliness of it all momentarily caused me to escape the pain that welled in my heart.

Just then, I could hear Andy's voice behind me. I would be sitting directly in front of him. My heart once more sank. I even wondered if Linda planned it like this, even though I knew she didn't. Kaufman spotted me and said, "Great!" referring to my close proximity to him. Next to him was Budd Friedman and his daughter and wife. We exchanged greetings, neither one of us letting on.

Also present was Marilu Henner and a few other celebrities. Their presence there to me seemed ridiculous and insulting. Some of them who had been so unsupportive in the past now came out to support the dying man. I wanted to scream at the top of my lungs: "You hypocrites! How dare you show up now?! Where were you when he needed you?" But I kept silent and could see that their presence did much to lift his spirits.

Robin Williams was also present, a true supporter and fan of Andy's work over the years. A gentleman and a major talent who had been unknown when first spotting Andy. He's headed for major stardom, probably a lot bigger than Kaufman, and, like him, never copping any attitudes about it.

The lights went down and I told myself it would all be over in an hour. My legs were locking on me already. But instead of the film starting right off, it seemed that some sort of pre-show announcements would be made. I could just scream.

Out walked the official Ringmaster from the Olympic Auditorium and did a stand-up routine that I'm sure was well intentioned but was excruciatingly painful, considering that some of the most respected minds in comedy were present in the room. After ten minutes of this very unfunny banter, I could feel the audience turning uncomfortably. Budd Friedman let out with a few sly remarks under his breath. I couldn't help adding a few back to him. I could hear Andy giggle behind me. It seemed like old times, only it wasn't.

I looked over, saw Estelle and Harold Ramis, also shuffling back and forth in their seats. I shuddered at the thought of them thinking I had staged this. Then I shook my head in disgust at the thought that such a vain idea would cross my mind at such a moment.

Finally, the Ringmaster wound to a close. Everyone applauded vigorously that it was over. The lights went down and the film began.

"My Breakfast with Blassie" was a low, low budget video spoofing the highly successful film, "My Dinner with Andre." Whereas "Dinner" took place at a posh restaurant with intellectual discussions between the two principals, "Breakfast" took place at a Sambo's restaurant and the intellectual discussion was changed to idle ramblings between its two principals, Andy and the famed wrestler Freddie Blassie (the man credited with the phrase "pencil-neck geek").

I myself appeared briefly at the end of the film and dreaded the thought that I would have to watch myself with this "Hollywood crowd" present. Especially since I did the whole thing on a lark one day after receiving a call from Kaufman telling me to meet him at a restaurant. When I arrived, I was greeted by a video crew and an assortment of what I thought to be students working on a project. At the time, I'm working on "D.C. Cab" over at Universal and consider myself pretty hot shit. In my mind, I'm thinking, "God, is this what it's all come down to for Kaufman?" Murray and Williams and Martin doing majors, and Kaufman fucking around with some kids on video, because "Heartbeeps" died at the box office.

Andy encouraged me to join in the fun. In the film I can be seen pulling straws out of my nose and vomiting. The film was actually reviewed by *Variety* and singled out as the most "idiotic and sophomoric" piece of shit. If that wasn't enough, the same review would be xeroxed and handed out to the audience on the way in. When it rains, it pours. But all of this took a back seat to my dying friend, who was seated behind me.

The first ten minutes of *My Breakfast with Blassie* was death itself, and I wished I were somewhere else. The blown-up video was washed out and fuzzy and the sound was even worse. I'm sure many in the crowd were wondering, *What is this shit?* I know I was. I despaired. This is what Andy's career had come down to: nothing.

As my depression was about to get the best of me, an interesting thing happened — a few people laughed. Then a few more.

It was infectious, and suddenly the audience began to enjoy the video. The laughter had a therapeutic effect on me, as I'm sure it did on the few others who were going through the same nightmare. Kaufman and Blassie were brilliant at times, and even my own cockamamie appearance was met with laughter. For a few moments we were drawn into the film, watching a happy and healthy Andy improvising wonderfully with Fred Blassie.

The film was a tiny masterpiece. Shot in no time for next to nothing, it was ultimately as insightful as it was entertaining. As the film ended, I smiled to myself, deeply relieved as the audience burst into heartfelt applause. I had made it through the evening. Andy was asked to take a bow, which he did. It would be his last.

The next afternoon, I drove Lynne and Andy to LAX, where they were to board a plane to the Philippines. The mood was serious — for us — and none of us said much. We were certainly hopeful, but I was less sanguine about the notion that a faith healer was going to put right my dreadfully ill friend. I wheeled Andy, now relegated almost exclusively to a wheelchair, down the terminal hallway to the gate. Suddenly, out of nowhere sprang a paparazzo who immediately began flashing away a few feet from Andy. "You *fucking parasites!*" screamed Andy. "What kind of people are you?"

The photographer quickly fled, and Lynne and I were left stunned, more by Andy's totally uncharacteristic swearing than by the sneak attack. Two weeks later the picture ran in the *National Enquirer*. It was payback for all those phony stories we foisted on them.

Now wary that the sharks were in the water, I decided to check Andy onto the plane myself and scan for any additional photographic sharpshooters. As we approached the portal into the plane, Andy pulled himself out of his wheelchair. Just as I was about to joke, "Andy, right foot first," he crossed the threshold of the plane with his left foot. At that precise moment I knew Andy Kaufman was a dead man.

As soon as I had him situated, the flight attendant put a hand on my shoulder and gently asked me to leave. I looked at Andy, a wasting shell of his former vital self, and my heart wanted to pour out how I felt. I wanted to say things that he probably would have laughed at but understood. I wanted to hold him, to hug him hard for luck and for all our years together, but instead I lamely said good-bye and got off the plane. Through the window at the gate I watched as the crew secured the plane's door and as the ground crew directed the aircraft away from the terminal. I waited until Andy's jet passed by again, this time streaking down the runway into the sky. I felt an anger at myself and a complete emptiness. I knew I would never see my friend again.

Disbelief mixed with the knife-edge of reality as I walked blindly back to my vehicle. I climbed into my car and just sat there for an hour before I could move, alternately slamming my head against the steering wheel, while wracking sobs consumed me as I cursed the gods. *Why didn't I tell him I loved him? What kind of pitiful specimen of manhood was I?* My misery knew no bounds as I beat myself up for missing the most important opportunity of my life. Together we had explored failure, and now I was finding mine, and it was bitterly complete.

The next morning I dragged myself over to Universal to continue my odyssey with Joel Schumacher. We had finished *D.C. Cab* and he had engaged me to develop a script for him, this time about a trio of teenage girls who drive to Ensenada, Mexico, with the intent of finding guys and parties. Tentatively entitled *She Devils*, it was light comedy — exactly the sort of thing I could not concentrate on given the terrible distress Andy was suffering. Joel was a workaholic and didn't understand my waning enthusiasm for our work. He had no idea what had been developing with Andy and mistook my low ebb for a lackluster work ethic.

That misunderstanding was endemic among everyone who knew me and Andy, for our "state secret" was known only to our tiny inner circle, and the rampant rumors about Kaufman were naturally relegated to the "boy who cried wolf" category. But in two weeks, the *National Enquirer* photo and accompanying article (which was surprisingly accurate) would change all that, with our family-held confidence becoming fodder for the public as well as for everyone in the industry, including some who would feel they had been left out of the loop.

Over the next few days I lapsed into a severe depression. Finally, on the third or fourth day after Andy's departure, my guilt and agony became unbearable, and I didn't show for work, without so much as a phone call to say I was sick. My manager and agent tried to reach me, but I couldn't have cared less. Schumacher messengered me a letter excoriating me for my "unprofessional" behavior and warning me he would not pay me until I delivered the script as promised. Perhaps this self-destruction was brought on by my guilt, the desire to suffer along with my dying friend.

Finally, bowing to pressure that included the death of my career, I threw together some utter shit and launched it over to Joel with the hope it would get him off my back. It didn't. He knew it was crap and called me on it, so I demanded my money. He dug in and said, "No way." I called the Writer's Guild and demanded arbitration. According to the letter of the law, the Guild determined that he had to pay me. The reality was I didn't deserve it, and since the community involved in the hiring of writers in Hollywood is very, very tight, my actions were nothing short of outright sedition. All I had fought to achieve, my career as a writer, could and would be snuffed out in a ten-minute flurry of phone calls over my actions, but I really didn't give a shit. Unlike Prometheus, I had chained *myself* to the rock to allow the eagle to eat my liver.

My depression deepened, and within a few days Connie Bryant, my sweet and beautiful girlfriend, had also been pushed over the cliff. She found me impossible to take, given the months of angst over the initial news of Andy's tailspin, coupled with the last few days of blackness, and we split up. I couldn't blame her. No one in their right mind wanted to be around me — I made Mr. X look like a choirboy.

The morning after Connie left I awoke to an epiphany: *What the hell am I doing here? When my best friend is dying in the Philippines?* I quickly packed a bag, jumped in a cab, stopped at the bank, then had the driver take me to LAX. Racing down the main promenade, I hastily searched for the airline that would get me to the Philippines the quickest. I prayed I wasn't too late.

I landed in Manila at 7:30 A.M. on April 7, and the stifling humidity nearly knocked me over. I checked into the Manila Hotel, the same one General Douglas MacArthur operated out of during his campaign to stave off the invading Japanese. The next morning I rented a car and headed out of the city onto the narrow dirt roads of the island of Luzon in search of Andy and Lynne. I knew they were in Baguio, a city in the low mountains more than 125 miles north of Manila.

About a half hour out of town I came upon a sight that will forever be etched into my mind: a man nailed — *crucified* — to a tree. I stopped and tried to help him down, but some of the locals approached and stopped me, saying it was Lent and this was his penance. Climbing back into my car, as jarring as the scene was I couldn't help but think the guy should move to Hollywood if that's what he wanted.

Farther down the road I came to yet another vision that was welcome but perplexing: at a dirt crossroads sat a McDonald's. With nothing around for forty miles but shantytowns, it was truly surreal. I went inside, starving and seeking a taste of home. After receiving my order of a couple of burgers, fries, and a Coke, I noticed I had no ketchup. "May I have some ketchup?" I asked the young counter girl.

She eyed me suspiciously. "Is it for you?"

I wanted to crack off some smart-ass comeback, but I knew, despite the two Big Macs in my hands, that I wasn't in Kansas anymore. "Of course, who else would it be for?" As she walked off to fetch the ketchup I wondered why the hell she'd asked me that. I expected her to return with some packets, but instead, as if she were passing on the crown jewels, she handed me a small paper cup half filled with the tomato distillate. Outside, I realized why she'd acted that way. As I walked to the car a half dozen adults crowded around me, begging for my ketchup. I asked them why. "We make soup," said one, swallowing his pride enough to explain to the American how it really was.

Feeling guilty about stuffing my face with two hamburgers and fries, I went back inside and asked for more ketchup. The girl refused, saying I could have it only if I bought another hamburger. I had her ring up a whole sackful and then had her load me up on ketchup. Back in the parking lot I gave all the burgers and ketchup to those grateful and hungry folks and drove away. I thought, *Nothing like visiting a third-world country to hammer home how lucky you are.* Then again, I realized, maybe they were the lucky ones: after all, they weren't on their way to help their best friend die.

The drive to Baguio was breathtaking, especially when I hit the mountains and began to ascend the dirt road and drive past lush jungles and deep valleys. Baguio is considered a vacation retreat for the wealthy of Manila when the heat and humidity drive them north into the cooler coastal mountains. I enjoyed the trip, reveling in the precarious, winding one-lane rut as I skirted vertiginous drop-offs. With no guardrails, one has to pay rapt attention to the track or find sky beneath the vehicle and forest hundreds of feet below. Every so often there was a turnout allowing slower vehicles to withdraw as the more aggressive moved past.

I slowly made my way up toward Baguio, carefully dodging the heavy foot traffic. I found it interesting that everyone seemed to be holding hands, even the men. My Western reaction was that they were gay, but that was just the custom and had nothing to do with sexuality. I yearned for another time, different circumstances, under which I could really enjoy that wonderful, gentle country.

I was told that I would know I was approaching Baguio when I encountered the Lion. The Lion is a magnificent sculpture, four stories high, reposing in a cleft of a mountain, much like Mount Rushmore. The Lion offers a grand salutation as you enter that magical and mystical city. As I drove down into Baguio, I figured that finding Jun Roxas's clinic would not be difficult. I assumed that every local could probably point it out.

I knew that psychic surgery was a lot of baloney, but I also knew that some of the doctors back at Cedars-Sinai, where Andy had been receiving treatment, didn't completely discount the possibilities. They acknowledged there were documented cases where someone "visualized" their tumor shrinking, and lo and behold, it did just that. But those instances were few and far between. Then again, Lynne, George, Andy's family, and I didn't see the harm in giving Andy hope. Perhaps with his mental resources and rich background in yoga, he could evict those life-poisoning cells from his body.

I found the Hyatt hotel where Lynne and Andy were supposed to be and checked in. It featured several fine restaurants, and its main aesthetic draw was a glass elevator that overlooked a picturesque courtyard. As I walked to my room I fantasized I was back on the road with Andy, on my way to the gig, with thoughts gelling in my head where we might later pick up the girls. After unpacking, I decided to venture out and try to find Andy and Lynne. As I descended the glass elevator I saw them coming into the court below. Lynne spotted me first, and her face lit up with a broad smile. We waved and she directed Andy's attention to me. He seemed so much smaller and lifeless, considerably more so than when I'd seen him less than two weeks before. I was shocked but hid my emotions. I waved as he looked up, and his face came alive at the sight of me. As I stepped out of the elevator and hurried over to them he kept repeating, "I can't believe you came here! I just can't believe you came!"

His reaction told me I had done the right thing. Fuck Hollywood, fuck everything else — my friend needed me, and that was the only thing I cared about.

On Wednesday morning, April 11, I drove Lynne and Andy to the session with Jun Roxas, the psychic surgeon. The clinic Roxas had established occupied what had been at various times a resort and a popular nightclub. Built into a mountain, it overlooked a vast valley, and its stunning setting gave one a sense that this might indeed be some sort of hallowed ground where medical science was regularly defied and miracles happened like clockwork.

As Andy was ushered inside, I tarried in the plaza to take in the view. After a few moments I struck up a conversation with the young woman who'd been assigned to drive or guide us around, should we need it. She had worked for Roxas for quite a while and seemed quite taken with him. "Oh, yes," she cooed, "Mr. Roxas is a good friend of President Marcos. He's even running for assemblyman of Baguio City."

I smelled shit. Being a friend of that crook Marcos was strike one, and running for office was strike two. Just as I was about to ask some probing questions about Andy's "surgeon," a big yellow Mercedes with blacked-out windows pulled in.

"There's Mr. Roxas!" said my new friend excitedly.

Roxas exited the car accompanied by several guards packing submachine guns. *Sure,* I thought, *just like any other surgeon at Cedars-Sinai.* I was informed that the firepower was necessitated by Roxas's running for office under the Marcos banner. If that wasn't Roxas's third strike, then nothing was. I feared for Andy, what this disappointment might do to him psychologically. My gut instincts are pretty accurate, and I had a very bad feeling about "Doctor" Jun Roxas at that moment. I hoped I was completely wrong.

I sat on the balcony, letting the sun warm me, and chatted with our driver. Given the nature of our trip to the Philippines, the conversation came around to human existence and its meaning. Though neither of us plowed up any new ground, it was a pleasant diversion from my concerns about my friend. After we'd gotten to know each other a bit, she lowered her voice conspiratorially. "If you want to," she said, "I can show you to certain places. *Special* places . . . that is if you get lonely."

I smiled to myself, assuming she was referring to the local brothels. Could it be that our reputations had followed us all the way here? I politely declined, saying I wouldn't be "needing" that during this trip. Then a man came out and informed me that Andy's surgery session was about to begin. I went inside, found Andy and Lynne, and we were escorted down a long hall, past a chapel festooned with religious artifacts and reeking of incense. The corridor was decorated with hundreds of framed photos of gory surgery sessions. It was almost as if the presence of so much blood in the pictures was meant as proof of the authenticity of Roxas's practice.

The main surgery chamber was separated from the visitors' area by a glass partition that allowed videotaping of the sessions without being in the same room. Also present were a number of other surgical hopefuls, all stripping down to their underwear and placing their outer garments in plastic bags to shield them from the anticipated spray of gore. The group ran a cultural and ethnic gamut, and the expressions on their faces were a mixture of anxiety, desperation, and serenity. I wondered if they all truly believed this would work. Since Roxas's clinic was like no doctor's office any of them had ever visited, there was a general sense of confusion, and after disrobing, everyone just milled around waiting for something to happen.

Then Roxas arrived and jumped into his work. As Roxas's hands writhed over and onto the bellies, chests, arms, legs, and heads of his patients, blood flew in every direction. He extracted great gobs of foul, blood-drenched tissue, which he laid in pans that his assistants took away. As I watched the procession and waited for Andy's turn, I counted about twenty-five patients in the room. I calculated that at an average of forty-five seconds per patient, at a charge of $25 each, Roxas would rack up about $625 in twenty or so minutes. Not a bad wage in a third-world country. I ballparked that an equivalent sum stateside was probably more like six grand. As I watched Roxas furiously tossing guts left and right, I thought of the money he was making and smiled cynically over the fact that the staff charged extra for photos.

Andy finally got his turn. He was there for a course of treatments, given the nature of his disease. Jun Roxas concentrated on Andy's head that day, removing all manner of bloodied items. Later, in a quiet conversation with Lynne, I cracked that had Roxas truly removed that much diseased tissue, Andy's head would've had to have started out the size of a basketball.

At one point I noticed Roxas palming the "sick tissue" — probably chicken guts — before he "removed" them from Andy's head. After what was the most bizarre twenty or so minutes of my life, Andy cleaned up, and we got ready to drive back. Andy asked Lynne to go with their driver and asked me to drive him back in the car we came in. Alone. On the way back he talked about the problems he and Lynne were having sexually. Andy had stopped taking his pills, and his speech was slower and slightly slurred. It was often a real struggle for him to complete a thought. That frustrated him tremendously.

"We're just not attracted to each other," he said. "She didn't think it was working out months ago, but then I got sick, and she couldn't tell me."

"How do you know that?" I asked.

"She just told me."

"How do you feel?" I asked.

"It's okay. I wasn't totally honest with her, either. We haven't really been attracted to each other for a while. She's here for me, and that's okay. I'm glad she is."

I liked Lynne a lot and felt she was a positive influence on Andy. Andy had always had strange relationships with women because none ever knew how to handle him. Until Lynne. "Maybe you guys should get some counseling when you get back home," I suggested.

"Yeah, maybe we should," said Andy, as he gazed out the window. For most of the drive back to the hotel, he just stared at the passing countryside. The sense of humor that had made him a star was nonexistent. He was bored with being sick and dreaded every moment to come, because there was only one thing to look forward to: dying. I wondered how much worse it could get.

April 12 — Baguio, Philippines

Something is happening to me. I can feel it. I am becoming aware of a certain peace within. An acceptance of the vastness of the universe and my insignificant position to it. It's almost as if I have been put in my place. I have slowed down. Much more contemplative, but in a nonverbal sense. I am content with just being.

Over dinner, some troubadours came to the table and played. Andy requested "(They're Gonna) Put Me in the Movies," which, under the circumstances, was quite surrealistic.

I find contentment in this solitude. It is what I needed. Perhaps I am on the road to monkhood, or perhaps I am just monkeying around.

Kaufman is confused and frustrated. One moment he believes himself cured, the next he doesn't. He sleeps poorly, the wheezing keeps him awake. His chest hurts him tremendously at times ("like a heart attack"). He believes it to be "the cure" working. If you told him to rub butter on both of his feet for a cure, he'd do it. He is desperate.

I walked through the hills today and got lost. I ran into two little girls gathering sticks and did a magic trick for them. They were adorable. The thought keeps crossing my mind of living here and doing my work, whatever that would be. What seemed significant before now seems silly. Perhaps I am maturing. A great change is taking place.

Friday the 13th

Called Kaufman's room to see if they have left yet for the clinic. Bad news. He had convulsions this morning. His left side is totally paralyzed, and he is incapable of moving. The people associated with the clinic say that that response was good. It's a sign that the healing is working. This is their answer to everything. This is madness. Just smiles and everything is all right. Will report more after going to see him.

Just came back from his room. He couldn't even sit up. Had to prop him up. I think it was a stroke (convulsions followed by paralysis). Lynne and I had to wobble him to the john and support him while he took a piss. I'm fighting that urge in me just to leave. Escape death and dying. There is no light at the end of the tunnel, but then why did I come?

I said I was going to look for a walker but ran off to the beach for a couple hours. When I came back, his condition hadn't changed. He cried and begged me to stay longer. He'd pay. I said nothing. A few more days of this and I'll go mad. I'm even considering leaving without telling him, but decided it was such a chickenshit thing to do.

I went to a Catholic hospital and borrowed a walker from a paraplegic for a couple of days. Lynne seems to think he'll be better then. I fear he will only get worse. I have no hope. Lynne is all hope. Her father died of "the cancer," she said. She knew he would as soon as it was detected. I wonder if this time her hope is based on her last experience ending poorly.

Kaufman continues to shake his head in disgust and disbelief that such a thing can be happening. I escort him around like a frail grandma. Lynne pointed out that he had gotten just like this when his parents were in town (L.A.), and perhaps it was somewhat of an act for us. I had wondered the same thought and took note of the coincidences.

It is truly a nightmare, except that I am wide awake. I was told today that Saturday the flagellations begin, where they whip themselves for their sins.

Death in a five-star hotel.

What I'm experiencing now is a dual emotion of both sympathy and disgust, with disgust winning out. Because of his illness, he is milking the sympathy and demanding more and more attention. More of an entourage. The illness brings out the worst of his personality. It is a greedy demon, this thing called death.

Saturday the 14th — Day
   Lynne said he's moving better. I don't believe it. He's confined to a wheelchair. I think he's mad at me because I don't want to stay . . . Fuck him. I make no man guilty and want no man to make me guilty.

Hell is the highest city in the Philippines.

If Andy was self-indulgent in life, in dying he is selfishness itself, but then selfishness is what death is all about. The ultimate and last selfish act. It's hard to be sympathetic to someone who is so selfish. He spits orders at Lynne, but who can blame him. The pain must be excruciating.

After recently rereading the last passage of my newly found diary I was convinced Lynne would think ill of me. Embarrassed to admit I had wanted out, that I couldn't take it any more, I was worried she might be appalled that I felt the whole experience of being around someone who was dying was also killing me. She knew Andy required a lot of hand holding, and we both witnessed, as death neared, his becoming nearly impossible to be around.
   I hated myself for thinking those things, but when I finally expressed them to Lynne she said she was relieved, because she also had been carrying the same guilt around all those years. Sharing those seemingly self-centered emotions helped allay the guilt for both of us by allowing us to see that what we had been thinking and feeling was a natural reaction to the death we were observing from front-row seats. The hopelessness and powerlessness of seeing loved ones fade as your grip on them slips away is perhaps the most frustrating experience one can endure. Andy's condition had driven him to the point where his will and energy could no longer filter the hurtfulness that came from his mouth, which

made it even harder to defend against both Lynne's and my own natural feelings of resentment.

Saturday the 14th — Night

Had a wonderful meal with Lynne and Kaufman in a Japanese restaurant in the hotel. I reminisced about the past. The time the football team threatened us. And the Hilton place that was an orgy. We all laughed.

We got him back to the room, and before I left, he signaled me to come near to him and we shook hands — I shook that paralyzed hand. He applied pressure. I said, "Hey, that's more like it," and then he did something quite extraordinary. He said, "That was nothing," and he jumped up and growled like he had done a hundred times before in a wrestling match. It was the most courageous moment I had ever experienced in my life. For one brief moment I thought that this had all been a put-on. Then he collapsed back on the bed, looked me straight in the eye and said, "I want you to know that I'm proud of everything we did together."

Those words were Andy's good-bye to me. A few days later I flew back to L.A. Andy and Lynne followed a couple of days later. Jun Roxas had pronounced Andy "cured" and fit to travel. He sent Andy home with a pat on the back, probably terrified that Andy would succumb in his facility and ruin future business. Andy and Lynne immediately went to Colorado, where Kaufman had heard about a new wonder cure involving crystals that might be his answer. After a short stay near the Rockies, they came back to town. The doctors at Cedars found that Andy's condition had worsened. He didn't want to stay at the hospital, so they let him go home to the place in the Palisades, but soon his body began to give out, and he was forced to return to Cedars.

Friday — April 27, 1984

Back from Philippines. Off to Denver. Acupressure on his head when he had a seizure, back for radiation. Might as well stay in the hospital. After a few days he leaves. More at home. He's back on the eighth floor. The vigil. The kidneys go. I go home for some sleep. The end is near.

Andy's parents flew out to be with him and his closest friends stopped in over the next few days to try and cheer him up. Robin Williams showed up, and in an act of kindness not unlike his character in *Patch Adams*, he brought a videocassette player and a box of Laurel and Hardy tapes. He was probably thinking of Norman Cousins and how humor had cured him. Robin is sweet and caring, but I don't think he knew how sick Andy really was. He never watched the tapes.

During those days my mind reeled with weird possibilities and options to the seemingly inevitable conclusion to the story. Had Andy planned all this? Was it the perfect ending to his personal saga? He was certainly aware that his early death would likely be just the catalyst necessary to propel him to the next level of fame: legend. As Andy lay in the hospital dying, I studied him very closely. Was this some spectacular put-on, making the illusion of Tony Clifton pale by comparison? Was this real? If so, was he hearing me? Was he cognizant of what was going on? Then I remembered what he had told me about doing Clifton, about conquering my fears, and about how he had conquered his through TM. And I realized he was doing it again, right before my eyes. Even as he was dying, he wasn't afraid — he was meditating.

It was Wednesday, May 16, 1984, and I had gone home from the hospital early to take a nap. Sometime after six or so the phone rang and awakened me from a deep sleep. I grabbed it, but there was no one there. I unplugged the phone and went back to sleep. I had not been sleeping well for some time, and I took any opportunity when my body allowed it. Finally, around eight-thirty that evening, I awoke and puttered around to clear my head. I noticed the phone was unplugged, and as soon as I snapped the line into the jack it started ringing. "Hello?" I said.

"Bob, hi, it's Linda." It was Andy's assistant, Linda Mitchell. Her voice was muted, and even from those four words I knew what her next words would be. "It's over," she said softly.

"Thanks," I said, and hung up. Mechanically, I got organized and drove down to Cedars-Sinai. I didn't really think about much on the way. At the hospital I ran into Stanley and Janice

Kaufman and then saw Linda leaving with Lynne and Elayne Boosler. We said some quiet hellos. There was nothing left to do, so the Kaufmans went to Nibblers to eat, and I joined the others at Linda's to watch the eleven o'clock news. The story about Andy was the lead, and it ended with reporter Tawny Little solemnly intoning, "He joked to the end." *Bullshit*, I thought.

On the way home I drove by the Improv, and the media were gathered out front. "Andy's gone. Go home," I said to myself as my car passed the throng. The next day I drove to the house in the Palisades, but there was no one there. I went to see the movie *The Bounty* and cried. I'm sure the people around me thought it was the film that so moved me. After the movie I called the Palisades house, and Linda answered and told me that George Shapiro and Jim Cancholla were there. I thought of happier times when Jim as "Jimmy the C" helped us pull the stunt on *Dinah!* I told Linda I couldn't talk to them at that moment but would see them at the services on the East Coast.

On Friday the eighteenth I flew to New York and checked into the Doral Inn. Joe Troiani arrived that evening. The funeral was scheduled for the next day. To blow off some steam, we went into the city to the Improv. Budd Friedman's wife, Silver, spoke with us for a bit, espousing her theory that the deceitfulness of Dick Ebersol had done Andy in. Then Joe and I went down to some of the strip joints on 42nd Street.

The next morning I rented a car and picked up Lynne at the airport. The three of us then drove to the mortuary in Great Neck. We were hours early for the ceremony but wanted to pay our respects to Andy in private. I really didn't want to go inside, fearing that the vision of seeing Andy in a coffin would be something I'd never be able to shake. Joe went in and looked, then Lynne did the same. She came back and said it was best I didn't go in, and that she wished she hadn't, either.

There was plenty of time before the service, so we went to breakfast and then over to the Kaufman home. No one answered the door, so, like family, we just walked in and sat down. After a few moments we heard a stirring in the bedroom, and eventually Mrs. Kaufman came downstairs. We hugged her and tried to make light of things. She'd been crying. A little later Stanley appeared with some letters from Carol Kane, Bob Einstein (Super Dave), and Judd Hirsch. Just before we were to leave, Michael and his girlfriend and Carol and her boyfriend arrived.

At the synagogue, I immediately reverted to being Andy's producer, worrying that not enough people would show. No one from *Saturday Night Live* came, nor did any of the agents, managers, or press. The only *Taxi* cast member to attend was Latka's love, Simka, Carol Kane. It was a simple affair, with just family and close friends and a few fans. A couple of the girls from the Mustang Ranch flew out to attend.

The rabbi was sensitive, and his words and demeanor were comforting. Andy's brother, Michael, talked and then played the tape of Andy singing "Friendly World," which had always been Andy's closing song. That did it. Everyone burst into tears, destroyed by the reality of it all. Next we went to the cemetery in Elmont, where we saw a *National Enquirer* photographer hiding behind a tombstone. I figured we'd used them enough over the years, so I thought, *Sure, go ahead, take your best shot.*

Back at the Kaufman home there wasn't much else we could do or say, so we said our good-byes. Michael, Carol, and Stanley took Joe to the airport, and I went back to the city and checked in to the Taft Hotel. I went up to my room, turned down the bed, climbed in, and cried myself to sleep.

When I woke up I dressed and went over to the Improv. I didn't laugh once, but just being there was soothing. I closed the place and then went back to the hotel and slept until noon. I checked the paper and found a small article about Andy. I thought they'd written a lot more on John Belushi when he died. Andy's producer to the end, I was still monitoring the reviews. I checked out of the hotel and, on autopilot, drove to JFK, dropped off the car, and left New York.

15

Out of the Ashes

I said, "He died? Really?" And at first I didn't want to believe it 'cause Andy was known for his outlandish comedy . . . his hoaxes.
PAUL RODRIGUEZ

How could this happen? A guy who didn't drink, smoke, or do drugs; who was a vegetarian; who was into holistic medicine, yoga, and transcendental meditation — in other words, a guy who was a complete health nut — how did he die at *thirty-five?* It didn't make sense, and given all the talk that surrounded Andy Kaufman, rumors began swarming like killer bees on a bad day. For months the speculations raged, and everywhere I went I heard them. I still hear some even today. These are but a few examples:

> *"It was Dick Ebersol . . ."*
> *"No, it was the TM movement, when they threw him out . . ."*
> *"It was actually the sugar, I heard he told Zmuda that . . ."*
> *"Sugar, my ass, it was a CIA hit, obviously. You can't come into people's living rooms and get away with that kinda shit without the government putting a hit on you . . ."*
> *"That's totally ridiculous. It was actually the makeup they put on him in* Heartbeeps. *I knew somebody on that picture, and they said he sat in a chair three hours every day while they sprayed a bunch of crap all over him. The makeup people wore masks. It was the carcinogens in the metal paint . . ."*
> *"Bullshit. Bernadette Peters had the same thing done to her, and she's fine . . ."*

"It was AIDS . . ."

"AIDS didn't even exist then, dummy . . ."

"Yes, it did, and that's what he had, AIDS . . ."

"Well, nobody dies of AIDS in five months . . ."

"It was all that crazy shit he did in his act . . ."

"No, it was simply because his career was over . . ."

"His career wasn't over. He still had a high Q rating . . ."

"That was his act. He himself told Letterman his career was over . . ."

"Okay, then what killed Andy Kaufman?"

"Nothing. He's still alive."

"How do you figure?"

"He told people he was going to fake his death . . ."

"So? You think he paid off everyone at Cedars-Sinai?"

"Why not? He was rich. Besides, he was a master of that kind of thing."

Had anyone read page 128 of *The Tony Clifton Story*, the screenplay that disappeared into obscurity at the behest of Universal Pictures, the fuel on the fires of speculation would have exploded. For on page 128, written by Andy five years before Andy died, Tony Clifton dies. Of lung cancer. At Cedars-Sinai Hospital. Coincidence? Perhaps.

It has been speculated that Andy Kaufman managed to pull off one last hoax, certainly the biggest of his life, with the man upstairs in collusion. Insane as it sounded, I clung to anything, despite having seen Andy wither away before my eyes. If Andy's death had been a scam, then it made Houdini's greatest illusions look like the coin behind the ear. When Andy died, so did I. For almost a year I spiraled down and down into a whirlpool of ever-deepening despair. I sought refuge with drugs, alcohol, prostitutes, and every other vice that could take me away and dull my mind as it overloaded on the pain of such loss.

One morning, a year after Andy's funeral, the phone rang at seven and jarred me from a deep sleep. I fumbled the phone off the cradle. "What?"

"You sons of bitches!" said a familiar voice on the other end. "I knew it! I knew it!"

"What are you talking about?"

"You know what I'm talking about!"

"Believe me, I haven't a clue."

"Have you seen *Variety*?"

"How could I have seen *Variety*? It's seven A.M."

"Well, get your ass out of bed and go down to the newsstand and get a copy — now!"

"This better be good," I warned.

"*Good?* It's unbelievable!"

I hung up, jumped into my pants and shoes, and drove to a 7-Eleven not far from my house. I knew they carried *Daily Variety*, so I found that morning's issue and groggily flipped through it. Then I saw it, a full-page ad:

TONY CLIFTON LIVE
May 16th
The Comedy Store
(All proceeds to go to the American Cancer Society)

May 16, 1985, was the one-year anniversary of Andy's death. At the bottom of the ad, in small letters, it said, "produced by Bob Zmuda." A small smile formed, the first to come to my face in a year. It was something I had never expected to experience again. I bought a few copies and drove home.

The news spread like wildfire among the Hollywood community: could it be true? The show sold out quickly, and on the night of the event the place was packed with entertainment-industry execs, producers, artists, comedians, fans, and friends. Five network camera crews set up positions, as well as most of L.A.'s major media. A lot of celebrities came out to see it with their own eyes: Whoopi Goldberg, Rodney Dangerfield, and Eddie Murphy were present, and Dan Aykroyd, Elayne Boosler, Steve Martin, Richard Pryor, and Robin Williams all lent their names to the program. Sitting in a corner was a struggling unknown comic named Jim Carrey.

Eight comics donated their time to the cause, but it was Tony Clifton whom the audience had come to see. Tony was scheduled to close the show, and when the eight other acts came and went, and no Tony showed, the crowd got restless, feeling they might have been had. Was *he* going to show? You know who.

The clock ticked away and there was no sign of Tony. Just when people thought they'd truly been had — typically, the last minute before the audience got up and left — the announcer spoke: "Ladies and gentlemen, in his first public appearance in over a year, please welcome . . ."

All eyes were glued to witness the stage entrance of a ghost, but instead a movie screen descended and a projector started up with clips of Tony on *Dinah!*, the Miss Piggy special, *Merv Griffin*, and finally *David Letterman*. Though it wasn't Tony live like everyone had hoped, they were still caught up in the nostalgia. When Tony began singing "I Will Survive" from Dave's show, they all smiled . . .

> *First I was afraid, I was putrified . . .*
> *Kept thinking I could never live without you by my side.*
> *Then I spent so many nights thinking*
> *How you did me wrong . . .*
> *But I grew strong*
> *I learned how to get along*
> *And now I'm back . . .*

Suddenly the announcer screamed, "*Mr. Tony Clifton!!*" and the projector stopped. The screen quickly ascended to reveal none other than Tony Clifton in the flesh. Microphone in hand, he stepped forward and, with hardly a loss of the beat, continued — as a live band kicked in — where the on-screen Tony had left off . . .

> *From outer space*
> *I just walked in to find you here*
> *With that strange look upon your face . . .*

Strange look was right. The audience was dumbstruck. In the back of the house, Lynne shrieked and fainted. Tony strutted the stage as the band followed his lead . . .

> *Were you the one who tried to hurt me with good-bye?*
> *Did you think I'd crumble?*

Did you think I'd lay down and die?
Oh, not I
I will survive
As long as I know how to love
I'll simply stay alive
I got all my love to give
I've got all my life to live
I will survive . . . I will survive . . .
I will survive!!!

As the song closed, the crowd leapt to its feet, giving Tony a standing ovation. It was so un-Tony, such wildly unqualified acceptance. But people were just delirious to have him back. Reporters scrambled out of the club to file their story before the others, and people went crazy that Tony Clifton had done the impossible and had returned. As I surveyed the wondrous scene, my eyes welled with tears, and I lifted a shaking hand to take a draw on my cigarette. No, I hadn't taken up smoking in my depression, it was just a prop — *Tony's* prop. I was Tony.

You see, a few weeks before that show, I heard another voice, the same one that had spoken to me in San Diego and persuaded me to toss off my apron and quit my cook's job. But this time it had a different message: *"Bring back Tony."* That was not an easily answered request — Andy's death had kicked the life out of me, too. To go in front of the entire Hollywood community as Tony was, at best, terrifying for me. Particularly when I knew whom they'd really be looking for. Also, I was in bad shape, having been lost in the bottom of a bottle for almost a year. But the voice was firm and I went back to some advice Andy had once given me, "Get over your fear and just go for it." He'd been right, inspiring me then to become Tony Clifton, and he was right again. Perhaps that is Andy's greatest legacy to us all: Failing is okay . . . not trying isn't.

Another extraordinary thing happened the night Tony wowed Hollywood. Sitting in that audience was the other half of "Albrecht & Zmuda, Comedy from A to Z," my old friend Chris Albrecht. Chris approached me after the place cleared and asked if

I had any ideas for shows. He was certainly looking for them, given he'd become one of the head cheeses at HBO.

I reminded Chris that "Tony Clifton Live" was a benefit for the American Cancer Society and that it was the first time anyone had ever brought together so many comedians to perform strictly for charity. Chris got where I was going, and "Tony Clifton Live" became the prototype for "Comic Relief." About a year later, HBO carried our first telecast of Comic Relief, hosted by Billy Crystal, Whoopi Goldberg, and Robin Williams. It raised nearly four million dollars. Promising the funds were to help soften the scourge on America's homeless men, women, and children, I reflected on the parallel between those unfortunate folks and another homeless individual named Foreign Man, who carried all his worldly possessions in a little suitcase.

Since that first production, coproducers John Moffitt, Pat Tourk Lee, and I have mounted seven more Comic Relief shows, raising more than fifty million dollars that has been distributed to Comic Relief project sites in twenty-three major cities to provide greatly needed medical care to more than 150,000 citizens who do not even have the minimal necessity of a home. Every major comedian in the United States has appeared on Comic Relief, and it is considered the single biggest comedy event in the world. I am proud of all the people who have generously contributed their time and talents to make it work. I would not have founded Comic Relief had Andy not pushed me to take on Tony Clifton and then left me the costume. That act not only saved many people but also saved me as well.

In 1992, on May 16, the eighth anniversary of Andy's passing, we held Comic Relief V and dedicated it to Andy as a tribute to the man who made it all possible, who was the catalyst for its creation. I placed a camera backstage to record all the comedians' reminiscences about Andy. Later, when I watched the tape, which had thoughts and anecdotes from Robin Williams, Jay Leno, Richard Lewis, Richard Belzer, Rita Rudner, and Garry Shandling, to mention a few, I was astonished at how many cited (with uncharacteristic seriousness) Andy Kaufman as one of their major influences.

I was so struck by the tape that I showed it to George Shapiro and Howard West (who were producing *Seinfeld* at the time), and we took it to NBC. There we showed the tape to Rick Ludwin, the executive in charge of specials for the network. We promised we could get more stars who would be happy to talk about Andy and the impact he had on them. Rick was intrigued, but I could see he didn't want to insult us. "It's been ten years," he said. "I don't know if kids today would remember him."

I jumped in. "R.E.M. has a song called 'Man on the Moon,' it's a big hit right now, and it's about Andy." Rick finally agreed, and we shot "A Comedy Salute to Andy Kaufman." It aired in 1995. The telecast was a critical success and, on top of that, garnered an Emmy nomination. Kaufman was back.

One night not long after the special aired, Danny DeVito, whose Jersey Films had a deal with Universal, struck up a conversation with Milos Forman at a party. Having not worked together since *One Flew Over the Cuckoo's Nest*, they kicked around the notion of presenting to Universal a biography of Andy. When the word got out, immediately every big-name actor wanted the role — Nicolas Cage, Kevin Spacey, Ed Norton, and Sean Penn, among others. Eventually, Jim Carrey got the role. Interestingly, Jim and Andy's birthdays are on the same day, January 17.

Principal photography on *Man on the Moon* was completed the day before Thanksgiving, 1998. I am proud to say I served as co-executive producer of the film, along with George Shapiro and Howard West, with Lynne Margulies serving as a consultant — a full circle for us all. The film is due for release late in 1999.

Epilogue

Andy's biggest fear was not that he would die, but that he would not be remembered. Given the perspective of time, I now know that did not happen, that Andy's name and work *are* remembered, and fondly. The things that he did will persist, on these pages and in the memories of those he touched.

To this day, I still suffer the loss of my best friend. All the movies and books about Andy will never fill the void. His life was a testament to those kindred artists who push the limits higher and higher through their art. If you get only one thing out of this book, I hope it is this: don't take your friends for granted. For whatever reason, they have decided to share their lives with you, so cherish them. I'm proud Andy was my friend, my best friend.

Finally, I've often been asked, "Had Andy lived, what would he be doing?"

The answer is obvious: I truly believe he would have faked his death.

Backword from Jim Carrey

INSTRUCTIONS: Hold this page up to a mirror and believe . . .

For those of you who are still puzzling about Andy Kaufman, I offer this simple thought: the microscopic organisms that feed off of decaying cell tissue make it possible for the Creator to regenerate new skin.

Are you insulted, angry, or even more bewildered than before? Good! That was always your purpose! You're still playing your parts brilliantly. After all, you were the stars of the show all along. Andy was the director and the audience.

Enjoy your meal.

Jim Carrey

Acknowledgments

I'd like to thank a number of individuals without whose support this book would not have been possible:

First and foremost, my friend and book publicist, Jodee Blanco, whose inexhaustible devotion to this project knew no bounds. I owe you lunch and dinner at Mooses.

Frank Weiman of the Literary Group, for bringing me to the attention of Michael Pietsch, editor in chief of Little, Brown, who took a chance on this previously unpublished author. Michael, along with senior editor Judy Clain, Beth Davey, Claire Ellis, and Sandy Bontemps, all made me feel right at home. Also, Michael Kaye, for designing the book's jacket.

Wordsmith Matt Hansen, my cowriter, whose easy manner and laughter encouraged me to remember incidents that I had previously forgotten.

My lawyer and friend, Roger Sherman, who, along with Peter del Vecchio and Kim Schwartz, dotted the i's and crossed all the t's.

Most important, Mike Miller, as he is the only living soul who can make out my writing, even when I can't read it myself.

Also my family, my mom, dad, and my two sisters, Carol and Marilyn.

My beautiful wife, Ranko, for her patience and funny dances. And my dog, Woody, who watches over us.

And finally, my friend Jim Carrey, who brought Andy back among the living and in so doing, brought me along with him.

Index

Agency for the Performing Arts (APA), 82
Albrecht, Chris, 20–22, 27, 28–30, 289–90
Aliens (film), 212
Allen, Steve, 62–63
Amadeus (film), 255
American Airlines, 177–79
American Broadcasting Company (ABC), 84–85, 95, 188, 189, 203, 205, 219, 227
American Cancer Society, 290
American Graffiti (film), 107
Amos, Wally "Famous," 144
Animal House (film), 190, 191
anti-Semitism, 233–35
Arkush, Alan, 194
As Good As It Gets (film), 223
Aykroyd, Dan, 58, 184, 219, 287

Bachelors Three, 57–58
Bad Seed, The (film), 245
Baguio, Philippines, 273–74
Baker, Rick, 212
Balboa Park, San Diego, 69
Bananaz, 91, 106
Barnum, Phineas T., 156
Bellew, Bill, 78–79

Belushi, John, 58, 90, 184, 219, 284
Belzer, Richard, 24, 111, 242, 243, 290
Benatar, Pat, 242, 244
Beverly Hillbillies, The (TV), 245
Beverly Hills Cop III (film), 191
Bewitched (TV), 157
Beymer, Richard, 75–78
Birth of a Nation (film), 53
Black, Clint, 157
Blackwood, Pady, 81, 82
Blassie, Freddie, 239, 269–70
Blues Brothers, The (film), 190, 219
Boosler, Elayne, 24, 103, 283, 287
Brando, Marlon, 228
Brillstein, Bernie, 241
Brooks, Jim, 99, 106, 132, 135, 223
Brown, Edmund "Pat," 245
Brown, Jerry, 245
Bruce, Lenny, 196
Bryant, Connie, 190, 272
Burns, Jack, 204–05, 206, 253
Burrell, Maryedith, 204, 206
Burton, Richard, 54–55

Cage, Nicholas, 291
Cahn, Sammy, 108

Cancholla, Jim "Jimmy the C," 168, 170, 283
Candid Camera (TV), 208
Carlin, George, 59
Carnegie Hall show, 145, 146–50, 154
Carnegie-Mellon University, 20
Carrey, Jim, 128, 217, 225, 287, 291
Carson, Johnny, 63, 85, 91–92
Carver, Randy, 106
Carvey, Dana, 184
Cash, Johnny, 162–63
Catch a Rising Star, 21
Catch a Rising Star Tenth Anniversary HBO Special (TV), 241–44
celebrity: limitations of, 108, 183–85; and sex, 108–09
Chandler, Raymond, 108
Chartoff, Melanie, 204
Chase, Chevy, 58, 184
Chase, Ken, 212, 214
Clifton, Tony, 50–52, 127, 132–37, 197–99; at Comedy Store, 287–89; creation of, 128; on *Dinah!*, 168–74; Kaufman as, 130–31; makeup of, 128–29; persona of, 137; role of in Kaufman's ethos, 185; on *Taxi*, 132; on *The Fantastic Miss Piggy Show*, 240; Zmuda as, 209–16, 217, 287–89. *See also* Kaufman, Andy
coffee houses, Greenwich Village, 14
college tours, 113–20
Comedy Salute to Andy Kaufman, A (TV), 291
Comedy Store, 102, 141, 287–89
comedy wars, 103–04
Coming to America (film), 191
Conaway, Jeff, 106, 131–32, 135–36
Coney Island, 53–54
Conversation, The (film), 107
Coppola, Francis Ford, 107
Cousins, Norman, 282

Creative Artists Agency (CAA), 61
Crowe, Richard, 122
Crystal, Billy, 242, 290
Cukor, George, 107
Culp, Nancy, 245
Curtin, Jane, 58

Daley, Richard J., 11, 12
Dana, Bill, 64
Dangerfield, Rodney, 73, 188, 196–98, 287
Daniel, Sean, 190
Danson, Ted, 20
Danza, Tony, 106, 135
David, Larry, 24
Davidson, John, 159–60
Davis, Sammy Jr., 63
D.C. Cab (film), 249, 271
DeVito, Danny, 106, 132, 135, 184, 291
Death Sport (film), 194
Denoff, Sam, 21
Dinah! (TV), 167, 168–73
Doumanian, Jean, 220
Doyle-Murray, Brian, 247
Dreesen, Tom, 103
Dubrow, Bert, 80–81, 91, 94–95
Duvall, Robert, 107

Ebersol, Dick, 58–59, 220, 248, 249–50, 264, 283
Einstein, Bob, 284
Elvis (Goldman), 86, 220
Endler, Estelle, 156, 267, 268
Equus (play), 54
Escaped Lions, 221–22

Fan Mail Sex Tours, 88
Farley, Chris, 184
Feldman, Marty, 151, 194
Fillmore West, San Francisco, 196, 197–99
Fitzgerald, F. Scott, 89
Flynn, Errol, 108
Ford, Harrison, 107

Foreign Man, 25–26, 27, 63–64, 127

Forman, Milos, 224–25, 254–55, 291

freak show, 7–10

Fridays (TV), 95, 203–05, 253

Friedman, Budd, 21, 24, 28–29, 77, 89, 268, 283

Friedman, Silver, 283

Frost, David, 102

Funt, Allen, 208

Gacy, John Wayne, 122

Gallery magazine, 240

Ghost Tour, The, 122–23

Giamatti, A. Bartlett, 255

Giamatti, Paul, 255

Goldberg, Whoopi, 287, 290

Goldman, Albert, 86, 220–21

Graceland, 97–98

Graham, Bill, 197, 199

Grahm Junior College, 14–15, 80

Grandma Pearl, 10, 147, 179–80

Grand Ole Opry, 162

Grateful Dead, 197

Gray, John, 260

Grease (film), 11

greasers, 11

Great Gatsby routine, 88–89

Great Neck, Long Island, 3, 14

Gregory, André, 239

Griffith, D.W., 53

Grodin, Chuck, 22

Group W, 91

Gumby, 220

Guru Dev, 15

Haight-Ashbury, 67

Hall, Monty, 62

Hall, Tom T., 163

Hamlisch, Marvin, 63

Harrah's Casino: Las Vegas, 152–53; Reno, 153; Lake Tahoe, 213, 215, 217

Harrah's House, 157–60

Harrington, Pat, 64

Harry, Debbie, 256

Hart, Jimmy, 238

Hartman, Lisa, 157, 159

Hartman, Phil, 184

Has-Been Corner, 76–78, 83

hatha yoga, 224–25

Heartbeeps (film), 194–95, 218, 244, 264

Heavens' Gate (film), 246

Hefner, Hugh, 111

Henderson, Florence, 63

Hendrix, Jimi, 197

Henner, Marilu, 106, 240, 268

Henson, Jim, 240–41

Herman, Pee-wee, 219

Heston, Charlton, 195

Hills Have Eyes, The (film), 263

Hilton Hotel, Las Vegas, 17

Hirsch, Judd, 106, 132, 135–36, 227, 284

Hoffman, Abbie, 11, 12, 19

Hoffman, Dustin, 45, 108

holistic healing, 259–60

Holly, Buddy, 118

Home Box Office (HBO), 227, 242, 290

hoodwinking the press, 154–56

Hope, Bob, 63

Hopper, Dennis, 12

Hormsby House, Carson City, 214, 215

Howdy Doody, 79–83, 146, 241, 264

Hubert's Museum, 10

Hughes, Howard, 224

Humperdinck, Engelbert, 16

Huntington Hartford Theater, Hollywood, 101, 141–44

Idle, Eric, 163

Improv West. *See* West Coast Improv

Improv, The, 21, 23, 24, 28, 184–85, 283

In God We Tru$t (film), 151, 194

Jackson, Michael, 224
Jerry Springer (TV), 95
Jersey Films, 291
Johannsen, Jake, 228
John, Elton, 225
Johnny Cash Christmas Show, The (TV), 162
Jones, Tom, 16
Joplin, Janis, 197
Jordan, Michael, 226
Jurassic Park (film), 212

Kane, Carol, 284
Kaplan, Gabe, 28
Karloff, Boris, 119
Kaufman, Andy:
–career of, 140–41, 193–94; development of material by, 74–75; dismissal from *Saturday Night Live*, 249–51, 264; to Hollywood, 60; at Improv, 25–26; influence of on other comics, 290–91; TV debut of, 59–60; as writer, 74–75
–early years of: childhood, 10, 226–27, 254; daughter of, 222, 225; and Elvis, 16–19
–health of: cancer diagnosis, 257; cancer treatment, 259–60, 264, 270–71; death of, 3–4, 262–84; hepatitis attack, 144–45; and sweets, 79, 263
–as performer: death of as hoax, 3–5, 252–53, 286; in flight, 175–79; as Foreign Man, 25–26, 27, 63–64, 127; photographic memory of, 45; relationship with audience, 75, 104; as Tony Clifton, 130–31, 132, 185, 240
–psychological makeup of: asceticism of, 202–03; black-and-white world of, 56; limitations of celebrity for, 108, 183–85, 200–02; love of confrontation, 43–46, 48, 56, 111–12, 192–93; and multiple personality disorder, 131, 155, 217; need for hand-holding of, 73–74; obsession with failure of, 56–57, 76, 137; and obsessive-compulsive disorder, 223–26; sense of history of, 121
–sex life of, 108–10, 113–14, 158–59, 161, 217, 240; and prostitutes, 161; on women, 165–66
–and transcendental meditation, 15–16, 61, 202, 206, 210, 222, 256; and levitation, 100–02, 105
–and wrestling, 86, 113–16, 164–65, 228–39, 256
–and Zmuda, 61, 73–75, 121, 222
Kaufman, Carol, 7, 126, 255, 284
Kaufman family, 179–81
Kaufman, Janice, 189, 226, 254, 256, 282, 283
Kaufman, Michael, 255, 259, 284
Kaufman, "Papu," 226–27, 254
Kaufman, Stanley, 180–81, 189, 226, 236, 254, 282, 283–84
Kerman, Rick, 126
Kerouac, Jack, 17
King Kong (film), 212
King, Alan, 14, 254
Kissinger, Henry, 109
Klein, Marty, 250
Klein, Robert, 262
Knoedelseder, Bill, 136
Kovacs, Ernie, 21
Kristofferson, Kris, 177, 178, 245, 246
Kutscher's, 179–81, 252

Ladd, Diane, 245
Lambert, Mimi, 165–66, 253
Lancaster, Burt, 260
Landis, John, 190–92
Late Night with David Letterman (TV), 214, 220–21, 236–37, 249, 254, 255

Laverne and Shirley (TV), 73, 107

Lawler, Jerry "The King," 97, 228–39

Lawrence Welk Show (TV), 205, 206–07

Lazarus (dog), 189

Lee, Pat Tourk, 204, 206, 290

Legend, Johnny, 239

Leno, Jay, 24, 96, 103, 127, 290

Letterman, David, 103, 141, 195–96, 228, 236–37

levitation, 100–02, 105

Lewis, Jerry, 218

Lewis, Richard, 24, 290

Light, Judith, 20

Lincoln Park love-in, Chicago, 11–13

Lincoln, Abraham, film of, 52–53

Little Hippodrome, The, 22

Lobster Survival Poll, 247–48

Los Angeles Times, 102, 136

Love, Courtney, 239

Lubetkin, Steve, 102–03

Lucas, George, 107

Ludwin, Rick, 291

Lynch, David, 77

MacArthur, Douglas, 272

McCormack, Patty, 245, 246–47

Magic Christian, The (film), 162

Maharishi Mahesh Yogi, 15, 102

Mailer, Norman, 137

Man on the Moon (film), 206, 217, 224, 228, 239, 291

Many Loves of Dobie Gillis, The (TV), 112

Marcos, Ferdinand, 275–76

Margulies, Lynne, 3, 111, 225, 239–40, 257–58, 262, 267, 270, 277–78, 280–81, 283, 288, 291

Marshall, Garry, 107

Marshall, Penny, 107

Martin, Steve, 64, 211, 287

Martindale, Stan, 258

Masked Hypnotist, 124–26

Maslow, Abraham, 111

Meadows, Jayne, 62–63

Men Are from Mars, Women Are from Venus (Gray), 260

Meredith, James, 7

Merv Griffin (TV), 214

Michaels, Lorne, 58, 59, 89, 90, 146, 182, 183–84, 252

Mid-South Coliseum, Memphis, 228, 237

Mighty Mouse, 59

Mike Douglas Show, The (TV), 96

Miss Vicky, 207

Mitchell, Linda, 168, 267, 282

Moffitt, John, 204, 205, 206, 253, 290

Mommy's Day (film), 245

Monty Python, 163

Mormon Tabernacle Choir, 143

Morton, Robert, 214

Mount, Thom, 190

Mr. Bill, 182, 184

Mr. X, 30–42, 43–48, 192–93

Mrs. Doubtfire (film), 147

Muhammad Ali, 183

multiple personality disorder (MPD), 131, 155, 217

Mummy, The (film), 119

Murphy, Eddie, 184, 220, 247, 287

Murray, Bill, 184, 219

Musso & Frank restaurant, 108, 130

Mustang Ranch, 157–59, 215

My Breakfast with Blassie (film), 239, 265–70

My Dinner with André (film), 239

Myers, Mike, 184

National Broadcasting Company (NBC), 58, 85, 195, 227, 291

National Lampoon Radio Hour, 58, 156, 271, 284

Newman, Rick, 21, 67, 241–44

Newsweek magazine, 102

Nicholson, Jack, 223

Ninety-Nine-Cent Tour, 258–59

Northeastern Illinois University, 19

Norton, Ed, 291

O'Brien, Edmond, 116

obsessive compulsive disorder (OCD), 223–26

Ocean Beach, San Diego, 69

Olde Spaghetti Factory, 144

One Flew Over the Cuckoo's Nest (film), 254–55, 291

On the Road (Kerouac), 17

Ovitz, Michael, 61

Oyer, Brenda, 18–21, 53, 138–39

Pacino, Al, 32

Paramount Studios, 227

Pardo, Don, 181

Park West, Chicago, 123–26, 221

Patch Adams (film), 282

Penn, Sean, 291

People v. Larry Flynt, The (film), 255

Peters, Bernadette, 194

Pikeville, Kentucky, 19–20

Piscopo, Joe, 24

political tour, 245–47

Posh Bagel restaurant, 200–02

Presley, Elvis, 14, 16–18, 96–99; Kaufman impersonation of, 25–26

Prinze, Freddie, 28

Private Parts (film), 255

prostitution, 161–62

Pryor, Richard, 151, 287

psychic surgery, 260, 274–75, 276–77

psychogenesis, 92–93

Radio City Music Hall Rockettes, 143

Radner, Gilda, 58, 60, 184

Rain Man (film), 45

Ramis, Harold, 268

Reilly, Charles Nelson, 172

Reiner, Carl, 21, 24

Reubens, Paul, 219

Richards, Michael, 204, 206

Rickles, Don, 91

Rock 'n' Roll High School (film), 194

Rock, Chris, 184

Rodriguez, Paul, 285

Rogers, "Nature Boy" Buddy, 182–84, 228

Rolling Stone magazine, 199

Roxas, Jun, 264, 274, 275–77, 281

Rubin, Jerry, 11

Rubin, Marilyn, 87–88

Rudner, Rita, 290

St. Valentine's Day Massacre, 122

Sambo's restaurant, 239

San Diego, 69

Sandler, Adam, 184

Satchidananda (Swami), 224

Saturday Night Live (TV), 58, 89, 90, 153, 163, 181, 220, 236, 247

Saturday the 14th Strikes Back (film), 245

Saving Private Ryan (film), 255

Scanga, Dick, 22, 28, 29

Scent of a Woman (film), 32

Schumacher, Joel, 249, 271

Séance, 121–22

Second City, 13

Seinfeld (TV), 24

Sellers, Peter, 162

Sex Pistols, 197

Shales, Tom, 227

Shandling, Garry, 103, 175, 290

Shapiro, George, 21, 61, 71–73, 102, 119, 138, 167, 199, 213, 231–33, 250, 267, 291

Shapiro/West and Associates, 61, 85, 214

Shawn, Wallace, 239

Shelly, 65, 67–71, 73, 138, 166–67, 200

Shore, Dinah, 63, 167, 168–73

Silverman, Fred, 85–86, 146
Sinatra, Frank, 178–79
Sinbad, 153
Slobodkin, Gail, 83–84, 87
Smith, Buffalo Bob, 80, 82–83
Snyder, Tom, 144
Sonny and Cher, 57
Soule, John Babsone Lane, 65
Sound of Music, The (play), 83
Spacey, Kevin, 291
Sparks, Nevada, 157
Spielberg, Steven, 190
Stapleton, Jean, 173
Steal This Book (Hoffman), 19
Steinberg, David, 218
Stills, Steven, 245
Students for a Democratic Society (SDS), 13
Sugar Blues, 263
Sullivan, Cathy, 205, 206–07
Sutton, Greg, 179
Swan, Billy, 245, 246

Tabitha (TV), 157
Tanen, Ned, 218
Taxi (TV), 99–100, 106–07, 123, 167, 218–19, 227, 254
Teaneck Tanzi: The Venus Flytrap (play), 256
Terminator, The (film), 212
Terminator 2 (film), 212
Terre Haute Express, 65
Thanksgiving at Kutscher's, 179–81
Thomopoulos, Tony, 85
Time magazine, 100, 101, 108
Tiny Tim, 207
Tom Cottle: Up Close (TV), 254
Tomlin, Lily, 58
Tonight Show, The (TV), 62, 63–64
Tony Clifton Story, The (film script), 194, 195, 265
Top, The (TV), 259, 267
Trading Places (film), 191
transcendental meditation (TM), 15–16, 101–02, 105, 223

Travels with My Aunt (film), 107
Travolta, John, 11
Troiani, Joe, 3–5, 67, 122, 126, 155, 217, 283
Turko the Half Man, 9–10, 147
Twin Peaks (TV), 77

Uncle Andy's Funhouse (TV), 188–89, 219
Universal Studios, 190, 228, 271, 291
Uttman, Kathy, 202

Valens, Richie, 118
Van Dyke, Dick, 62
Van Dyke and Company (TV), 62
Variety Hour (TV), 62
Variety, 102
Vertigo (film), 212
Viet Cong Confession, 94, 205
Vinton, Bobby, 7

Wagon Train (TV), 7
Walker, Jimmie, 28
Walters, Barbara, 102
Warhol, Andy, 145–46
wave-over, 91
Weinberger, Ed, 106, 132–35
Weintraub, Jerry, 96
West Coast Improv, 29, 58, 77
West Side Story (film), 77
West, Howard, 61, 257, 291
Westmore, Wally, 212
Willam Morris Agency, 61
Williams, Cindy, 73, 107–08, 109
Williams, Robin, 75, 103, 147, 208, 211, 242, 268, 282, 287, 290
Winston, Stan, 212
Wood, Natalie, 77
wrestling, 56, 113–16, 164–65, 181–84, 228–39
Writer's Guild, 272

Youth International Party (Yippies), 11

Zmuda, Bob:
–and Andy Kaufman: and death
    of, 262–65, 272–81; meets,
    27; relationship with, 61,
    73–75, 121, 222; and TM,
    223
–to California, 64–65, 67–73
–career of, 254–55; as Clifton,
    209–16, 217, 287–89; as Dr.

Zmudee, 92–95; and John
    Landis, 190–92, and Richard
    Burton, 54–55
–early years of: in Chicago, 1968,
    11–13; childhood of, 7–10,
    121–22; at college, 19–21; and
    Mr. X, 30–42, 45–49
Zmuda, Marilyn, 121
Zmuda, Sophie, 122–23